Nobody's Child

KATE ADIE

Nobody's Child

Who Are You When You Don't Know Your Past?

HODDER &
STOUGHTON

Copyright © 2005 by Kate Adie

First published in Great Britain in 2005 by Hodder & Stoughton
A division of Hodder Headline

The right of Kate Adie to be identified as the Author
of the Work has been asserted by her in accordance
with the Copyright, Designs and Patents Act 1988.

A Hodder & Stoughton Book

1

A CIP catalogue record for this title is available from the British Library

Hardback ISBN 0 340 83800 0
Trade Paperback ISBN 0340 840307

Typeset in Plantin by Hewer Text UK Ltd, Edinburgh
Printed and bound by Clays Ltd, St Ives plc

Hodder Headline's policy is to use papers that are natural, renewable
and recyclable products and made from wood grown in sustainable forests.
The logging and manufacturing processes are expected to conform
to the environmental regulations of the country of origin.

Hodder & Stoughton Ltd
A division of Hodder Headline
338 Euston Road
London NW1 3BH

To my family

Acknowledgments

To all the foundlings and their families who so generously gave me their time and told me their stories.

I'm grateful to Louise Greenberg, my agent, Brenda Griffiths and Ariel Bruce for their advice and support. I gained much information and help from the staff of Norcap and the Foundling Group, especially Pam Hodgkins and Anne Caffari; and Rhian Harris at the Foundling Museum in London and Micky White, the Pieta, Venice.

To Anna Portugalova and Downside Up in Moscow, Tim Jaccard in New York and Mike and Jean Morrisey in Boston.

To my editor Rowena Webb and Juliet Brightmore at Hodder and Stoughton, Esther Jagger and Kerry Hood and all the Hodder team.

Contents

Turning Wheel: 'A revolving cradle or device to aid the anonymous abandonment of infants'

My passport contains a lie. I've had several well-thumbed examples which have been scrutinised by polite border officials, drunken militia men and crazed revolutionaries. Everyone has been presented with a page on which it states that I was born in Sunderland. This is not true. I was brought up in that north-east town, but I first saw the light of day somewhere on the coast of Northumberland, within sight of St Mary's Island. The discrepancy is not so great as to amount to a deception of polite border officials etcetera, the distance along the coast to Sunderland being a mere ten miles. Nevertheless, it's a fib which started when I was a teenager.

I've only once met someone else who changed their place of birth – she was born in Belsen in 1944, and was understandably tired of comment and curiosity about a place she thankfully didn't remember.

In a world in which form-filling has become the norm for almost every transaction, the standard questions about name, age and nationality pose little trouble for the majority of us. Even those whose nationality may have shifted through marriage or residence can usually put down their place of birth with confidence. My own deception originated as a device for continuity. I was a teenager in a town where the Adies had been settled since their forbears left the Shetland Islands and came south at the end of the eighteenth century. Claiming the town as my birthplace simply did away with any need to invent a story about a detour to a house on the Northumbrian coast. A house? Or a nursing home? Or a farm? Or a hotel? Surely not a field . . . I didn't know. Nor did the Adies who adopted me.

Just after World War II had ended, adoption societies were rigorous in their reticence and conveyed only the barest of facts to prospective clients about their charges. They were acutely interested in matching what they knew about a child's background to the circumstances of couples wishing to adopt. Religion dominated their decisions, in the quaint belief that an infant should inherit spiritual continuity, if nothing else. What they learned about the circumstances of the birth, they determinedly withheld from the new family. A few details demanded by law – name of mother, place of birth – were swallowed up in their records, never thought proper to be revealed.

I started my life with a Certificate of Adoption, having been carried into court in Sunderland and deemed properly processed, while yowling loudly. Later, I acquired a Short Birth Certificate, a discreet document which did away with the need to provide any details other than those of the adopting parents. And I continued to write 'Sunderland' on every document which demanded PoB. Am I racked with complex feelings about this little quirk of inaccuracy? No. I don't give a hoot. However, I don't underestimate the significance that such discrepancies can have for others.

I was a fortunate child, and fortune must have smiled on me in 1945 – give or take a few days in October when the Northumberland and Durham Adoption Society waved me goodbye in the arms of a fine Catholic couple, apparently from Cumberland, who whisked me off towards Carlisle; only to return me five days later. I'm happily ignorant of what I did at the age of two weeks to deserve such treatment, and ended up with the Adies very shortly afterwards, a good little Methodist.

All through my childhood the subject of adoption was not of great significance, and never a problem. For a start, I was part of a surge of unexpected pregnancy which in itself was part of the 'Baby Boom' years. The end of the war brought reunions for many separated by military conscription and overseas service; and it brought disruption as well. Years apart and lives changed by war wrecked many marriages. Relationships forged in the crucible of 'tomorrow we die' were confronted by the gentle tedium of peace.

Uprooted folk sent hither and thither on errands of war to towns they'd never heard of returned to familiar neighbours and clacking tongues. Men shed uniforms – and lost some of their warrior glamour. Women who'd held down jobs in what had previously been male-only territory were exhorted to return to home and hearth – and get cooking. After six years, peace was wonderful – but having been through so much, 'getting back to normal' wasn't unalloyed joy.

And six years of war had seen sexual attitudes influenced by the pressures of conflict: 'Up with the lark, to bed with a Wren.' Far from being a calm progression towards the sunny uplands of peacetime, the emotional landscape echoed to the sound of lives being rearranged. The divorce rate went through the roof. And there were also those of us whose very existence attested to things 'getting a bit out of hand'; as the official statistics would have it, 'Illegitimacy peaked.' In 1945, 9.1 per cent of all births were illegitimate – double the rate before the war. As ordinary folk would say, a lot of women were 'in trouble'. And shame hung over many pregnancies.

Formal adoption was the middle-class response (working-class children were much more likely to be absorbed into the wider family, often as a sibling to the erring daughter). The agencies were efficient and respectable, with most babies being healthy, white and immediately available. I grew up with several childhood friends who were adopted – it was nothing out of the ordinary, and attracted little attention. The only question which frequently arose was: 'Aren't you curious about – you know . . .?' Those who had no notion of adoption were far more inquisitive about our roots than we were; though there was always likely to be more yearning among those who found less happiness in their adoptive family. Nevertheless, with age came more introspection for most. And at some time or another – often at a rite of passage such as marriage or the prospect of one's own new family – there were questions to be answered about roots.

In the past fifty years, the law has been changed several times in response to the view that both children and parents have rights in respect of knowledge of each other. It has become more accepted, and there's been official encouragement, for adopted children to find a parent. The system is still cumbersome – and can throw up brick walls. Permissions and safeguards are built in, and there is still debate as to how easy it should be made. Even so, with determination most adopted children can now make some head-way towards finding out about their past. We do have a past. We know it's there; there's merely a gap to be closed, a leap across to information on the other side. We are not foundlings – the infants who from earliest times have been exposed and abandoned to an unknown fate, often placed in a wheel or cradle – 'a Turning Wheel' – at the gate of an institution. When the wheel revolved, the child disappeared inside and lost all contact with its mother. Today the Turning Wheels across Europe have been gone for nearly a century and, though adopted children like me have many ques-tions about our past, we do not have that void which faces foundlings: the near-impossibility of discovering anything about your roots and why you were left – hopefully – to the care of complete strangers.

I

What is your name?

Where did you come from, baby dear?
Out of the everywhere, into here.

I heard it as a child – a Victorian song, perhaps one of the tea-
coloured sheets in our music stool, sandwiched between Stainer's
Crucifixion and 'To A Wild Rose'. To a child, roots are hidden and
not very interesting. Occasionally a friend would talk of a grandfather who'd been in India or an auntie who'd married a missionary and gone 'somewhere hot where lions eat you and termites
eat the mission piano'. However, in suburban Sunderland life was
mercilessly conventional, and most people appeared to be of good
Methodist stock with nothing more exotic in the past than a nasty
accident in the shipyards.

Heritage? 'Twas of no account. Grand family trees belonged in
romantic historical novels borrowed from Boots' Lending Library.
The name Adie was uncommon in England, though a clutch of
them could be found in Aberdeen, and these hardy creatures all
lived in the box in the corner of the atlas marked 'Shetland'. Fond
family musing brought forth the claim that Robert the Bruce had
had a faithful lieutenant called Robert Adie. Frankly, I thought
Robert the Bruce had come down through history possessing not
an Adie but a spider – perhaps it was called Wee Robbie. . . . Only
royalty seemed to have those curious diagrams of descending
generations; ordinary folk remembered no more than three or
possibly four layers of ancestors. The two world wars had carried
off large numbers – and curiosity about them seemed tinged with
wincing reflection about those who had failed to live their full lives.
Search for those who were married at the close of Victoria's reign,

and there were those mildly embarrassing crosses, instead of signatures, on the official certificates which betrayed illiteracy, even among the skilled and relatively prosperous. Photographs were jumbled in large boxes on top of the wardrobe: tiny prints of unknown Edwardian ladies with cottage-loaf hair-dos, sleek men on bicycles, and children with frilly pinafores above awful boots. They were things past, with no great connection to the present. I never felt any twinges of need, of the desire to have an unbroken line going back centuries – especially if it ended up with a ruddy spider.

Anyway, I was an adopted child. Not that there was much made of it. Adults cooed, 'Don't you look like your mother!', and my failure to grasp the mystery of chemistry at school was put down to wilful rejection on the part of a pharmacist's daughter. And so many others were adopted too: at least five of my school friends, and numerous others who were mentioned without any comment or tone to suggest that it was unusual.

The official variety of adoption involved the full majesty of the law: it was years before I realised that I had made my first appearance in court as a babe in arms. There were papers to be filed, health examinations, and the rules of the local adoption society to be complied with – frequently this was a religious-based organisation, absolutely heaven-bent on placing children with the 'right' denomination. A mother giving up her child for adoption was quizzed about faith, often to the exclusion of any other details, which perpetuated the age-old religious insistence that a soul should never be lost to the Church – as long as it was the right Church, of course. Foundlings presented a frightening dilemma: a spiritual blank page, perhaps tinged with a lack of virtue because of the circumstances. However, over the centuries sheer competitiveness for souls usually got the abandoned child shepherded to a specific flock.

Official adoption wasn't celebrated very publicly – it was another thirty years before the newspaper columns included proud adoptive parents' notices next to the birth announcements. Adoption was a rather private affair, despite the court hearing: a matter of quiet satisfaction for those involved, but not quite on a par with other hatches, matches and dispatches. And the papers pertaining to the transaction disappeared into an official steel trap, buried from view, nearly impossible to access.

Then there was the unofficial variety. In the days of larger families (or, as an elderly Wiltshire schoolmistress recalled to me about turn-of the-century procreation, '*long* families – took 'em twenty years of pregnancies before they got a bit of a rest'), unofficial adoption was commonplace. Poor families farmed out their offspring to better-off relatives; widowers transferred their children to their sisters; illegitimate children were tacked on to the young mother's siblings. The last was a classic way of avoiding shame, or the attentions of the Poor House, or the opprobrium of an employer; and families of a dozen or more could absorb another infant without the neighbours noticing. Unofficial methods were the only solution for the illiterate and the impecunious. And they worked, in that they operated in an extended family, with the law and the Church kept from interfering.

I was official. I'd been to court. And somewhere in a dark vault were bits of paper which I was certainly not welcome to inspect. The line was drawn, the judge had pronounced, and the past was sealed off.

There were always hints. The occasional remark. But all very subsidiary to the oft-repeated and sincere words: 'We chose you. You were the one we wanted.' And adoption was not something to be ashamed of – perhaps one needed to be just a little discreet, for there was an implication that the people who had chosen you could perhaps not have their own children. This was to raise the unspeakable matter of sex, something which did not occur in polite society, and when it did, was to be either condemned or spoken of in cryptic language. (Sunderland magistrate to woman on soliciting charge: 'And were you intending to do IT?')

Attempts to deal with infertility were rarely discussed, and then only in whispers. Any idea that the male of the species might somehow be at fault was ruled out by many a specialist and many a husband. It was 'woman's trouble', and ignorance and embarrassment went hand in hand. So any suggestions that these awkward matters might have arisen in one's own family were better not mentioned. Your adoption had been a considered gesture flowing with welcome, an embrace which was lawful and above board, and from which all the messy details had been trimmed off. The hints and the occasional remark were all that remained of the messy details – the tiny footprints back to the *accouchement.*

There was the birth certificate, of course; but with the introduction of the Short Version in 1947 the messy details were omitted, specifically to avoid embarrassing the illegitimate. And somewhere in St Catherine's House in London lurked a huge set of volumes wherein you were actually registered. Not as Adie, however, but under whatever name your birth mother had written. Another obstacle course with few signposts.

Natural curiosity arose in my teenage years. By then I had (only just, for this was the 1950s) grasped a few of the fundamentals about procreation – nothing elaborate, it has to be said. Having failed to choose biology in the Fourth Form, I missed out on the thrilling and much-awaited lesson on the Frog, which was what the Church High School deemed a suitable vehicle to explain the Mystery of Life. It was not an illuminating session, I later gathered, and at least one desperate girl was left staring into the loo-pan expecting tadpoles to drop out. Nevertheless, we were a gossipy lot, and slowly enlarged our knowledge of forbidden things via rugby club songs, odd books (not occasional odd, but ODD odd) and jaw-dropping sessions in the gloom of the Lower Library with a school chum who appeared to have a different life from the rest of us. At the time none of us had a concept of 'going off the rails', but we were getting reports from this particular runaway roller-coaster, and we absorbed the factual and acrobatic bits with ravenous appetites.

There was also the rare instance of a girl's elder sister going on holiday at an unusual time of year. Whisper, whisper again: not so much IT, but a question of being SO. However, the piece of information which seemed to be relevant to the teenage adopted child opening her eyes to a wider world was that there were women who made a living out of IT, and therefore ended up SO and had children to spare. Of course: prozzies. We couldn't even bring ourselves to say 'prostitute': it was another un-sayable word, and our parents would go spare if they heard us use it. But surely it was the terrible thing that lurked in those messy details? Every adopted child I knew jumped to this conclusion.

I grew older, and the teenage fantasies faded; and my curiosity ebbed away as I embarked on an odyssey of boyfriends. They never asked, 'Where did you come from?' It didn't matter. I had had a sunny childhood and loving parents. I was embarking on a life which I would make for myself.

Nevertheless, at least I had had a grounding in the fog of ignorance, prejudice and embarrassment which surrounded the question, 'Where did you come from, baby dear?' And I also knew – through hints and the occasional remark – that there were some little footprints which had led to the court appearance, and which could possibly be retraced. Was this a comfort? Or a necessity? Or a tiny, threadlike lifeline to – to what? And what would it be like if there had been absolutely nothing? If you had been a foundling?

Let us begin with names. Your name in this country is what you are known by – give a cheer for dotty English law. Deed polls, certificates and documents, baptisms – all are secondary to people who know you calling you by a certain name. Tough if they all call you Fatty. However, if you don't like your name you can change it, as long as you get your family, mates, neighbours, colleagues and everyone else who delights in calling you something to use that name, and you have no intention to deceive or defraud. I wish more people realised this. Names are not immutable.

I've given up counting the number of people I've interviewed who, in response to the formal 'What is your name?' question, have looked rather distressed and replied sadly along the lines of, 'Well, I'm actually called Aloysius.'

'But we arranged this interview with me calling you Mike.'

'Yes, because that's what I call myself. My mother had a rather different take on life to me.'

'So what do you want to be called – when we put this on air?'

Again and again people hesitated, fearing that a failure to use their baptismal name would somehow be improper or even fraudulent.

I even had a colleague who went through life shuddering with dislike when he introduced himself as Norman. He didn't want to be a Norman. He didn't feel like a Norman. Come to think of it, he didn't look like a Norman. When the subject of change was broached, he said wistfully that he thought it a bit late – and anyway, that was the name he'd been given. I once interviewed a man who said his name should be Gerald, but the vicar had misheard and christened him Harold. He seriously thought it would be a sin to alter it.

But for innumerable other people, names are floating labels – much to the ire of those who believe we should all be classified and codified and identified immutably. Some change their own names on a whim, but have to be ready to explain to others that they are not arch-criminals running for cover or debtors fleeing creditors. More seriously, it's not surprising that there should be a desire for change when adults realise they can slough off something which has caused them misery and humiliation throughout their child-hood.

Apart from those burdened with 'Moon Tunes' or 'Peaches Features' by their (usually rich and loopy) parents, there are those saddled with family enthusiasms: when I worked in regional television, I once spent half an hour before an interview for a news programme trying to find out why a monosyllabic mum and dad had called their minute new-born by the surnames of the entire Plymouth Argyle football team.

'Like footie,' said the new father, while mother cradled the eleven-strong infant.

'Have you given him a Christian name?'

'Nope.'

'Is one of the names your favourite?'

'Nope.'

To mum (in desperation): 'What'll *you* call him?'

'Dunno. Don' like football.'

A very brief interview took place on the programme, the news editor cutting it short after I had read out the team for the third time.

Single or multiple, names convey a message, if only to evoke an era: my adoptive mother was Ethel Maud, and loathed them both, blaming some distant Victorian-era great-aunt and the Queen of Norway. On the other hand, the alternatives seemed to be relatives sporting names just as period in their own way: Nellie, Nessie, Dolly, Violet and Lily. And in Britain, of course, class rears its head at the font. As one of my friends once mournfully remarked: 'Have you ever heard of a Princess Doreen?'

Others make the change because of a need to fit in. Much of America owes its names to the desire of immigrants to identify with their new land, contrary to the folk-tale that they were given an approximation of their European name by immigration officers on New York's Ellis Island. All those Polish consonants and Russian patronymics were carefully noted on the paperwork by officials who were almost always conversant with the mother tongues (immigrants themselves some years earlier). It was when the new citizens began to prosper that they altered their names, sometimes for pure ease of pronunciation, sometimes to reflect the pride they felt in their new land.

Yet others have a name change thrust upon them. Religious outfits, governments, even employers all at times take arbitrary decisions to rename. A millennium ago, Saxons began to borrow Norman names in order to fit in with the regime which arrived with William the Conqueror. Centuries later, Huguenots fleeing persecution in France found the British welcoming but stubborn when it came to the French language, so the LeBlancs became the Whites. And in recent times, whole ethnic groups still find themselves bullied into taking on something 'more compatible' with a nation's image. Everywhere, illiterate folk find that poor pronunciation results in a new written identity. Married women lose a surname. Actors discover that on relinquishing a Fluck or Scroggins they cannot acquire their chosen stage-name if someone else treading the boards has bagged it already.

So your name is what you are known by. To do what you like with – as long as others know. It usually links you to the past – but not always. I think I may have the use of four surnames. Well, it balances the rather shocking moment in St Catherine's House when I discovered that I had no Christian name. In the Register of Adoptees, I finally found the entry, and written in the space were the words: 'No Name'. Standing bent over a heavy red volume surrounded by a weird swirl of people who couldn't possibly have been involved with sensitive discoveries about their past, and seemed more like a posse of ferrets chasing bail-jumpers and missing persons via the Official Registers, I had my first doubt.

Having been adopted, I was vaguely aware that names were a little arbitrary. For a start, my surname was obviously not the one I would have had had I not arrived as the result of a love affair instead of being born into wedlock, as it is quaintly known. Had I had a name and lost it? Maybe it was somehow removed, sliced away the moment adoption became an option. Perhaps bastards are nameless? Shakespeare has that wonderful stage direction, 'Enter a Bastard', and a long scene in which the matter of names and inheritance is argued, mostly in the light of Elizabethan England's view that the weight of shame from illegitimacy was dumped squarely on the child. And even though, courtesy of dramatic licence, the young man in question is knighted when he's acknowledged as looking rather like his dad – no less than King Richard Coeur de Lion – Shakespeare determinedly refers to him the whole way through the play as 'The Bastard'. Medieval bastardy is a complex subject, with Church Law and Common Law at odds with each other over the definition of marriage and wedlock, and a differentiation between bastards and illegitimate children. As usual, the English language is rich in terms: base-born, misbegotten, spurious, natural, imputed (father doesn't admit it), reputed (father does, or at least there's proof), filius populi (son of the people – but taken to mean an unidentified local man), filius nullius (son of a stranger – no one's son) and ignotus (unknown).

Clerics and lawyers fretted over people who insisted on producing children while they were betrothed, then later got married; also those who for some reason failed to get married, men who fathered children on married women, impregnations by a man of a woman who subsequently married someone else, and so on. The permutations of coupling confounded the Church and the courts. And because of the lack of hard evidence, it's possible that the recorded cases which reached the authorities may only have been the unusual ones or those with a significant problem attached. In other words, people got up to what was natural, and although levels of tolerance and disgrace yo-yoed up and down according to social and economic pressures, it was generally regarded as the result of frailty, rather than of outright sinfulness – until the Victorian era.

In Puritan times, in the 1600s, there was a great to-do over whether illegitimate children should be allowed to be baptised. Parish registers recorded the births – and often specified if they were foundlings. They fell into the same category as the 'offspring of unbelievers' and there were grumpy references to the 'child of a strumpet' and its dubious religious status. At least the German tradition was avoided, of recording such names upside-down or sideways in the register.

Inheritance was the knotty problem, with Dr Samuel Johnson acknowledging in the 1770s the need for female chastity: 'Consider of what importance the chastity of women is. Upon that all the property in the world depends. We hang a thief for stealing of sheep, but the unchastity of a woman transfers sheep, and farm, and all from the right owner.' Most of those arguments, however, were confined to the upper classes – the small proportion of the population who actually owned something to pass on to the next generation. Everyone else was relatively indifferent to titles and estates. Keeping the wolf from the door was much more important:

children were a burden on either the parents or the parish, and for many centuries the parish was none too keen on shouldering yet another infant.

So the main concern of the law – and the authorities generally – was perennial: who was going to pay for the upkeep of the child? In 1610, during the reign of James I, the law stated that 'Every lewd woman which shall have any bastard which may be chargeable to the parish, the justice of the peace may commit such women to the house of correction, to be punished and set to work, during the term of one whole year.' But if the father was prepared to support the child, no offence was deemed to have been committed. To this end, one of the tasks which officially befell midwives, mid-labour, was to worm out the father's name. But what name did the child take – and did it matter?

In Britain legitimate children tend to take their father's surname, a practice that first appeared somewhere in the twelfth century among the nobility. But it took time for the idea to catch on – almost five hundred years – and peasants in small villages were happy to acknowledge their identity through their job or appearance (hence the proliferation of Smiths and Redheads), or eventually their dwelling or place of work (giving us the people living near sheepfolds, the Shufflebottoms).

But in time it became common for bastards to take their mother's name: a letter from Earl James, writing from the Isle of Man in 1643, points out that 'It is very true, there be many bastards here in this Isle . . . but sure it would be very well if that law were here as in other places, that all known bastards be called after their mothers' names.' Manx law not only conferred fathers' names, but removed illegitimacy and the threat of disinheritance from some of those who were born out of wedlock: 'If a man get a young woman or maid with child, and, within two years after the birth of the child, marry her, that child, though born before the marriage, shall possess his father's estate, according to the custom of the Island, as amply as if that child had been born in wedlock.' This law stayed on the statute book until 1929.

The English parish registers are a patchy record of illegitimate children and foundlings: some never made it on to the registers, concealed from official view through shame or fear. Not surprising, when some entries had additions from clerks and clergy which expressed their views: base, lamebegot, scapegoat, byblow, merrybegot and chanceling. The mothers fared no better, being inscribed as harlots or fornicators. Father's names did appear sometimes, alongside the mothers', leading to the emergence of a number of double-barrelled surnames – not as posh as sometimes thought, then . . .

As society has become more literate, signatures and consistency have gained more importance, though it still puzzles some people that family names can vary so much. We had relatives called Fambely – or Farmbely, or Famelly, or Famebely, or . . . it's as if every generation had been dealt a limited set of Scrabble tiles and had come up with a different solution.

My own set of surnames gives me pause for thought. I'm known as Adie, my adoptive father Wilfrid's name. (Please note, not Wil*fred*; his father spent a lifetime trying to inculcate a teensy bit of Anglo-Saxon into people, to no avail. At least Wilfrid was spared a shortened version: Freds there may be, Frids there are not.) However, do I have a claim on – well, my mother's married name? Or perhaps I could revert to her maiden name, because no husband was involved? Should you have a claim on the father's name? After all, children appear to take their father's name when people are married; so can you lay claim to the father who's a father but not married to your mother? It was merely an intellectual curiosity. I wasn't bothered particularly, and I was never interested enough to dig into the legal details when I was older, merely accepting that names were tags that got attached for a variety of reasons, many of them to do with inheritance and some to do with 'respectability'. Anyway, I didn't mind Adie at all (even though letters still arrive with eleven variations on the spelling). I was at the top of the form register at school, which had a few disadvantages (always the first and most noticeable late-comer), but according to Penelope Wood, who lived at the other end of the register, being last was monstrous (especially in a posh but parsimonious school with not enough books to go round).

Not much use, though, if you start off as No Name.

Andy McNab is Andy McNab to the millions who have read his books and imagined that they too could join the Special Forces and command Bravo Two Zero, the patrol that went behind Iraqi lines in the first Gulf War. That's the name he's known by. There is another Andy McNab – a character in a Scots cartoon strip – whose name just happened to occur to the SAS sergeant when he needed a pseudonym under which to write his account of being captured and tortured by the Iraqis in 1991. And it's the fourth name he's had – though his first probably disappeared with the carrier bag in which he was found.

There's a family memory that it was a Harrods carrier bag – but you never know. However, it was left with Andy inside it in the Emergency Department of Guy's Hospital in central London. An ambulance crew is thought to have found it – and their collective names were showered upon the new-born: Peter, George, Fred, David or Roy – whatever – the story was never very sharp in anyone's memory. For a surname, the little scrap in the bag was called Body.

Andy himself knew nothing about his arrival at Guy's until he was sixteen years old – he'd also been unaware of his adoption, though, as his elder brother had been adopted, he was not particularly bothered when he was told. He'd been fostered, then adopted, by a south London couple who'd given him their surname, and he'd never asked about his status.

At sixteen, the certificate was handed over to him in the kitchen when he was about to join the army. His elder brother by eleven years had also served in the Royal Fusiliers, and there'd been a right fuss trying to get his papers organised – in the course of which their dad had found out that his *own* birth date was wrong. He was a year younger than he'd thought, and was mightily hacked off at having to work another year before retirement. Dad came from a Traveller family – caravans and greyhound-breeding and no shoes until he was seventeen. Mum was from Bermondsey, rag and bone trade, and originally from Ireland. They married very young and thought they couldn't have children, so adopted two boys before their own son finally appeared. Andy and the Harrods bag appeared in 1959 – round about 28 December – and thus he narrowly avoided being called Noel, deemed highly appropriate by hospital staff at Christmas.

Throughout his early adult life – as a young soldier in the Royal Green Jackets and then in 22 SAS Regiment – thoughts about his origins never crossed his mind. His childhood had been lively verging on delinquent, but he was streetwise and resourceful, having delivered coal, nicked handbags, mopped floors in Mc-Donald's and indulged in small-time burglary. Once in the army he was well blooded in action in Northern Ireland, where I inadvertently came across his handiwork. In the relentless stream of bombings, shootings, riots and incomprehensible hatred that was the daily menu for Belfast-based reporters, certain stories get lodged in the memory.

In the late seventies, waiting in the Catholic cathedral graveyard in Armagh as a funeral procession approached, I had taken up a strategically discreet position behind a large tomb. The mourners included a goodly number of people you wouldn't want an argument with: indeed, when a prayer-book was thrust into my hand by a warty-faced man filling the cathedral door I had not been reassured by my cameraman's hiss of 'Provo bomber'. Going to his final resting-place was an IRA double-murderer. The burial went a bit pear-shaped when an army helicopter decided to sit over the open grave and annoy everyone while the priest shouted his prayers. A swift movement with the rotors created a sudden down-draught, and the prayers and the priest disappeared into the deep, newly dug hole.

The entire episode had been prefaced by my finding the expired Provo in a cottage hospital over the border in the Republic, to which he and other members of the IRA had retreated after a major gun-fight with the British army in south Armagh. An extremely hostile nun at the hospital's front door had reacted to our polite enquiries about possible casualties by leaping at my cameraman and raking her nails down his face. Having reacted with due impartiality – why should nuns get away with violence? – I thumped her and hared off to inspect the hospital morgue, where I duly found a stone-cold terrorist. When I joined the BBC News Division, I had, it has to be admitted, no notion that 'pinning down the facts' involved GBH with nuns and blundering round morgues in the dark, searching for the obvious. Nor do you expect to meet the person who despatched the corpse which is lying in front of you. A decade later I interviewed him and learned that this was the first man killed by the then nineteen-year-old Lance-Corporal 'McNab'.

After Northern Ireland and several more postings he focussed on Selection – the gruelling tests for admission to the SAS. Life opened up for the lad from south London, where a good job had been considered to be 'getting on the print or the docks . . . or next level down an Underground driver or a panel-beater'. The SAS beckoned with travel, adventure, lots of crawling through mud, revolting insects, loud explosions, comradeship and hard encounters with people who may want to kill you. He persevered and thrived – and along the way managed three marriages which he fully admits didn't quite get his full attention.

The birth of his daughter gave him pause for thought: 'You know all that stuff – does your family have a heart condition and so on – I hadn't got a clue. So I wrote to Norcap [the National Organisation for Counselling Adoptees and Parents] and got their magazine – but then didn't really do anything about it.' Nevertheless, he had noticed the considerable number of young men who join the army 'in order to find a family'. 'When I became a training corporal in the Green Jackets for two years, I noticed guys turning up at the depot with just a carrier bag with soap and a toothbrush – and their stories – adopted, or from care homes . . .'

Years of adventure saw him all over the world and thoroughly immersed in the world of Special Forces, culminating in heading for the Middle East after Saddam Hussein invaded Kuwait in 1990. Afterwards, he thought about writing a book. The extraordinary saga of infiltration by the men of Bravo Two Zero into enemy territory in the Gulf War ensued: a blistering tale which delivers the realism of war and subsequent imprisonment and torture. While thousands fantasise about crawling around suburban undergrowth and leaping out to vanquish the dastardly foe while sustaining a scratch or two on the cheek, the genuine experience delivers something rather different: the bullets, the kicks and punches, the smell of fear and the churning gut which have to be endured if you want to live.

For someone who was nigh-illiterate at the age of nine and failed his basic English and maths test when he first tried to join the army, Sergeant McNab's description of events in the desert and Baghdad was an unexpected tour de force. *Bravo Two Zero* sold – and continues to sell – by the shed-load. More books followed when he left the SAS to take up full-time writing.

Only recently has he begun to look for his roots: talking to his daughter, who's now at college, he finally had the 'where we've come from' thought, and he's been to an American university which specialises in DNA testing. To his complete fascination, they've already told him that in among the standard markers of Indo-European heritage is a strand of Native American Indian: 'Wild Bill's come to town,' he says joyfully, and roars with laughter. He feels little desire to discover his birth parents: 'I've got the ones I've got – they did all the nappy-changing and the rest of it, and they're fine. They're all I've known.'

There's no self-doubt or regret. He radiates an easy confidence and doesn't carry the past with him – except as recollections of a tough environment, but one which eventually shaped him to come through a huge adventure relatively unscathed. He's a diligent writer, with novels flowing on a yearly basis, and comfortably anonymous still under that fourth name. The curiosity about his roots manifests itself as an interesting sideline in what is clearly a very sorted life. 'I like to think the reasons why I was left was the 1950s' "shock-horror – an illegitimate child" – at least I wasn't put in a skip! I was left at a hospital. How *lucky* I was picked and adopted – I might have been shipped off to a Catholic school in South Africa or wherever. But here I am, and I feel lucky.'

2

What is your mother's name?

The foundling's reply: 'If only I knew.' Usually the official question is: What is your father's name? Women traditionally change their name on marriage, and bureaucracy is much more interested in the male line, with visa applications for Middle East countries demanding your grandfather's name as well. Discussions on genealogy involve a zigzag course in the hunt for female ancestors. The man has a family tree with his name in every branch; women join those trees like Christmas ornaments, having lost their origin on the marriage certificate.

But foundlings aren't so interested in the maiden name: it's any name. Their mothers may have used their maiden name, if they were married and attempting to conceal the birth through a ruse which could be described as mildly economical with the truth. A single mother might use a false name. But most foundlings' mothers are only recorded as a blank or 'No Name'. A running theme in foundlings' lives is the possibility, however remote, of that day when someone surely familiar will walk through the door. Some dream of it, a few fantasise about it, some have already formulated what they'll say when she comes in . . . and others are wary of the whole business.

Most adults who were adopted learn to rationalise their feelings and adjust to reality, calling the woman who brought them up 'Mum'. With luck, there will have been love and protection, interest and pride – all that a child craves. Even if the experience was none too happy, there is still an understanding that a relationship exists. And if, to outsiders, it's odd that someone can talk about 'Mum' and 'my mum' and it's not at all clear whether they're referring to their adoptive or birth mother, that's just what it is: an oddity to outsiders. In their own minds there is no confusion. Two people have had a role, and the attitude to both involves deep emotions but different thoughts.

For children who have no mother figure at all, the consequences last a lifetime. To have a flock of bright-eyed little children running towards you to cling to your legs, all repeating the same word over and over – 'Mummy, Mummy', in whatever language they speak – as happened when I went to see Russian orphanages, is a moment of very mixed feelings. They love the idea that someone might respond to them. There is in each one some innate spark which will ignite into a flame of affection if only the right person can be found. You hug them and wonder how anyone could have abandoned them. Yet the institutional staff are relatively unmoved: as they said with a shrug, but not unkindly, 'They call everyone who comes here "Mother".'

That children should be shunted into institutions rather than placed in a family seems insensitive to the highest degree; then again, poverty, a faith in the state or in a religious body have all given rise to huge buildings and systems into which the abandoned have been placed, often with the added inference that they'll be *morally* better off there, since they have either been conceived in unsuitable circumstances or are bereft of a 'responsible' parent. And down the centuries in such institutions, after that first moment of compassion when the foundling is scooped up, there has been a finger of accusation waved at the growing child that he or she will have to be extra-careful not to stray into bad ways – with the whisper of 'old sins cast long shadows' and 'bad blood will out'.

These days, large residential homes are not in favour, at least in the UK. Religious bodies no longer automatically assume that they will take care of those with no home, and the mammoth institutions run by the Catholic Church throughout Europe and further afield have diminished; they were run, it might be noted, by those who had forsworn parenthood. Added to this, in recent years the standing of the Catholic Church has crumbled in the face of constant and widely documented cases of child abuse.

Those organisations such as Dr Barnardo's which tried to

produce a semblance of family life, often with a 'house mother', have had to implement drastic reform in the last few decades. Other societies and Homes have retreated, leaving the state to manage the problem. The state does what it can, and finds that in a society where women have the right to contraception and abortion there is only a tiny number of new-born healthy babies available for adoption. The state is left to cope with the handicapped, the socially disruptive and the mixed-race children who end up in care, though there are determined efforts to have these children taken out of Homes and placed in welcoming foster-families.

So today there's an emphasis in social work on keeping a family together, if at all possible. Therefore a reunion of a foundling with his or her mother is surely the most desirable event?

'My image of Mum was someone lovely and loving and warm and kind. And I got quite a shock.' It's a warm day and we're sitting in Fatima Whitbread's garden, an impressively manicured lawn that seems to go on for ever, edged with a riot of shrubs and trees – 'I designed all that,' she says. A boisterous six-year-old whacks a football again and again in professional style, as befits the son of an Olympic athlete.

Fatima has given hundreds of interviews in her role as a champion javelin thrower, but she also talks about her personal history with considerable concentration, using some of the vocabulary of those who've had to 'work through' their difficulties. That's not surprising when you hear her story.

'There are lots of first memories, but the one which stands out is, when I was a youngster, about two, I can remember being in a couple's arms, being passed from one to another. And I later learned that I was being viewed for adoption or fostering. But it didn't work out.

'I was abandoned in a flat in Islington in the spring. I don't know the date. Some would say, "That baby was left to die." I was wrapped up in sheets and left in a cot, and a neighbour heard it crying for two days or so and saw no one coming or going to the flat. So she called the police and they came and broke the door down and rescued the baby. It was taken to hospital and then made a ward of court.'

Fatima has dropped into talking about herself in the third person – it's easier for her, when looking at the past.

'I was hungry and had nappy rash. In fact I was a case of malnutrition, so spent several weeks in hospital. I don't think anyone could say my age – a few weeks – a few months? Anyway, I was found on 3 March 1961 and that's now my birthday. All I know in retrospect is that the biological mother was perhaps under extreme stress and strain – maybe it was too much for her, she couldn't cope, just left the baby, hoping the problem would disappear.

'After the police sorted things out they took me to a nursery in Hertfordshire, an old house with about twenty-five other kids. And then I went to a Home in Harpenden until I was five. I was OK – as OK goes. When you've got lots of kids in one place, they're on their own, parents come and go and there are a lot of emotional disturbances. It was very stressful for me: often I would ask, "Where's Mum? Where's Dad?" No one gave me any answers to that. Suddenly, when I was five, I was told to be ready and waiting in the foyer – because my mother was coming to take me to a new Children's Home!

'I sat there waiting for about an hour, and it was awful when I actually saw her. I'd been desperate to be loved and have My Mum, as all children do, and also I wanted to know why she hadn't made herself known to me earlier. In the hallway I watched the other children queue for the bathroom – because it was about six in the morning. About two dozen of them with the usual temper tantrums and arguments. And I sat there, having been told I was leaving. I didn't have much with me, for we had communal clothing, so I was wearing a little dress salvaged by one of the "aunties" and that was about all I had.'

The 'mum' who arrived was nothing like the image of a warm, loving person that she had dreamed up.

Five-year-old Fatima was about to be introduced to people who were the very opposite to her fairy-tale dream of a family.

Considering her foundling status, she had every reason to think that a magical transformation was about to happen. Even adult foundlings dream of this moment: the years have gone by, and suddenly there's a mum coming to see you. 'My image of Mum, as I sat there, was someone warm and loving and kind. And I got quite a shock.'

Through the glass door, Fatima spotted the matron bringing someone in. 'She was a rather large lady and she had very strong perfume on and she had a gold tooth in the front and was foreign-speaking. And she didn't show any emotion at all. She acted as if it was all a bit of a nuisance that she'd come to collect me. The Social Services had told her it was the right thing to do. She didn't talk to me – she just stood in the foyer and talked to the matron. Then the matron introduced me and I burst into tears. I was leaving the only home I'd known. It was horrendous. I was told I was going to join my sister and brother. I didn't know I had any. I later learned that they were my half-siblings, and for some time they'd actually lived in the same home as me – and I hadn't known them!'

Acquiring a mum who hadn't existed hitherto (except, it seems, to the police who investigated Fatima's abandonment), along with two siblings who also appeared to be in care, was overwhelming for a five-year-old who was briskly popped into the front of a car with a social worker, while this strange new 'birth mother' person clambered into the back, for the trip to another Children's Home.

'The Social Services took us to Essex. Through all the journey not a word was spoken. But at the end of the trip the childcare officer said, "You'll be fine – you'll enjoy this Home. It's a little bit smaller, but you'll be with your brother and sister."'

'Interesting. Interesting,' says Fatima, clearly not using the words which express her real feelings. When talking of the Turkish Cypriot woman who abandoned her in the Islington flat as a baby, she says 'she' and 'her' with a very deliberate emphasis and avoids saying 'my mother'. It's plain that she's been over this day many times and the dreadful feelings have been dealt with, up to a point.

'I went into the new Home, feeling very disappointed to have had to leave all my friends. And "she" came in too. The House-mother, "Aunt Elizabeth", introduced herself and we sat in a small TV room and then they brought in the other two. It must have been something of an ordeal for them as well. They spoke Turkish Cypriot very well and they ran in and had kisses and cuddles from their [real] mum. My whole perception of that left me feeling rather empty – an outsider. We were asked to go into the garden where there were a few other children. I stood looking and watching and the next minute the mother – the biological mother – came out and she grabbed me by the throat and said, "*You.*" "*You,*" she said in her broken English, "You look after your sister and brother, otherwise *I. . . .*"' Fatima draws a finger across her throat and makes the noise we all associate with cutting it.

'And that was it. My introduction to having a new start in a new Home, with a new brother and sister who communicated with each other in Turkish – *and* had cuddles from their mother. And there was nothing for *me*.

'I never really had a relationship with them. Anyway, they left soon after and went to live with their mother. This was a few weeks later – she came to take them and said that I was supposed to be going with them. When we got down the road she reached into her bag and gave me half-a-crown and whacked me on the shoulder and said: "Take this, fuck off, we don't love you, you're not part of the family. We don't want you, you go back."

'I was quite relieved!' Fatima breaks into gales of laughter. 'I got half-a-crown for it. But it was . . . quite an experience. I cried all the way back and when I got to the Home they asked: "What are you crying for – c'mon, get out into the garden and play with the others."

'When I was eleven I was told that I had to go back to my biological mother. It was very much against my will. The police had tracked her down after I was abandoned, but she'd had several children – there were five of us in the end – and looking back, the father was a Greek Cypriot and she was Turkish Cypriot, and there was a lot of tension at the time between the two communities . . . so . . .

'The birth certificate names me as Fatima Vedad – it had the biological father's name on it as well . . . they later found out he was her half-brother. . . . But at least the date was right – 3 March, 1961.

'Going back wasn't a pleasant experience at all. When I went, it was one of the most disturbing experiences I've ever had. My mother's lover was in the flat where we all stayed, and I had to try and get away from him all the first evening. It was horrendous. There were no locks on the door. Only one room in the flat had a lock. And my half-brother, who was also there with his girlfriend – and a lot older than me – said, "Try to lock yourself in that room – or hide behind the sofa," . . . but . . . .'

Social Services did nothing after she was raped. 'I became more difficult to handle at school. I was constantly in trouble.'

But one small lucky moment also happened that year. She watched the Olympics on television and saw Mary Peters. 'She was my heroine. So I decided to concentrate on sport, because I had no support in the Children's Home for anything else. I became a "lovable rogue" at school, playing football with the boys and so on. And I got lucky at the Home. We had a Mrs Peat – a "thirty-hour lady", one of our aunties – they come in during the daytime, helping with cleaning and cooking and washing and so on. She taught me "In giving, you receive", so she taught me to look after the other kids and she was also very kind to me. I used to wait in bed in the morning for her to come and wake me up – with a little tickle. She meant a lot to me.

'Sport is a level playing-field for everyone, isn't it? You *can* shine and achieve. At eleven I was playing netball and Mrs Whitbread was one of the PE mistresses. In a close game with another school, I was giving my team all the "support" I could and the whistle went and she said: "Any more cheek from you, young lady, any more noise, and you're off." So I gave her some verbal abuse back and one of my team-mates said, "Oh, Fats, Mrs Whitbread's quite strict – she *will* send you off" – and I just carried on. About a month later, I'd decided I wanted to do Track and Field Events: I'd been at the local track a couple of times and I saw this very handsome young man, David Otley. Though I didn't know this at the time, he was the British record holder in the javelin. I wandered over to him and said, "Hello." Then, cheekily, "I'd like to throw the javelin." He said I'd have to wait for the coach to come – she wasn't here yet. So I sat and waited impatiently in the stands and this Mini pulls up into the car-park and this little person comes across – and suddenly, I saw it was the same lady I'd been told off by on the netball court. So when someone at the track said, "This girl wants to throw the javelin," she replied, "I know who Fatima is . . . and if you want to throw, there'll be no more of that cheek."

'And I promised I'd be good. And that was the start.'

For the first few months, having asked her to 'get Mum and Dad to come up for a talk, because you've got quite a bit of talent and we'd like you to get a javelin and some boots' and got no response, Mrs Whitbread thought that Fatima was ignoring her. Eventually a colleague told her that her protégée was from the Children's Home. The following week Mrs Whitbread said, 'Would you like these boots and javelin? One of the girls has retired.' The boots were two sizes too big, but when they were stuffed with paper they were 'fantastic'.

All through this story Fatima has never said 'Mrs Whitbread' – she's automatically said 'my mother'.

She took the javelin back to the Home and was so excited that she decided to show it to a German student who was helping there. 'There was this vegetable patch at the end of the garden – hmm . . . a couple of little throws to get that . . . and then I turned round and gave it a really big throw – and smashed the French windows! So I got banned from going out for a month – and Mrs Whitbread thought I'd chucked up the sport. I wrote to her and explained, and said that I wanted to be the best javelin thrower in the world. Not long after, I started back at the track and she asked me if I would like to come and meet her family. She had little two boys – one four, one eighteen months – and because I'd cared for the younger ones in the Home, the boys took to me at once and it was very nice. And I visited, and I stayed – on and off – and then Mrs Whitbread said, "Would you like to come and live with the family?" "Oh *yes*," I said.

'I began calling her Mum almost straight away. I'd always wanted a mum, although for her it was probably a strange period at first . . . .

'I was fourteen and we had to wait for a while before I could be adopted. They didn't consider I was old enough to give my consent, and also my biological mother fought against it – though she wasn't fit to be called my mother. So it was all very difficult. I was fostered first, and during that period I had calls from my half-brother, verbal abuse: "They're not your family, you're *our* blood." Then there were visits from him, threats, he followed me – it was very disturbing. And then I was adopted, and it stopped.'

And that was it from the family from hell – until she began to make a name for herself in the athletics world. The phone calls started up again. When she really hit the big time, a journalist on a Murdoch newspaper acquired one of her own photographs and headed off to see her birth mother, saying, 'This is your daughter. How about we do a nice little article?' The spectre of her none-too-loving relatives rose again in lurid headlines. 'I felt a bit let down,' she says, with a nice line in understatement about the tabloid press. Then she laughs: 'We all have our problems, don't we? Even in loving families things can go wrong.'

She says she's found out a lot about her own personality as she's grown up and especially now that she's started a family, emphasising time and again the need for love and cuddles and stability. 'I was very nervous about taking on the responsibility. It was very daunting – although my mum says I do a good job!'

She also feels that you are tested as you face more challenges and go up the ladder of success. 'Maybe I had more stumbling-blocks – but perhaps they were stepping-stones. Being a foundling made me more determined to succeed. Sport has been my saviour over the years – and my family is everything. Life is what you make it – but it's also a series of coincidences . . . .'

As we're talking, Mrs Whitbread bustles out from the house and offers to get us both a sandwich for lunch. 'Thanks, Mum,' says Fatima.

3

When were you born?

As a very junior technical assistant in local radio in Durham in the late sixties, I was constantly being imbued with the spirit and ethos of the BBC. The important bits – such as truth, accuracy and decency – were never actually written down; you were meant to absorb them by a kind of osmosis. The rest were to be found in what was known as the Blue Book: in true BBC fashion, it was actually yellow – a large ring-folder with pages of Do's and Don'ts, compiled as a result of on-air disasters and faux pas. It covered everything from how to address a bishop correctly to what to do in the event of fire in the studio: 'Do not broadcast this fact.' The name of the actual organisation we worked for was also dealt with: 'The preferred term is The BBC' – presumably arising from a historic moment on the original Home Service, when a programme was introduced from the British Broadcorping Castration. There were also a number of admonitions in the matter of music: 'Take care over musical introductions, such as Bach's Organ Works.' (Lucky old Bach . . .) 'Listeners' requests are sincerely intended: respect their choice and do not comment'; this caused some guilt on the part of the young staff in local radio who'd had difficulty understanding the general public's affection for Vera Lynn and George Formby. Royalty was to be treated as – well, not at all: no one in the BBC in London trusted anyone in local radio to behave properly should Something Befall a Royal. We were instructed to 'join the network' rather than attempt a local angle – 'the Princess, who's never actually been to Durham . . . .'

The strongest advice was reserved for certain programme ideas which were deemed to deceive or mislead the public: UFOs caused the BBC a lot of bother. The local radio audience liked Unidentified

Flying Objects. They were always sighting them and ringing the radio station to deliver awe-filled reports about huge cigar-shaped glowing thingies floating over the town hall. Or twinkly lights hanging around misty woodland at midnight. The radio station I worked on in Bristol had a particularly keen bunch of spotters who were evidently convinced that someone out there had a message for us: every so often the news editor would despatch an unwilling reporter to spend a chilly night with a lot of fish-eyed people in bobble hats who gathered on a bleak hilltop in Wiltshire to dangle tinkly equipment somewhere in the direction of Mars. Any reporter who suggested that the army also spent chilly nights practising low-level helicopter flying and occasionally got up to odd things on firing ranges was met with outrage. We were judged a highly insensitive and unsympathetic radio station.

Local television came off worse. At least a radio reporter could record the sound of thermos flasks being unscrewed and weird little metal tripods being erected to receive important communications. TV cameramen are a breed unimpressed with spending Saturday evening on a bald hillside being scolded by the bobble hats if they put a camera light on: 'It will send the WRONG SIGNAL to THEM.' And when they reach the cutting room the next day and – unsurprised – view half an hour of tape which is entirely devoid of lights, twinkly, glowing or otherwise, they have to prepare themselves for major complaints from Enthusiasts for Aliens that their equipment is not sensitive enough for inter-galactic activity.

However, the Blue Book always insisted that we treat people politely: a considerable test of BBC character when faced with several score calls on the subject of a 'mysterious man with pink eyes and in a silver suit at teatime on the Winchester by-pass, who caused my car to lose control and I came over all funny'. Our viewer was adamant about her facts when interviewed on the regional news programme, and expanded into the realm of inter-planetary travel, only to be treated with just a touch of scepticism by the presenter. The switchboard lit up in a way that it never did when we broadcast stories about politics, education, health, transport – oh, everything else. I fielded a number of calls, but began to lose it when a well-spoken lady from Bognor Regis chided me – and all my colleagues – for not being a Believer. I thought better of getting too deep into religion or philosophy, but the caller was determined that I should agree to visit Bognor with a film crew on a Wednesday afternoon – any Wednesday. I ventured to ask why.

'Because that's when I get my proof,' came the reply.

'Er, who from?'

'Well, the Angel Gabriel, of course. He just loves Bognor Regis Promenade.'

UFOs and allied things that go bump in the night were only just tolerated by the Blue Book. Astrology was not. A grim fate (clearly not foreseen in the stars) awaited anyone with the temerity to rabbit on to our listeners about Jupiter in Sagittarius giving you a better love life or an opportunity for travel. It never crossed anyone's mind that the sort of columns that appeared in the cheaper women's magazines at the time would ever have a place on air. Times have changed. However, today I'm still brought up rather sharply when, having just met someone, they determinedly squeak, 'Star sign?' That broadcasting is now littered with people dispensing anodyne generalisations which mainly act as gentle encouragement or common sense caution, but are based on picky bits of astronomy and a midwife's timing, still seems rather odd to me. It's even more curious when you realise many people haven't a clue about the precise time they were born (labour is remembered by most mothers not for the minute and second of arrival but for the time it took to get there).

So all those charts and calculations based on the exact position of some distant planet while you're in the Delivery Room would seem to be slightly iffy. And never mind the forgotten minute and the hour – what if you don't know the day? Does it matter that you don't have a birth-day? A birthday? What about the cake and presents and cards and balloons? What if it's the wrong day? Think of the mortified apologies which have to be made when someone says: 'Actually, it was yesterday.'

Never mind the officials who care passionately that you shouldn't squeeze your child into school until a precise birthday has been passed. Never mind the rites of passage which seem to have such symbolic weight, even though we increasingly never feel a year older. . . . The day matters to officialdom; think of the number of times it's now demanded: you don't give your age any more – far too imprecise; it's the d.o.b.

Most people rarely give a thought to its accuracy. Surely your parents don't get it wrong? Well, maybe they're just a bit vague at times. As you grow older, you hear from friends who have been to merry celebrations of their parents' silver wedding anniversaries, only to have a nagging thought somewhere after the second glass of champagne that their twenty-fifth birthday is only three months away . . . .

But what if your parents are not so sure – the people who brought you up, that is, whom you regard as parents? What if you suspect they just plucked a date out of the air, or based it on a vague estimate made by those who found you? Is it an annual puzzle? And if so, is it one that matters?

'I had my second birthday two days after I got to Barnstaple – but I've no idea if it was the right day.'

Lady Cottesloe is thinking back nearly eighty years, while her Jack Russell Tom Tom scrabbles up the sofa, coming to rest neatly round her shoulders. He's a sleek, intelligent animal as befits one belonging to the author of the official history of the Battersea Dogs' Home. A torrent of memory pours from the widow of John Cottesloe, whose name graces one of the stages at the National Theatre. Gloria Cottesloe is energetic and perpetually busy, living in an elegant house crammed with intriguing memorabilia, and she thrusts on me the newly printed pamphlets about her latest venture, a charity to help children orphaned by Aids in Africa.

Shortly before that 'birthday' Gloria was in a hotel in Kensington, the result of bizarre goings-on which would give today's social workers a fit.

'The first thing I remember was looking out of a window, the top window of a big house, and I'm told it was the hotel to which my adoptive parents came. All I know is that I had been brought into the headquarters of the National Adoption Society in Ladbroke Grove in Kensington and left there by two women who then hurried away. What they said, what the circumstances were, I have no idea at all. But moments after they had rushed in and out, my adoptive parents came up the steps – and they saw these two women going away. They came into the Adoption Society and said to the woman behind the counter, "We want to adopt a baby boy." And she replied: "We've got measles in our Home, so we've no children available at the moment. The only one we have is this child who's just been brought in by those two women you may have seen." And there I was, aged two, sitting there. Imagine – a two-year-old, nobody looking after me or doing anything as far as I know. And without any references, without anything at all, my parents took me off that very minute. There were no formalities at all. My mother told me this on her death-bed. She wouldn't talk about it before, but she poured it all out when I said I had to know a little bit more.

'I think it colours my whole attitude. Although I give the impression of being self-contained and poised and so on I'm quite shaky inside, and I've always been terrified of being let down – and of abandonment.

'My adoptive parents were in their early fifties and originally from Staffordshire – and I think it was all a whim. They'd never thought it through. My mother was inclined to have impulses. She'd probably read an article somewhere, and they'd come up to London, and they got me and took me off down to Barnstaple.

'My father had two or three shops and a lending library and a bookshop – a kind of mini-Harrods but room-size – and everything he sold was in very good taste. He used to get Czechoslovakian glass and things like that. What is so good is that he had a tremendous love of books, which was the right home for me, for I could read before I was three . . . .

'They sent me off to nursery school at two and a half, because my mother said she didn't really know anybody with small children – and it was good for me to meet other children. I went to this dame school in Barnstaple run by Mrs Lyell. She was absolutely amazing

– she had about thirty children aged from two to seven, and we all learnt the catechism every day, and to read and to count with shells. Later I went to Barnstaple Grammar School, where there were two Miss Curries – Plymouth Brethren, very tall and straight with hair in a neat bun. Then I went into the big school and after a year got ungulant fever, with TB glands in my neck and chest. It's a form of brucellosis called Malta fever, and there were hardly any known cases in this country, so I was lucky to survive. I was away from school for about a year and listening to the radio and reading the papers – it was the Munich crisis, all about Neville Chamberlain. Funnily enough, I know his granddaughter now . . . .'

Gloria pauses for a moment. Her childhood is keenly remembered, right back to that first moment in the hotel in Kensington in 1929. It was just a couple of years after the Adoption Act had come into force and procedures were still – well, flexible. No one had enquired after the sort of household that Gloria was taken to.

'The atmosphere at home was of intimidation, rather than affection. My mother was a very dominant character, my father a very gentle and loving man, but completely under her thumb. But I loved her, although she was a very difficult woman. Was she glad she'd got me? Let's say, she would have been sad if she hadn't. She told me nothing about my origins at all. She had various *stories* – I listened to her telling people various stories. She once told me that she was looking after me for a civil engineer and his wife who'd gone to India to build bridges – in Bombay. The only place she knew in India was Bombay. And she actually used to send me Christmas presents from them for the first two or three years, and then they conveniently "died". But I also heard her telling someone that she was looking after me for Lady Mary Teck – who eventually became the Duchess of Beaufort (whom I later knew very well, because I ghosted her husband's book on fox-hunting. But I never told her that – she would have been absolutely horrified!). My mother had this sort of false grandeur. She had to make someone rather special out of me, so I had to do all the extras. I had to learn to ride – but I mustn't tell anybody, so I had to take the bus to Croyde so the locals wouldn't know. I can't understand it. Then I had to learn to dance, and had to dance better than anyone else, and I remember going to summer school and dancing with Beryl Grey, who was a year younger than me and a very nice child too.'

Although Gloria acquired all the accomplishments, there's no doubt that even the fledgling Adoption Society might have had something to say about the several tales which her mother broadcast about how she came to live in Barnstaple. Nor was she adopted for many years. Nor did she have their surname. One of the odder aspects of her arrival at the Adoption Society was that her full name somehow came with her – Gloria Jean Irene Dunne – and that was how she was known.

'You see, I kept my name – they never called me by *their* name and I never called them Mother and Father. I always called them Uncle and Aunt – Cunkie and Nantie. They did eventually formally adopt me, but this bigoted old solicitor said to them, "Bad blood will out" and he probably persuaded them not to give me their name.

'After the illness, the fever – it did something to my brain and I was never as bright and quick afterwards. Back at school, the war had just begun and now we were full of evacuees. I was absolutely swamped, so my parents took me away and sent me to a private school which had been brought down from Hendon in London. We had prayers in the morning and a lot of girls went out of assembly and I followed them, to find out they were Jewish: I'd never met anyone Jewish before. That school folded after a year and I went to another little dame school. It was academically hopeless, and there were only twenty-seven senior boarders, but Joan Collins was there, an evacuee from Ilfracombe – so her age is really true, it's what she says it is, because I have a school photograph with her in it.

'At the end of the war my parents were not prepared to send me away to university, because it would mean more money, so I did secretarial training with journalism at Stanway House in Gloucestershire. And that house had an enormous effect on me – it was such a beautiful place – it gave me that feeling for grandeur . . . .

35

'I wanted to become a journalist and a woman came to talk to us to say how difficult it was and that we should join a local paper. But not me. I came up to London and went on *Vogue* – as a dogsbody, which I hated, wrapping parcels and writing envelopes for the managing director's Christmas cards. And I knew I was Little Miss Nobody from Nowhere and I would never get anywhere. Strangely enough, my daughter worked at *Vogue* forty years later and became Fashion Editor without telling anyone what her origins were, so she did it – she was obviously much better stuff than me!

'Anyway, I left and went to work for an ophthalmic surgeon, having met his wife at the City Lit where we learned to write short stories. But he chased me round the table so I left rather abruptly and went into publishing. I had a series of jobs: I answered readers' letters at *Popular Gardening*, though I'd only ever planted bulbs as a child, and so on. Then the surgeon's wife asked me what my politics were, and I said, "I suppose I'm a lukewarm Tory." I wanted to get to know people in London, so she invited me to a canvassers' meeting. I went along with friends and listened to this very nice man talking about the London County Council – and this was my husband. We actually did fall in love across the room – because I became a Young Conservative, which is quite out of character. He started haunting YC do's.

'I met him in 1946 and we finally married in 1959 – he'd always said he was too old for me, but in the end I was thirty and the time had come to do something with my life. I intended to go off to Canada and I lined up a job out there with a literary agent. I'd got my ticket and John, who didn't really believe I was going, said, "Let me see your ticket." Then I knew that he believed it, for he said, "Ohhh, yes . . .", for I'd put on the ticket "Miss Gloria Dunne and Cat". The next night he said, "You're not going to Canada, you know."

'I said, "Are you trying to propose to me?"

' "That's what I'm trying to do," he said – and he did it in the Travellers' Club, so I wouldn't make a fuss. But the gilt was taken off a little bit when I found out he'd proposed to his first wife there too!

'We had a very happy marriage. He said, "One dog, one cat, no birds, no children" – he'd already got two children. So I gave away my two free-flying budgerigars because he was frightened his pictures might get pecked! But nine weeks after we were married my cat had kittens and my dog had puppies, and eventually we had three children.'

Her story is told with gales of laughter and sharp observations and all kinds of gathered memories: journalism on *Country Life* and the *Field*, among others; several books, lots of interests and three children – a son who's a racing correspondent on a national newspaper, a daughter who writes, having been on *Vogue*, and a younger daughter who travelled in Africa and married an African tribesman. 'Not quite what we had in mind' – she laughs uproariously – 'but he was lovely, enchanting, a very good batik artist. But sadly, after two little girls, he died of Aids. So I started this charity, Visions of Glory, to provide education for Aids orphans.'

Her own origins were much of a mystery until her mother talked to her at the end of her life. However, when she was twenty-one a friend who was a medical student suggested that she had to find out more. So she got her birth certificate from Somerset House.

'The certificate set it out as: mother – Constance Mary Dunne; father – blank, and that was all. Presumably those two women must have taken some sort of document to the Society, because it was known that my name was Gloria Jean Irene Dunne, but as far as I know my parents never had a birth certificate. And because it was in 1929 and everyone was terribly uptight about illegitimacy and adoption, anyone who was adopted was ipso facto illegitimate in those days. I think I was frightened of knowing anything more, frightened of what I'd find. I could have gone back to where I was born, in the workhouse in Vicarage Road in Watford. It didn't say "workhouse" on the birth certificate, but I threw it away anyway – I didn't want it any longer. I got the shortened form for use later. I was just frightened of what I'd find.

'The fear that must have been around it all – and the impossibility of bringing up a child . . . how that woman managed to bring me up until I was two . . . there was nobody to help. I've never hidden it from anybody, always kept it out in the open, because there was so much secrecy when I was a child, so many lies told. It's always easier to tell people than to hide it. My husband was never interested, never really wanted to know – and we never really talked about it. Remember, I married a man old enough to be my father – I was always looking for a father and he also had, deep down, a lot of those prejudices.

'It's one of the things that is *there*. I take it out and look at it, but as I get older – I'm seventy-seven – I can't really waste the time. But it does mean that I understand other people . . . and I've always been an opportunist – a terrible word – but I'm always ready to seize anything that comes along.

'I didn't talk when I turned up at the Adoption Society offices; I could only say Cunkie and Nantie. But when I eventually talked, I talked perfectly and in a completely different accent to my parents who spoke with a Staffordshire accent. How about that? All the speech was in there, and it was probably trauma . . . and I also remember that I was terribly cunning. When I was taken back to Barnstaple and I was left alone for a moment, I peed on the floor. And when they came back there was this terrible wet patch on the floor, and I pointed away from it and to some pictures and tried to speak. You see, I knew what was wrong, but I was cunning: I had learned to survive.'

Tom Tom careers around the room and Gloria hunts for more literature on her charity project.

4

Where were you born?

Having been less than truthful about my place of birth for the whole of my life, for relatively trivial reasons, it's curious to know why place of birth matters so much. Perhaps initially because the only right accorded the child, illegitimate or not, under the United Nations International Covenant on Civil and Political Rights is the right to acquire a nationality. Not an entirely simple matter, when you consider the complications of borders, ships and aircraft. There are volumes of legal advice on how these apply in different nations, but even then there are arguments as to exactly how you become a little citizen waving a particular flag: the nationality of the mother, of the father, the place where she gives birth, the status of that land, the place of registration.

A group of elderly farmers in the mountainous border territory between Turkey and Georgia were highly suspicious when I was filming in the area and wanted to know if they were Turkish or Georgian. Their eyes began to resemble those in their flock: that round, blank sheep's eye which gives nothing away (though in the case of sheep, because there's nothing much there). 'Why do you want to know?' they asked.

I was curious about their allegiance. They ran their flocks over a vast area which appeared, even though it was a NATO border between the West and the then Soviet Union, to be bereft of a meaningful line or fence or frontier. A bleak place fought over by just about every warlord and invader for many centuries. They weren't at all keen to talk about it and eventually replied to the question about nationality with the word: 'Depends.' It seemed to depend on who was asking, why and with what intention, for most of them had swapped nationality officially at least three times in their lives, depending on the political claims to the area. There were times in their lives when it wasn't at all wise to be frank: nationality can be a dangerous right. One thought he'd been born Russian but with Turkish parents. Another insisted he'd been born Turkish but had unwillingly acquired citizenship of the Soviet Union for some years of his life. A third said he didn't recognise such a thing, because his parents were Georgians. Yet another took little interest in the proceedings, and the rest said, 'Oh, he's a Kurd.' They were all born in the same village.

Follow any stream of refugees, frightened people often heading for a place called safety rather than a named promised land, and you will meet pregnant women who are doubly worried. Will the end of the journey be a good place to bring a child into the world? And will it mean the child is cut off from its roots?

In the war in the Balkans in the early 1990s, the issue of ethnic identity was paramount. Yet the actual ethnicity of the Serbs, Croats and Bosnian Muslims was pretty well identical, especially compared to the maelstrom of DNA shared by British TV crews with Scots, Welsh, Irish and English ingredients.

Does where you were born define you? There are Yorkshiremen who would go to the stake rather than say No. On the other hand, there are millions born in anonymous suburbs from where their parents took off for pastures new well before the child became aware of its environment. The notion of roots goes deep – however, roots are not always defined by where you first appeared and may well depend on where you feel you have flourished. Perhaps information about where you were born is most useful to those who are trying to verify your identity. Someone must remember a baby arriving here? Neighbours, the postman, the milkman, the local vicar, the midwife? Then there's the paperwork: registration of births is one of the older bureaucratic habits, with religions keen to add souls to their flocks as soon as possible.

For most foundlings, the place is another unknown. They may only be aware of the place where they were discovered, which seems to be of passing relevance: apparently a strong clue in the search for more information about their parentage, but in reality more often a random choice by someone desperate. Nearly all foundlings go back to the spot, once they have learned where they were left. And having seen it, there are sometimes questions to be asked of the older folks who live nearby to see if there are more traces to be found. If the building is gone, or the geography of the streets has changed, foundlings can experience genuine disappointment at not being able to walk to the place and think how it might have looked when their mother came there. However, many of the locations don't yield any clues – maybe they were chosen for that very reason.

'I was found in a paper bag in the back of a London cab. It was parked in William IV Street near the Strand. There's a big white building there which is now a police station, but it was then the Charing Cross Hospital. This was 8 December 1949, and I was wrapped in a green woollen cardigan. I was described as "a few hours old".'

Christine Simm recounts the circumstances of her discovery with some enthusiasm, getting the details right and happy to discuss the matter. She works at an Oxford college and lives with her second husband and two daughters in the north of the city, a world away from her beginnings.

'The newspaper account said that the taxi driver had left his cab to have a cup of tea, and he'd left the window open. He got back in the cab and he heard me – this baby – and he turned round and lo and behold, there I was. I was taken to Charing Cross Hospital. There was an article in the *News of the World* and the *Evening Standard*, but nobody came forward. I subsequently found out, via a researcher who got hold of the police records at the time, that the police said a woman of about forty was seen to place this baby – or this "parcel" – in the cab and hurry away. And obviously it must have looked an unusual thing to do, but I suppose nobody looking on would think, "Oh, there's a baby in that parcel."

'I stayed in the hospital for a few weeks, then went to live in the LCC's St Margaret's Home in Kentish Town.

'I was adopted when I was about one by a couple called Stan and Margaret Sheppard, who lived in Wallington in Surrey. They'd both been brought up in Forest Gate in east London and my dad had a wholesale fish company in Billingsgate Market, as his dad before him, and Mum didn't work.

'I can't even remember being told I was adopted – I've always known. My childhood was a bit difficult – I was an only child and I wanted to grow up soon. They sent me to a little private school when I was seven or eight, in order to pass the Eleven-Plus exam – which I did, getting into Wallington Girls' Grammar, after which I went to Hull University to do Social Administration.

'The only thing that my mother told me about being adopted was: "Your mother would have been too poor to look after you", and I accepted it. To be honest, it wasn't so uncommon at the time – and I looked so unlike my family. Then I got older and in 1979 I was in Oxford with my first husband and had my eldest daughter – and by then the law had changed. I was very busy, but I was interested and sent off for some forms for information . . . but it took me another fourteen years to actually go to St Catherine's House. And what I thought I was going to find out at that point was the name of my mother. I'd thought of all sorts of scenarios, but it had never occurred to me that I was a foundling. It wasn't something I knew about, never mind had thought about.

'I went with my first husband, and you have to see a social worker (which I was also training to be at the time). She was really inept and didn't understand what she was saying to me. She had this exceedingly thin file and said, "Sometimes they aren't very thick, because they are found." And I was wondering: what's found? Files found? And so she told me that I was found in King William IV Street – and that's all she told me.

'I was very passive at the time and I didn't think to question her authority. But she did tell me what my name had been, which was Mary Cross: Mary because it was near Christmas time, I expect, and Cross because of Charing Cross Hospital. So Mike and I walked along the Strand from St Catherine's House to the street, and we thought, right . . . OK . . .

'I came back to Oxford where we were in the middle of an election, and I was running the Committee Room, and I remember telling my colleagues in the Labour Party about it that evening over a drink. In fact, one of the first people I told was the man who was standing as the candidate – and he's now my second husband. But I suppose, in a way, it made me think I'll never resolve anything in my life going on this way, so I might as well . . . just get on with it. So I left Mike and ran off with Adrian!

'In 1993 my adopted mother died – Dad was already dead. That night I was talking to my aunt Frances, Dad's sister, and she said, "I expect that with Margaret dying it makes you think about your own mother." So I said, "Yes, I know I'm a foundling but I don't know anything else." And she said, "Ooh, but it was all in the papers. When Effie [another sister] went with Stan and Margaret to choose you, they told them you'd been found in the back of a taxi." Frances used to be a civil servant and she was very precise, saying, "I remember that, I remember the story – it was in all the newspapers." So this was a huge chunk of information.

'Next day our best friends came to dinner – Andrew Smith, who was my MP, and his wife Val, and she offered to help. She rang the Colindale Newspaper Library and took on a researcher, Beatrice. Nothing much happened initially – I felt that she didn't believe my story. But finally we got the cuttings – and THE photograph.'

THE photograph is in the next room: a black and white newspaper snap of a bonny baby in the arms of a nurse.

'Beatrice then tracked down the nurse in the picture through the Charing Cross Retired Nurses' Association, and the nurse wrote to me saying she remembered me. We then tried to find the driver via the *Taxi Driver* journal, but no one came forward.

'I did get my records from the LCC Children's Department. They're quite hard to read because they're mostly handwritten, but they're quite touching. About, for instance, the amount of clothes they gave you when you were adopted, like three vests and two rompers and that sort of thing. I was wrapped only in a green cardigan, left to be found . . . whether she waited until the taxi driver returned, I don't know. I was just a new-born baby, wrapped up in something warm and left to be found. I used to think it was a coincidence that she left me next to a hospital . . . and

I think I was probably born in London . . . that I hadn't arrived via the nearby railway station. The woman who left me might have been my mother . . . or perhaps grandmother . . . or maybe a friend helping out . . . we don't know.

'The Sheppards did try to give me a good education – and I have got an extended family, through cousins and my aunt and so on. I feel I have a family.

'It was completely bemusing when I found out I was a foundling. Then I joined Norcap and I met other foundlings and this fleshed things out a bit more . . . that we were different from adopted people in that we weren't going to have these reunions, and the search was almost certainly going to be fruitless. And then I began to think about other things that are important to foundlings – like the photographs. And what was with you, and who found you. This is all part of you – the link to the past. It matters hugely – I mean, when I got this photograph I was just completely enthralled. It was just fantastic – though it took me a long time to have it framed. I was looking at it one day and asked myself, "Why have I got it hidden away? It's my baby photograph – I should have it on my wall." I like it above my desk. I feel it's in a kind of private space, so it's not "public" – it's for me, private. It's like the tokens at the Foundling Hospital, isn't it?

'But I haven't got that place or date of birth – and there are health issues as well, which are so important these days. What about donor babies, sperm and eggs? And all the ethical issues? Because there's more emphasis on genetics in predicting what you might have. I mean . . . when you don't have a family medical history . . .

'Norcap has a Foundling Group – and the foundlings *are* a disparate group and there *is* something different about us – which only we can understand – that is good and positive. I noticed the huge satisfaction the other foundlings took in their children and, in some cases, their grandchildren. And there was quite a high level of anxiety – higher than you'd find in the general population – about whether they were good parents. You are the *first* person in the family tree!

'And there are those odd moments when someone tells you they've seen someone exactly like you. That happened to me quite recently. My cousin was at a Catholic school parents' evening in Ealing and she said to her husband, "I'm sure Christine's Irish", and her husband said, "You're looking at that woman over there, aren't you?" She said, "Yes, she not only looks like her, she talks like her and she *dresses* like her." And she apparently had the sort of clothes on that I would choose. . . . So I think: I want to see that woman. And it really tears my heart-strings, the thought that there's someone out there that might be related.'

Christine has tried most of the routes to discovering her past – the newspaper cuttings, the official records, and publicising her story. She's been interviewed on *Woman's Hour* and local radio, appeared on the *London* TV programme and been the subject of an article published in *Marie Claire* magazine in the hope that someone's memory might be jogged. But she's not obsessed by the search.

'I suppose I've constructed my life quite existentially and I feel strongly that I have created myself. I look at my husband and in the past few years he's got more and more like his father, even though they've had very different lives. At least he's not looking at me getting more and more like my mother!

'I've had to make my own way – and I quite like that, so I think there are positive aspects. It is a tragedy for a child and a mother to separate in that way – it's awful, awful, awful. But given that it *has* happened, it doesn't have to be a tragedy that ruins your life.

'I *would* love to know who my mother was, and I know I shan't. But you get over it and you can't let it ruin your life – so I don't use it as an excuse for what happens in my life now.'

Christine doesn't think that any more information will emerge – and she's content to accept the situation. Others feel that they can't let it rest, often having spent decades either not knowing they were foundlings, or indifferent, or perhaps unwilling to pursue the trail.

'I feel passionate about it. I feel I've got a hole inside of me.'

The speaker is an ebullient man in his sixties, with a sheaf of files on the table in his flat in London Colney, Hertfordshire. Letters, e-mails, articles, photographs and notes spill out, and Tony May's own story is woven into a closely typed manuscript full of thoughts about his attitudes and the effects on his life.

What makes an outsider blink is evidence of the relentless desire of those who have the initial care of abandoned children to name them – in a suitable but plonking manner. I am talking to a man originally called Victor Banks. One guess as to where he was found . . . .

'Why,' he asks, 'was I left *there* – on the Victoria Embankment? Was I left to be found? Was I left from dry land – or brought there from the Thames? I've looked for the first reference to me in the newspapers, and I couldn't find a sausage.' Nothing more has emerged about the circumstances of his birth, or being found, despite a very long time spent on the trail: there don't seem to be any clues. He's been to all the relevant points in his earliest journey as a baby and written countless letters:

'I was taken to the Chelsea Institution – I've been there, but it's flats now. It was attached to a women's prison, I believe, and that was where I stayed "while enquiries were made". Then I was moved to the LCC Children's Home in Ware in Hertfordshire – and I've been there. Fantastic place – and I thought: amazing – I really won the gold medal there then, it was lovely! And I put an article in the local paper, saying was anybody still living around there who knew what life was like there – Easeneye, it was called. And I got some lovely letters back from old ladies – I was in tears reading them – saying, "Ooh, it was lovely. I don't remember you exactly, but Matron looked after us and it was just wonderful." But I wonder, of course, how much actual hugging and that sort of thing went on. The pictures are of babies in baskets . . . and there were up to fifty-four of them to look after.'

All Tony's recollections are peppered with questions. He would love to know the detail, love to fill in the background.

'My mum and dad came from Barnet – they must have travelled over to Ware and my sister thinks that it was arranged through some kind of moral welfare association. Maybe Dad qualified to adopt because he was a lay preacher. He was a rather old-fashioned parent. He had flat feet and couldn't go into the army in the war, so he was an air raid warden – but I wanted a war hero. . . .

'I knew I was adopted. My parents told me a nice little story that I had been "selected" by them from a hospital, but I was too busy when I was young to ask questions – school, sport, then a family. And we never talked about it – my parents never discussed it once with me, never at all. I had the short birth certificate, the one you have to pass up to the front when you're at school, while everyone else had the long ones.'

Tony was acutely conscious of having parents a good deal older than those of his school friends, and wanted to avoid being seen with them. He still remembers being 'fantastically annoyed' when his sister told other children that they were both adopted, though the nervousness and anxiety he felt when he was younger he never put down to his origins. Always looking for respect – and feeling the obligation to impress his parents – he excelled at sport, having disappointed his father academically. He became, he says, a 'parent pleaser'. Looking back, he feels that he might have been considered to have 'won the jackpot, living in a very nice house, in a very nice town with a senior commercial bank official and his wife, full of Christian values, devoted parents who had no money worries . . . and everything sounds so cosy and perfect and sometimes it was, but inside – due to no fault of theirs – I mostly felt anxious, lost, lonely and afraid, and could never talk about it to them or anybody else'. However, he didn't ever want his parents to know this, as he always felt it was not their fault. *They* hadn't abandoned him – they'd taken him in.

Tony was twenty-three when he decided to leave home and get married. On the day of his departure his father suddenly handed him an envelope containing some documents, with the words: 'You'd better have these, lad.' There were swimming certificates and a few O-Level certificates and so on, then he suddenly said, 'You'd better have this Adoption Order – I hope it's not too upsetting to see the word "foundling".' When his son asked him what that meant, he replied, 'Er, er . . .'

'I hadn't known about that, but it's incredible how I never asked *more*. I think it was that you didn't ask your parents any embarrassing questions at all. And that was that – except that I learned my name was Victor Arthur Banks and that I was found a week before Christmas 1942 on the Victoria Embankment "around one month old". But isn't it pathetic that I then just got on with things and didn't think any more about it?

'It never even occurred to me until recently to wonder why they adopted me. My sister – who was also adopted – said that Mum had lots of miscarriages and she left it right until the last minute to adopt: she was forty. After my parents died, there was no one else in the family to ask – they were both only children. Friends whom we called uncles and aunts – I talked to them, pointing out that I must have made quite an impact when I turned up, and they said, "Your mum and dad never mentioned it." So I must just have appeared one day . . . and no one ever said anything about it.'

Once he was married, with two children, the subject receded into the background again. Then, at fifty, when he was divorced, his son told him that his father-in-law had said, 'Well, Tony started on his own and now he's back on his own' – and two days later he heard a radio programme about adopted children.

'It all started then. I just suddenly thought that maybe I'd been given the wrong information and there might be more to find out. I was advised to speak to a social worker who would try and find out if my stuff was held in the Greater London Records Office. She told me that there were two files in the office and we went there together. *She* was shown in. I was excluded. Those are the rules. I had to sit outside for an hour and a half "because there are other interested parties". I thought: who the hell are those people, then? I was adopted over fifty years ago, both [adoptive] parents are dead, and as far as I could see no one else would be an "interested party".

'She had to sit in this room with a pencil and write it all down, in pencil – what *she* thought I'd be interested in, mind you, not what *I* wanted to see. I wasn't allowed then to see them in their original form – though I later got hold of them. So she took a stab at what I might be interested to know about and we went round to the pub next door, where she read the notes to me. To be honest, I didn't find out much – for instance, I hadn't known that I was in the Children's Home in Ware for a full year. After that, I stirred things up a bit and the archivist finally agreed to send the files to me. Initially I'd wondered if my parents had kept bad news from me, so I was quite glad when I read things through and I realised they hadn't. At least Dad was honest: he *didn't* know any more.'

He is full of questions about reasons for being abandoned – and also about straightforward facts, such as why he was given a birthday on 9 December when he was found on the 19th, apparently one month old. But after radio interviews, newspaper articles and letters nothing more has emerged, and the questions remain. The publicity attracted letters from other foundlings who'd had similar experiences to him, angry or despairing that the authorities had refused them information and seemed not to understand how important *any* scrap of information is.

'I had a bit of heart trouble a few years ago – might it be hereditary? I have a son who's a solicitor and a daughter who's a teacher – amazing kids, top at everything they do, but their looks, traits? Other foundlings I've met don't seem as questioning as me. It's as if you've been cast adrift – and the thing I really want to know about is the effect on me. Has it affected me emotionally, or in my relationships? Friends of mine think I'm so demonstrative and so passionate about things that I can't be English!

'After I'd appeared on a TV programme I realised that I also wanted to know more about my own father. What sort of person left that poor little creature? And when I've felt panicked or stressed, I've always felt that maybe I was like that in the womb. Maybe I was born tense – or was, when I was left. I wonder about the psychological effects on my life: I've always felt unconnected and lonely – I *presume* this is why.

'Despite all the hunting, I've never really felt that I've been on the scent and I've more or less packed in the search now . . . you feel the likelihood of finding something is very small. I know that I'd never be angry at all: I understand what the climate was in those days, and I would love to forgive the person. If they wanted it, if it was arranged and someone said, "Your Mum's in the next room", I would love to say, "Don't worry about it." I'd love to meet my parents.

'One of the answers might be to get on with life and forget the past, but sometimes it just rears up and I feel I've got a hole in me . . . at the end of it, I can't tell what the effect of it has been.'

5

Title or form of address

At some point in my life I became Ms. A Form of Address, and one which I don't care for particularly. Nevertheless I espoused it as a working woman because I was utterly fed up with being sneered at as a Miss.

As general dogsbody on my first radio station in Durham, I was the farming producer, brass band producer, *Thought for the Day* producer, and a cricket and rugby commentator when the newsroom was absolutely desperate. I trotted around County Durham trying to look like a professional interviewer, trailing tape and microphone wires and wearing a micro mini-skirt. As local radio was a novelty and the BBC had given us about two quid for publicity, we had to explain ourselves to everyone we met.

'Good morning, I'm from Radio Durham, the BBC's new radio station. No, not the Home Service – that's now called Radio 4 and it's in London. We're from Neville's Cross. Actually we're in a former manager's house in a field near Neville's Cross just outside Durham City – do drop in if you're passing, we're *your local station*.' People thought we were a bit bats. Before we were across someone's threshold we'd be into the second part of our mantra, explaining why they hadn't heard us on their radios.

'We're on VHF – 96.8 kilohertz – no, don't worry about that – yes, it's new but I'm sure your radio will have it, it's just a matter of twiddling the knobs. Ah, I see yours has Third Programme and Hilversum on the dial. Never mind, I'm sure your local dealer will be pleased to help you. And never mind if you hear police broadcasts sometimes – we've got a little problem with interference.' We omitted to mention that some listeners thought the police chat far more exciting than our broadcasts. Having gone through this rigmarole at the start of every encounter, it was time to introduce yourself.

'I'm Kate Adie.' Thirty-odd years ago, this met with the reply: '*Miss* Adie?' – with a very definite stare at the mini-skirt. Sometimes it was nuanced to suggest that courtesy was involved, and that we'd both feel better if formalities were observed. Although those of us new to the media had discovered that the use of Christian names was *de rigueur* in the BBC at all levels, this was still considered eccentric outside the Corporation and rather 'arty'. But frequently the 'Miss' was uttered with condescension, implying that you were yet to gain any status in the world of work. A 'Miss' was a shop assistant, a waitress, someone to summon or give orders to. That a nice middle-class girl wasn't yet a respectable Mrs, quietly at home, was a cause for comment, all contained in the intoning of 'Miss . . .?' The fact that my unmarried male colleagues were never spoken to as 'Master' only compounded the irritation. So I chose the only alternative, however much I thought it ungainly and something of a statement.

Forms of address are always changing, and since those days in local radio it's now become very common to use only the Christian name, much to the discomfort of older people patted awake in hospital beds to the sound of 'Come on, Margaret', when they think it proper that a teenage nurse should call them Mrs Smith. Phone conversations routinely begin with 'Is that Kate?' when someone you have never met – and never wish to – is trying to sell you double-glazing late at night. And everyone in a call-centre has been surgically deprived of their surname and is confused by the question 'Darren who?'

Nevertheless, the BBC was determined to maintain a Reithian continuity, and outside the confines of its staff it was a stickler for proper Titles and Forms of Address. It bought us a book on the subject, rescuing us from the terrible social faux pas of not being able to introduce an archdeacon properly.

An added quirk in Britain is the plethora of titles which survive, indeed are increased every year. Much of Europe may still have a clutch of Principessas and Vizcondes hanging on to their Bourbon and Hapsburg handles, but the British have a Christmas tree of titles which few can be bothered to get in the right order: just hang the title somewhere and it'll twinkle, even if you haven't the foggiest where a marchioness comes in order of precedence. Then, twice a year, the newspapers carry a long list of new Lords and Sirs and a few Dames. The best way of understanding the system is to try and explain it to an American. It's a bit like cricket, perfectly comprehensible until people (Americans) ask sensible questions about it. 'He's just been made a Lord? So he's Lord Andrew?' No, he's Lord Lloyd-Webber. 'His friend's just become a Knight? So he's Sir McCartney?' No, he's Sir Paul. Computers are not title-friendly: letters arrive to Mr Sir and Mrs Dame. There is a logic in there somewhere, but it's shrouded in sentiment, ambition, just reward, snobbery, honour and envy – and quite a lot of unseemly pestering in the back corridors of power. But nothing that should trouble a foundling. The law has seen to that, making the inheritance of titles near-impossible for those not of the blood. Even if the twenty-first-century foundling were to establish his kinship to the Duke of Greatacres through a DNA test, if he wasn't born after a legal marriage he can't inherit.

Nevertheless, should you wish to acquire a coat of arms, you will discover that bastardy and adoption are no strangers to the exotic world of cross crosslets fitchee, gules and besants. Among the unicorns and shells and lions and stripes and coronets lie the clues to origins. Should you be an adopted foundling who actually follows the fairytale road, and find yourself in the castle rather than the cottage or workhouse, the College of Heralds will happily handle your request for the coat of arms and issue a licence, signed by the Queen and published in the *London Gazette*. The reason you can't just stick the family emblem straight on to your notepaper, or wherever else you were thinking of displaying it which isn't too naff, is that the Heralds will have made a tiny alteration to the design. In amongst the paws and foliage will be two neat interlinked chains: to the initiated, this is the heraldic language of adoption. Bastards – there being numerous aristocratic acknowledged by-blows right back to medieval days – get the coat of arms unaltered, except that it's surrounded by a wavy border. . . . And don't ask about titles: the law is still being tweaked and nudged; in the past few years, the concession has been made that the younger adopted children of peers of the realm can acquire a courtesy title, but the bottom line is the Shakespearean view: Enter a Bastard, Exit a Bastard.

All this will not trouble most people. But, as many a foundling has dreamed, it might be useful to know. . . . And dreams and myth and fairytales are very much part of the foundling story: outside of the family experience, back to ancient times, the foundling has exerted a great pull on the imagination. The child from nowhere, the gift, the surprise, the mysterious, even the romantic.

Those hard-headed citizens of ancient Rome paid tribute to foundling founders – Romulus and Remus. The myth of abandoned twins, the offspring of a god and a Vestal Virgin, set adrift in a river, to be suckled by a she-wolf and taken in by a humble shepherd, is a classic version of an ancient tale found in numerous literary and oral traditions – the 'hero exposed at birth who attains success and salvation'. It turns up regularly in ancient Greece, for example in the tragedies of Euripides, in Rome's Daphnis and Chloë and in the Bible with Moses – abandoned in the bulrushes and taken in by Pharaoh's daughter.

There are many variations on the theme, but the idea of redemption or rehabilitation runs through a good many stories – the foundling has to try harder than most, prove himself, face many challenges, and succeed, in order to wipe away the stigma or the disturbing element of chance in his or her origins. But the other theme is that the foundling already has certain innate talents and qualities which will inevitably prove his worth; however, this often relies on the discovery of his true parentage, when everyone can sigh with relief that the mystery has been solved and the ties of blood have shown that perhaps '*good* blood will out'.

Through Grimm's fairy tales, Fielding's *Tom Jones*, seventeen-year-old Charlotte Brontë's *The Foundling*, and her sister Emily's Heathcliff in *Wuthering Heights*, the foundling's tale, whether of rehabilitation or virtue, runs counter to the reality of the time. The abandoned child may have been shown charity and provided for, but the expectations were not of great deeds, virtue and wisdom. The child's future was usually either to be disciplined in an institution or to become a creature of charity, trained for a prosaic occupation, always bound up with the idea of service – a notional fine for having appeared improperly.

Nevertheless, a vast array of writers has been attracted to the notion: while Foundling Hospitals flourished and the workhouses filled up, Victor Hugo created his abandoned monster child, Quasimodo, Jules Verne wrote *Foundling Mick*, George Eliot *Silas Marner*, Thackeray the *Lamentable Ballad of the Foundling of Shoreditch*, and Balzac *Jean-Louis or the Foundling Girl*. *Our Nig* was the first-ever novel by a black American, published in the United States in 1859 – a semi-autobiographical story of a 'free Black foundling'.

Charles Dickens took the less romantic view, being familiar with the Foundling Hospital in London and knowing the actual fate of the poor. However, his foundlings also embark on that search for their true parents and usually have a fortunate outcome, as in *Oliver Twist*. And Thomas Coram, founder of the Foundling Hospital, is remembered in *Little Dorrit* with Hattie, the foundling maid to Mr Meagles' daughter Pet.

'Why the fact is,' said Mr Meagles, 'Mrs Meagles and myself are, you see, practical people. . . . So on one day, five or six years ago now, when we took Pet to church at the Foundling Hospital – you have heard of the Foundling Hospital in London? Similar to the Institution for Found Children in Paris? . . . And that's the way we came by Tattycoram.'

'And the name itself –'

'By George!' said Mr Meagles, 'I was forgetting the name itself. Why, she was called in the Institution, Harriet Beadle – an arbitrary name, of course. Now, Harriet we changed into Hattey, and then into Tatty, because as practical people, we thought even a playful name might be a new thing to her, and might have a softening and affectionate kind of effect, don't you see? As to Beadle . . . whenever I see a beadle in full fig, coming down a street on a Sunday at the head of a charity school, I am obliged to turn and run away, or I should hit him. The name Beadle being out of the question, and the originator of the Institution for these poor foundlings having been a blessed creature by the name of Coram, we gave that name to little Pet's maid. At one time she was Tatty, and at one time she was Coram, until we got into a way of mixing the two names together, and now she is always Tattycoram.'

Tattycoram is very much the object of charity and benevolence, but not seen as deserving of equality; and the jolly games with her name reinforce the 'arbitrary' nature of her roots.

The fascination continues in Kipling's Mowgli in *The Jungle Book*, and with George Bernard Shaw, Georgette Heyer, Isabel Allende, Terry Pratchett, Peter Carey and Jeanette Winterson, as well as countless fantasy and sci-fi novels. Perhaps the greatest moment for the fictional foundling centres on the famous 'A handbag?' enunciated by decades of formidable actresses in Oscar Wilde's *The Importance of Being Earnest*. Jack Worthing, left in a large black bag at Victoria Station, gets the ultimate unsentimental put-down: 'To lose one parent, Mr Worthing, may be regarded as a misfortune; to lose both looks like carelessness.'

So if you can't inherit, why not earn a title the hard way? And there can be nothing grander than rising from the waiting room of a railway station to the mayor's parlour.

John Hilton is the kind of man who embodies civic pride and joy as the thirty-second mayor of a town which received its first royal charter in 1246. In the large parlour of Wigan's Edwardian town hall, he wears immaculate morning dress and is passionate about his borough. He and his wife Margaret are a delight, with three daughters, six grandchildren and six great-grandchildren. Downstairs John and I tour the borough regalia, with the gigantic mayoral chair and the medieval silver-gilt maces; upstairs we have sandwiches and chips with Margaret, the mayoress.

Perhaps the only hiccup in the progress from railway baby to parlour is that John was found 25 miles away in Oldham, on the wonderfully named Oldham Mumps Station. One of the origins of the name may relate to land at the meeting of two streams, but there's also the possibility that it comes from an old word for alms – a mumper was a beggar – and there was once a nearby workhouse. Fortunately, it had closed by the time John appeared in May 1940. 'I was roughly about fourteen when Mum and Dad got me round the table and said, "We've got something to tell you." They seemed a bit upset. Then they said, "You're adopted." It'd never dawned on me, even though they were somewhat elderly – they'd been forty-eight when they adopted me. They were very, very sober people. My father was a teetotaller, he smoked a pipe and was an ex-professional footballer, first for Skelmersdale, then for Wigan. He went into the army in World War I and played one of those infamous games of football in No Man's Land in France. He had a bit of a rough trip – he'd also been in Italy and at Gallipoli and he got gassed in France. He was demobbed in 1918 and he spent a few weeks at Everton, got a serious injury, then took up cricket. *Superb* parents – a heroic sort of dad, and Mum was a manageress in a sewing factory that made rugby jerseys. But they were sober, religious people, great Christians.

'I had a happy childhood – I was the only child in school to have a holiday every year! Father was no longer a cricketer and he was a guard on the railways – the Great Central Railway. The house I was brought up in was a great big detached railway house in the railway goods yard. So all my life, from the age of three, I knew nothing but railways. I was firing steam engines by the age of seven! There were steam engines and shunting engines all day and all night – and when I got married and moved away I couldn't sleep at night, it were so quiet.

'Anyway, I was getting ready to leave school at fifteen and my parents thought it was the right time to tell me about being adopted. It didn't mean a great deal, to be honest. I'd had such a good life – well, if it's not broke, don't mend it.

'They didn't tell me about being found at this point. It just sort of crept out in the next eighteen months: "You know, you were found abandoned. . . ." And I had a sight of my papers, saying "born on or about May 19th". It was an adoption certificate and doesn't say where I was born.

'Honestly, once I was told the story I just got on with it. What's the point? I never even thought of looking for who my parents were. They didn't want you then – they won't want you now.'

John was told by George and Elizabeth that he'd been found on Oldham Mumps Station, but he didn't know by whom. He was taken straight to Boundary Park Hospital – now Oldham Royal – and there was a brief article about him in the local newspaper. He was wrapped in a shawl and wasn't in a very good state – critically ill, in fact. He was named John Westwood Oldham: John because the man who found him liked it, Westwood being the area where he was found, and Oldham for the town. He thinks he stayed in the hospital for about three years rather than going to a Children's Home – probably because of the war.

'While I was in the hospital in Oldham, a young nurse called Marion Sutton who came from Wigan had to return to the town – and she couldn't leave me! So she went to my father and told him about me – I was nearly three by then – and she said she couldn't leave me, but she couldn't adopt me because her mum was very ill. So she asked him if he could do something – and there was a little family conference and off I went.

'In them days, our parents didn't like to talk about these things. They'd tell you so much, then let your imagination run riot. They actually told my wife Margaret more when we started courting.'

'His mother,' adds Margaret, 'asked me, "Did John tell you he was adopted?" And I said No. So she told me about the shawl and the cardboard box "on the railways". She didn't say anything else. I think she told me because when I was eighteen I had had a baby and kept it. And when John and I were courting, I told him. And when we were already engaged, he said he wanted to adopt Denise. Then he told me about himself – and I already knew from his mother. And I can honestly say he's treated Denise like a daughter – and like our two daughters.

'I can also say that I had a good mother and dad – and they treated me well. Mum used to look after her and they said, in 1957, "When this baby comes along, we'll look after it when you're working, and when you come home – that's your pleasure – you'll look after it! I didn't get to go out dancing – all that was stopped. When I met John, I told him I'd got a little girl and he said, "So what? I've already found out from my mate who was with me when we met."

'John's mother and his dad were brilliant with Denise and his father said, "If John's prepared to take Denise, he's got to give her all the love and care that he's had. And they used to treat her wonderfully, as their own granddaughter."

In the mayor's parlour there are many plaques and certificates and gifts, but out comes the prized trophy – a model train. 'Most of my friends went down the pits, but I spent forty-seven years on the railway.' John was first an engine cleaner, spent thirteen years as a fireman, then became a train driver in 1968, and finally got involved in local politics. As mayor of Wigan, he found himself being interviewed. He saw no reason not to talk about his start in life, and realised that he'd never talked about it before. There was quite a burst of publicity, including an interview on the late John Peel's *Home Truths* programme on BBC Radio 4. Out of the blue came a letter. Sisters Maureen Hopkins and Avis Scofield recognised the baby their father Arthur had found at Oldham Mumps, and Avis wrote: 'My father and mum could have adopted you, but my mother was already expecting a baby and dad was waiting to be called up to the army. My mum often wondered what happened to you. They said they'd called you John Westwood Oldham. They knew you went to a good home eventually.'

'A *lovely* letter from the lady in Oldham,' chorus John and Margaret. And John adds that there were details he hadn't known. 'She wrote this beautiful letter saying that it was well known in her family that her father found a small baby boy on Oldham Station. So we went to see her and her sister and had a superb day with them. They filled in a blank bit. Even though I was abandoned at two days old, there was always a little doubt – was the story true?

Now I know it is. Arthur Ripley was a porter at the station and he heard my cries and found me when he came on duty in the afternoon. I was in the corner of the waiting room in a cardboard box, wrapped in dirty rags – but 81b 4oz with blue eyes, and fairly healthy; though a bit distressed, not having been fed. They say I was two days old, and on the birth certificate it said, "Born on or around May 1940", and I was found 20th or 21st. They were over the moon to meet me. They hadn't realised until it was published in the local paper. "This is that young lad," they said. The line that goes through Oldham Mumps goes from Manchester Victoria, through Failsworth and comes out at Rochdale. As a train driver I used to pass it most days! I felt a bit different when I'd met the two sisters, though . . . the eldest remembers it quite clearly, she was eight years of age – all that excitement in the family – then it was gone. . . . Finding the real link made the story true for me.

'Being mayor has been superb – and meeting all the children has been the icing on the cake. And I chose my charity for the year because of what happened to me – the Start a Life Appeal. It's for equipment for the Special Baby Care Unit at Wigan Infirmary. I was found at two days, and looked after for three years, using only love, dedication and care – no machinery available then. And these days you get babies born prematurely, and some that aren't healthy when they're born, so I asked the local hospital's paediatrician at the new unit about their equipment. He showed me the ventilator and said another one would be on his wish list – at £25,000. So I said, if I raised that, would you like one? And having worked on the railways all my life, I know that when you get something built new you put all the old equipment in it! So I set about it. It was because I was well looked after – without the machinery.'

The mayoral year is nearly over, but the ex-mayor won't be sitting around; he's just back from Sinaia in Romania. 'I went with the Epiphany Trust – it's run by a local man, Bill Hamilton, a freeman of the borough, and he's concerned with orphanages. He's building a halfway house for them at the moment. And we met one young man who'd walked 300 miles at the age of seven from Moldova – from one orphanage to another. . . . Bill's seen some horrendous sights . . . and . . . I don't know how they can abuse children so . . . so whether it's because I was in hospital all that time – when I've finished this year as mayor, I intend to go back and help.'

Wigan's coat of arms is a typical intriguing mixture of rampant animals and a three-towered castle, with leafy bits held in the lions' paws – a mountain ash branch, known in local dialect as the Wiggin Tree. This is known as a joke in heraldry, which is an ancient and curious business. However, it has a serious purpose: it encapsulates identity.

Among the many odd beasts that turn up on shields and signet rings and mayoral cars are gryphons, perhaps best known in Wonderland where Alice encountered a rather energetic, bouncy one who performed the Lobster Quadrille with the Mock Turtle – not easy, when you have a lion's body and an eagle's head and wings. The gryphon represents courage unto death, combined with intelligence and vigilance (and a dozen other things, should you wish to research the mad world of gryphonologists who mutter on about gryphons' nests and flying properties . . .). And a coat of arms was the medieval announcement to a wider world of who you were: an ancient identity card, its claims and accuracy a matter of both political importance and social status. Blazon the arms of England on your furniture and servants' coats when you're Mary Queen of Scots and married to a Frenchman – and decades later, your use of symbols appears in the evidence against you when facing execution.

The College of Arms is a busy place, even today: new coats of arms are still granted, through a complex system involving peti- tioning the monarch. Henry is a banker in the City and started life in a Children's Home in south-west England, from which he was adopted; he doesn't know where he was born or the circumstances of his arrival there. He speaks with great thoughtfulness and precision, distilling his reasons for approaching the College of Arms.

'I suppose it was because I wanted to reinforce my own identity. It was a conscious decision to go back to the pre-adoption life – to reach back to one's forbears, rather than one's adoptive parents. So I petitioned for my own arms, in my own right.'

He wears a signet ring on which there's one of those gryphons: 'I suppose the main features on the coat of arms are a number of gryphons – I'm not sure how many exactly – bearing lances. The lances represent some form of military symbol – I'm connected with the military, and the lances seemed the right sort of thing. There's a motto underneath in Latin, and it translates as something 'combative'.

A reminder of the City world of long hours and intensive work, the phone, the pager and the mini-computer bleep and ping while we talk, the phone nearly bouncing off the table such is its urgent fanfare. Henry thinks long and hard about the time, just over forty years ago, when he was left in the Home.

'I know very little about it, but I did try some degree of tracing.' This was in the early eighties, when access to records was relatively new, and the policy at the time was to exercise the utmost caution when revealing information to adopted children. As Tony May also discovered during his research, there was a sense that it was not wise to deliver too much and that anyone who wanted to have access to their records should attend a compulsory interview with the counsellor – usually a local social worker. The general feeling for many years after the law was changed in 1975 was that everyone was walking on eggshells and that people could be hurt as a result of the search. Many of the foundlings I spoke to had been very irritated by this treatment, coming up against social workers half their age who seemed to doubt the searchers' ability to deal with details about their own origins.

'I went to the Home,' Henry continued, 'in order to identify my father. They gave me some information about him, and about my natural mother. The social worker with whom I spoke then discussed it, apparently either with my father or his sister. She came back to me and said that she didn't think it was "in my interests" to pursue making a contact. And she refused point blank to give me further information. . . . This was over twenty years ago now, and I suspect that the legal situation may have changed. One did somehow feel there was this attitude: "Oh, I know better than you do." I got the impression it was all rather . . . "locked up".' In fact the law has not changed, but more recently procedures have, for experience has shown that it's much better to provide far more information than was originally intended: adopted children are much more competent at dealing with what they discover than was thought by those who framed the law. Also safeguards for the vulnerable were often applied to robust adults such as Tony May by inexperienced social workers.

Henry got the bare minimum in 1983: 'I've no details about how I came to be in the Home – except that they were familiar with the identity of my natural mother and my father. I don't know whether my arrival there was pre-planned or whether my natural mother had nominated me for adoption. I have a birth certificate, and it only has my mother's name on it.'

Henry hasn't taken this any further. He sounds pensive and tentative: 'What marginal benefit does it achieve? There are other priorities in life. I'm much more interested in tracing my natural father – perhaps it's a male thing that one is curious about one's father rather than one's mother. The social worker mentioned that he was a chemical engineer . . . I don't know, I suppose I didn't actually have a perspective on it . . . there are many worse things! And it sounded not dissimilar to my character – he was a Dr Something or other. Obviously some intellectual capability. . . .

'My childhood, if I look back – well, I wouldn't say I looked back on my childhood with any great sense of . . .' He hunts around for a word, and when I suggest 'joy' he nods agreement. 'Yes, perhaps. I made some decisions when I was about eleven years old which were poor – just how to manage my life and so on, choice of school subjects, what I did in my spare time. I was always a shy, sensitive child – some sort of a loner, sort of drifting along. And in retrospect it didn't turn out desperately well, though hindsight's a wonderful tool! For example, I was never particularly active in sport at school

– I was always the last person to be chosen for the team, and sport was quite critical to social life.'

We talk about work in the City and the fact that there are still quite a lot of 'Captains of Cricket' and 'Prefects' who glide up the ladder. 'Which I wasn't,' he says with a laugh, and adds that he felt comparatively immature when he went up to Oxford. However, once there he took off into the sporting world like a champion, discovering that he enjoyed it enormously and ending up playing rugby, soccer, hockey and cricket. He does wonder why he didn't do it earlier.

'I read science at Oxford and then headed for the City – the traditional route – with a stint in the services. I think I always knew I was adopted – I can't honestly remember not knowing.' The phone chirps, the banker confers briskly with one of his team, and then there's another wistful thought about his background: 'I was in my twenties when I began to search – it was sort of tucked away in the pending tray, something which I wanted to look at one day, and which I eventually got round to doing. I didn't tell my adoptive parents – I don't want to offend them . . . but now I wonder whether perhaps I should search again. . . . I know I've got some half-brothers – that's what I'd like to know about.' The hand with the signet ring grasps the phone and the tiny golden gryphon glints, a reminder of courage and strength.

6

Is there anything in your past
we should know about?

Whereas many countries regard their ancient buildings as large fossils to be preserved emptily and visited by a troupe of tourists, Italy takes a more robust view: as a reporter on the trail of a supposed medical scandal, I found myself hunting for the neurological unit of a hospital in Siena. After an hour, trying to ignore the glories of the central piazza, I declared myself baffled. Not a single building in the centre looked remotely like a hospital. Sitting on the worn steps of an exquisite building, I stared at a tiny ambulance beetling over the cobbles. It nipped neatly into an equally tiny archway and disappeared under an ornate façade of centuries of weathered stone. It took a couple of minutes for the penny to drop, whereupon I went to discover a gleaming modern intensive care unit buried in the bowels of an architectural confection from the Middle Ages.

In Bologna, collating information on a terrorist attack on the railway station, I spent an entire morning marvelling at medieval pillars and carved ceilings in the coroner's office. Most of the city's administration, humming with modern equipment and stylish contemporary lighting, appeared to be accommodated in a Harry Potter Hogwarts location. The equivalent of the town clerk seemed to live in a gothic crypt – though one with discreet central heating and a coffee machine on what looked suspiciously like a tomb. But it all worked, and a good many Italians take the view that they'd be camping in a vast museum if they didn't keep using their heritage in a useful way.

If you're looking for the UNICEF Research Centre which houses the data to be used by the United Nations for twenty-first-century policy-making about children, then head for one of the great masterpieces of the Renaissance, Santa Maria degl'-Innocenti in Florence, opened in 1445. The Centre focusses on fundamental human rights for children today: policy is child-centred and children are seen as individuals. It works from a building which contains echoes from times when children were regarded in a very different light, but its creation was the result of new thinking in the fifteenth century, which overturned a millennium of established practice in the way foundlings were treated.

Children have always been abandoned, and the reasons have never strayed far from poverty, shame, inheritance and indifference. The existence of extensive legal statutes about abandonment attests to a continuous problem from Greek and Roman times onwards. In Europe, infanticide, slavery, castration and the sale of children walked alongside abandonment. The notion that children are individuals with rights and that their welfare should be a priority is entirely modern. Nor were parental responsibilities viewed in the same way as today: children were property, rather than a responsibility, and therefore could be disposed of by their owners as they wished.

However, there's little evidence to support the idea that hearts were harder and parents cared less for their children: sheer circumstances dictated abandonment. Poverty led the charge, when there was little knowledge of how to limit families and the majority of the population had poor defences against food shortages and famine, war and illness. Those with assets worried about how to divide their riches: too many children, and strife ensued about inheritance. And illegitimacy, once the Christian Church began spreading its influence and refining laws about sexual behaviour, became gradually unacceptable – a sin for both mother and child, rather than just a social shame and embarrassment.

Leaving a child in a public place – often at a temple at dawn – was common practice in ancient Rome. In country areas, for centuries children were found in woods hanging in bags or slings from tree branches – to protect them from wild animals, and to enable them to be easily spotted by passers-by. Tokens were often left with them – a scrap of material, half a coin – sometimes to indicate the status, rich or poor, sometimes to create the possibility of reclaiming the child at a later date, and perhaps in some instances out of pure emotion – a little leaving present, maybe a wish for luck to go with the child.

And though the law dealt with all kinds of complications regarding inheritance and whether a child was raised as a freeborn citizen or a slave, right up to medieval times no particular shame or criminal prosecution was attached to parents who gave up their children. The life of these children was that of servitude – at several levels. In a world of manual labour there was always work to be done, and foundlings constituted another pair of hands, often free labour. Admittedly, with the exception of a small ruling class, most people were beholden to people who had land, power or learning. However, even when foundlings were taken into a family in circumstances we would now describe as fostering or adoption, the implication was that they were 'not as good' as those who were related by blood.

Prostitution was a traditional avenue for the unwanted child – leading to the clerical worry that men might visit brothels and commit incest with their unknown daughters, a serious preoccupation of the Church in the Middle Ages. Slavery was also a possibility and the sale of children was commonplace, with the Venerable Bede, in his *History of the English Church and People* of 731, telling the tale of Pope Gregory coming across a sale of boys in the Rome marketplace. They had 'fair complexions, fine-cut features, and beautiful hair', and Gregory was told that they came from the 'island of Britain, where all the people have this appearance'. On learning that they belonged to a race called Angles, he delivered himself of the statement that has turned into the one great misquote passed on to schoolchildren to represent the millennium between Julius Caesar's arrival and the Norman Conquest: 'These are not Angles, but angels.' (Bede actually writes that he said, 'Angles . . . that is appropriate, for they have angelic faces' – but it's not quite so catchy.)

Pope Gregory was not concerned about the status of these boys as goods for sale; but he was horrified that the people of Britain were ignorant heathens, and in 596 despatched St Augustine on a mission of conversion. Bede, over a century later, seems not to have seen anything unusual about such a trade, nor is there any indication if these children had been abandoned or sold by their parents – or possibly kidnapped. However, he himself was the product of another kind of abandonment. One possibility for offloading children was to give them to the Church. When their son was seven, Bede's parents had done just that: 'With God's help, I, Bede, the servant of Christ and priest of the monastery of the blessed apostles Peter and Paul at Wearmouth and Jarrow, have assembled these facts about the history of the Church in Britain. . . . I was born on the lands of this monastery, and on reaching seven years of age, I was entrusted by my family to the most reverend Abbot Benedict and later to Abbot Ceolfrid for my education. I have spent all the remainder of my life in this monastery and devoted myself entirely to the study of the Scriptures.'

Having been brought up with St Peter's church at the centre of my home town on the banks of the River Wear, I've always wondered why such a young child should be in a monastery – well before the concept of regular schooling from the Church was established; certainly not much notice would have been taken of a seven-year-old had he made the unlikely announcement that he knew what he wanted to be when he grew up. It's much more likely that his parents were offering him as a permanent gift to the Church – an 'oblation'. This was both a religious gesture as well as a practical solution when there were too many mouths to feed. For centuries children were donated to monasteries and convents, a system that seemed to suit everyone: the Church gained clergy or workers, unwanted children were looked after, and parents felt they had done the best by their 'offering'. The only fly in the ointment was the regular complaint that the children could never leave: there were frequent disputes about whether the 'gift' was permanent, with a lifetime of obedience and celibacy ahead.

However, with hindsight it might be argued that the alternative for foundlings could have been much grimmer.

Girls were offered to convents: unsurprisingly, as one of the commonest threads which runs through the history of abandonment is the preponderance of female children. It is a discrimination which crosses the centuries and the continents, from the families of ancient Rome to those of modern China. And the shunting off into religious institutions of unwanted daughters or women who had in some way offended against the conventional notions of dutiful behaviour continued right to the end of the twentieth century, with the notorious Magdalen laundries in Ireland serving as a disgraceful hangover of medieval prejudice operating in a modern nation. That the virtual incarceration of women who had had illegitimate children or were considered to be 'wayward' or 'in moral danger' continued into the 1990s in Ireland sends shivers down the spine. Admittedly some were sent by their families and others found no support and much hostility in Irish society, but many were sent to the institutions by priests. That the Catholic Church ignored physical and psychological abuse and treated the women as sinners in need of continual repentance while working them like slaves reveals attitudes that were still deeply embedded at the close of the twentieth century.

Another thread of discrimination which runs right down to present-day eastern Europe, and specifically Russia, is drawn from the early days of the Christian Church and has been twisted together with pagan superstitions. Disabled babies, or those with unusual birth-marks, were primary candidates for abandonment – the Spartans threw them over precipices and the Romans drowned or strangled them without much concern. Even acknowledging that in precarious societies the survival of the fittest might be an instinctive pressure, the numbers of children consigned outside a family because of physical or mental handicaps – or unusual appearance – far outweigh Darwinian explanation.

Many cultures have superstitions based in ignorance, however. From the early days right through to the Reformation, the Church added to family pressures by increasingly insisting that all sexual relations were for procreation rather than recreation. And various Councils and pronouncements on the subject were refined into a set of rules which ordinary people were expected to observe. Abstinence was demanded of married couples during Lent, Advent, Whitsun and Easter weeks; and while a woman was breast-feeding or menstruating; and on feast days – which were numerous – and fast days – of which there were quite a number. And on Fridays – Christ died on Good Friday. And on Sundays – the Lord's Day. Somehow Wednesdays and Saturdays also got added to the list. If you observed the rules, sex in marriage would be allowed on average on fewer than four days a month.

If you didn't observe the rules any offspring of such copulation would be misshapen, a belief spelled out by Gregory of Tours in the sixth century as he looked at a severely deformed baby: 'He was viewed by most people with derision, and the mother, who was blamed for having produced such a child, tearfully confessed that he had been conceived on a Saturday night.' Saturday night couplings – and all the other forbidden times, according to Gregory – produced handicapped, deformed and leprous children; he was a man who believed that children were born corrupted because of the pleasure experienced by their parents in conceiving them. The seed had been planted, and from it has grown a widespread belief that children who are not perfect at birth are the symbol of sin – and they are cast out as a result. Their very existence points the finger at their parents, and the children themselves carry 'the mark of sin'. The references to sex on the 'wrong' days have drifted into history, but the consequences of the belief have resisted erasure.

But perhaps the most important condition of a child's existence, in the days when the Church ruled everyday lives, was whether or not it was baptised:

> The bairnie she swyl'd in linen so fine,
> In a gilded casket she laid it syne,
> Mickle saut and light she laid therein,
> Cause yet in God's house it had'na been.

Putting 'saut' or salt in the cradle next to the candles as described in this old Scottish ballad was one of the traditional magical ways of warding off evil before baptism – the Devil was thought to hate salt. And from the fourth century, salt appeared at the font in Catholic churches as part of the christening ceremony. A child unbaptised had its mortal soul in danger, so new-born foundlings were scrutinised for any evidence of baptism or lack of it: for should they succumb to death unbaptised, they didn't even make it into consecrated ground for burial. The sign was often a smear of salt on the infant's neck – showing that the mother had wanted to ward off evil, but that she hadn't had the child baptised. It was a superstition followed across Europe, where babies found in Florence in the fifteenth century, and in England in the sixteenth, all bore the same sign, as recorded in the Harleian manuscripts in the British Museum: 'It was uncrisned, seeming out of doubt, for salt was bound at its neck in a linen clout.'

The worry about a child's soul has accompanied decisions about foundlings right up to the present day. Baptised or not? Christian or other? Which denomination within the faith? In more recent times it spilled over into the selection of adoptive parents, with a feeling that to sustain a religious continuity was more important than the immediate welfare of a child.

Until the Renaissance there was little provision for orphans and foundlings who were not taken in by their own families or by the Church, the latter either as 'oblates' or deposited in a marble shell near the church doorway to be placed with willing families or to work for the Church in a menial capacity. There were a handful of 'hospitals' and 'orphanages' across Europe, the first one usually credited to the Italian city of Milan in 787. From the beginning of the thirteenth century comes a tale about Pope Innocent III converting the Santo Spirito Hospital for the sick into a foundling institution, after he'd had a dream and instructed fishermen to drag the River Tiber. When the bodies of 87 babies were found the shocked Pope ordered a second trawl, which yielded 340 more. As with most tales involving a dream, there's not a lot of solid evidence; however, by the end of the century the Santo Spirito Hospital is thought to have had some foundlings in it.

The next century was to see the creation of a number of specialised buildings throughout Europe, particularly in Italy, which were intended to deal with foundlings rather than with the poor and ill. One of the earliest was in a house opposite one of Dubrovnik's architectural gems. During the wars in the Balkans in the early 1990s, the whoosh of tank fire and the bang of mortars echoed round the stone-flagged streets of this city on the Adriatic. The Franciscan Friary took a number of hits, particularly on its library. It's been on the broad main street, Placa, since 1319, when Dubrovnik, then called Ragusa, was emerging as a thriving trading port. While the gracious Friary was still being added to, a century later, the building across the street was acquired by the city's Council: they had decided to deal with the perennial problem of foundlings in a new and practical manner: '. . . considering what an abomination and inhumanity it is to cast out little human beings who, because of poverty or for some other reason, are thrown out around the city like brute beasts without knowledge of their parents, for which reason they often die without the sacrament of baptism, or come to some other ill – and for reverence of Jesus'.

All the basic elements which would be employed in the next four hundred years in foundling hospitals were put in place. A revolving wheel – two in Dubrovnik, flanking the building – was intended for use day or night. A baby could be brought and placed on the wheel, effectively a simple turntable, which then, with one turn, delivered the child into the building. The question of anonymity, debated at each institution century in and century out, was decided here to be essential: there was even to be a penalty of imprisonment for anyone who questioned the mother handing in the baby. Baptism had to be quickly provided by the authorities, and wet-nurses organised to care for the child. Charitable gifts and a little public money supported the project, and children were brought up in the hospital, wearing distinctive white uniforms, until the age of five, when they became available for adoption.

There was also provision for the mother returning to claim her child; however, she had to pay back the cost of care.

In 1432 the wheels started turning; and within a few years other cities were also installing them, with the Italians leading the way. The *ruota* was in business until the twentieth century, and no country took to the management of foundlings quite like Italy. The wheel and the organisation attached to it could be seen as a humane gesture to those without support. Basically, the new institutions tidied up society: there would always be abandoned children, and now it was time to sort out the random way of dealing with them – and bring a bit of order to the community. A classic solution of the administrative mind was to take the messiness off the streets and put it behind the respectable façade of an important building. Out of sight, out of mind. Add a few rules and regulations, and the irritating problem could be safely kept inside and regulated. And prostitution – another intractable problem – would at least be free of the threat that the sin of incest might be committed: the foundling daughters would be discouraged from any such career.

In Venice, Padua, Naples, Siena and all other major cities both the civil authorities and the Church were involved in these new ventures. But the greatest – in both numbers and fame – was the Innocenti in Florence. Decorated with images of swaddled infants, and originally run by members of the Guild of Silkworkers who were immensely conscious of the social statement they were making, the building was designed by Brunelleschi and patronised by powerful local nobles. The first infant was left in a basin on 5 February 1445, ten days after the local bigwigs had attended a grand opening ceremony, all duly described by a contemporary chronicler:

'In the beginning, children who were not handed over directly to hospital officials were abandoned in a sort of basin situated on the right side of the front portico, beneath a window that opened into an inside room where a woman was on permanent duty waiting for an infant's first cry. This basin was removed around 1650, when a wheel was built on the left side of the same portico.' (It remained in place until 1875 – and was only taken away because of the unmanageable number of *legitimate* babies that were being left on it.) Once inside, the children needed feeding, and the system which was used throughout society was recorded with appreciation: 'Customarily they are first given over to a wet-nurse for breast-feeding. When they are weaned, they are diligently cared for within this institution. Boys are sent to learn their letters, girls learn womanly things. And when the girls are grown, they are all married off, and the males are taught a trade, which is a wonderful thing.' There was even the suggestion of a dowry being provided by the Hospital – and it would all have been 'a wonderful thing' except for the fact that survival was not built into the system.

As hundreds of children began to be taken in, the meticulously kept records reveal statistics which came to characterise Foundling Hospitals everywhere: appalling mortality rates. Another interpretation of the *ruota* was as the symbol of an institutionalised infanticide machine. But considering that life expectancy was not what it is today in Western countries, and that infant mortality was a commonplace, the figures may not have seemed immediately shocking. And, as the deaths took place within four walls, or with wet-nurses out in the countryside, it did not constitute a public scandal. The reasons were manifold: a dearth of wet-nurses, a lack of hygiene, overcrowding and epidemics of plague, smallpox and intestinal diseases. And something never considered until recent times – the almost complete absence of cuddling and affection, of regular warm human contact. In the first year of the Innocenti's operation almost 20 per cent died; forty years on 90 per cent didn't make it through their first year. A century later, to leave a child at the Home was thought to be the equivalent of 'consigning a child to death'.

Nevertheless, the idea was catching on in Catholic Europe. Protestant countries at this time were much less keen on the institutional involvement of the Church, preferring to rest responsibility for unwanted children on the individual parents, whereas the Catholic Church took in foundlings because it generally thought that their mothers were unfit to look after them, such was their shame. Belgium, Spain, Holland, Portugal and Ireland were also addressing abandonment with new buildings and a policy which gathered together hundreds of little children in the centre of none-too-salubrious cities. France too was sprouting Hospitals, with Paris gaining L'Hôpital des Enfants Trouvés, partly due to the energetic activities of Vincent de Paul and the Sisters of Charity, who had noticed the numbers of children abandoned on the steps of the Cathedral of Notre Dame. A monastic order had provided care in rural areas for abandoned children since the 1300s, but Paris had missed out except for small charitable efforts. By 1638 these had dwindled to a rather un-savoury centre known as the Maison de la Couche in Rue St Landry. Its failings were catalogued in the *Mercure de France*: the Maison was run by 'a widowed and charitable lady' and two servants. Its reputation was such that the two maids were de-scribed as 'annoyed and tired by the cries of the infants'. There were allegations that these 'vile and mercenary souls' sold children to beggars who then used them as a lure for alms, and that laudanum was used to get babies to sleep. The wet-nurses were said to have tainted milk and there were charges that they sub-stituted children who died. There's also the allegation that they used infants for '*opérations magiques*' and the writer names the price – 'twenty sols'. The result of this behaviour was that throughout the city the place was known as the Maison de la Mort.

With the help of the French Queen, Anne of Austria, money came from the King's royal purse along with some buildings near a forest on the outskirts of the capital. Unfortunately, the survival rate in the new setting was none too impressive and, rather more unfortunately, ascribed at the time to '*la vivacité de l'air*' – fresh air being considered somewhat poisonous. So the surviving children and their carers were moved to the centre of Paris. Again, Vincent de Paul and his charitable assistants were much moved by the plight of children, but also driven by the horror of their 'defect of Baptism', worrying about 'the loss of these young subjects, for Religion and the State'.

For those who managed to survive childhood adoption of a kind occasionally took place, and girls were often placed with widows or unmarried women; but overall, the impression is that such children were usually found a place where their labour was appreciated – and came cheap. The lives of the rest were considered by many to be only a step or two above 'begging and theft', for they were described as having no more than meagre education and were commonly believed to have inherited the sinful tendencies of their 'immoral' mothers. Some are mentioned as being employed in collecting alms at mass, in accompanying funeral corteges, or in knitting.

However, another opportunity was being created as European countries began to expand overseas into virgin territory. The French were as avid as others to send useful bodies to populate new lands, and Louis XIV had spotted a solution in 1670 to justify his mother's support for the Paris foundlings: '. . . considering how advantageous their preservation really was, since some of them might become soldiers, and be usefull in our Armies or Troups, some to be Tradesmen, or Inhabitants in our Colonys, which we are settling for the advantage of the Trade of our Kingdom'. This was an idea seized with relish by many empires in the next three centuries. However, as a breeding ground for sturdy young empire-builders the Foundling Hospitals were dismal failures: in Paris a century on, in a new building described as having 'space and light and with regular visits from 'doctors and surgeons', only 10 per cent of the inmates reached the age of five.

Back in Italy, those who took pride in the new institutions made little analysis of their success or failure. Babies had a place to go where records were kept in an excellent state, and, although there were endless disputes about funding, there was considerable moral satisfaction to be gained from the very sight of a handsome building embodying public-spirited endeavours. And if the infants appeared not to thrive – well, infant death was an occurrence in the best-run households, and wasn't the alternative to the Hospital a much worse fate, possible infanticide or fatal exposure in the woods or streets? There was also the virtue of reinforcing religious views on illegitimacy: by the middle of the sixteenth century it was becoming increasingly difficult for unwed couples to raise children – the Church was preaching ever more strongly against all forms of sex other than procreation within wedlock.

Greater problems were facing those women who'd heard the promise of marriage from a heavy-breathing suitor, and believed that he meant what he said . . . 'Twas ever thus. But the informal acceptance of a bastard conceived in those circumstances was diminishing. Instead, such women were becoming more isolated – their 'honour' had been lost and they were culpable of sin. Keeping the child and rearing it was an affront to the community, according to the clergy, and there was no alternative but for the mother to relinquish it. After all, she might encourage others to think they could 'get away with it'. What was missing from the argument was the father. Rarely are fathers mentioned in the context of responsibility – all the onus for what had happened fell on the mother. Legal and official pronouncements usually just refer to the importance of preserving the father's anonymity. And names reflect that: one of the more common surnames in Italy is Esposito, and I had never thought to wonder about its origins despite having worked for years alongside an Italian-American film editor by the name of Sposito. It means 'exposed' – the traditional term for a foundling.

The Foundling Hospitals began to be the only answer available to both a pregnant single woman and a married woman bearing a child who was not her husband's. Poverty was still an element in the pressure to abandon, but shame and sin had been added in bucketfuls. The Santo Spirito in Rome had imposed, by the eighteenth century, a method of distinguishing foundlings from other orphans. The moment the child arrived via the *ruota*, the Hospital's symbol, a cross, was incised in the infant's right foot. When an official Visitation was carried out in the 1740s, the main intention was to ensure that those being looked after bore the relevant scar; otherwise the staff were suspected of having substituted children for those who had died or been sold.

Foundling Hospitals began to bulge at the seams. Once the

concept had spread throughout much of Europe it delivered far and wide the general impression that this was an excellent and modern solution to abandonment, with travellers from St Petersburg to Dublin to Vienna commenting on the large buildings and impressive statistics relating to children received. There was meant to be a strict religious atmosphere, with emphasis on piety and obedience. The girls might be heading for a lifetime in domestic service or within a convent, and the boys would be learning a trade if they were lucky. What was not widely mentioned was that every single institution killed far more children than ever survived.

However, the public image of Foundling Hospitals was bolstered by seeming success in some instances: the Pietà in Venice had a busy niche in its wall, called the *scaffetta*. A mother, or someone who had found the child in the street, might ring the bell, or just leave the child, but there was also a spyhole so that a gate-keeper inside could observe. Anonymity was a much-disputed issue. Once inside, the infant was inspected for disease and lice, then taken to a table where the *Medico Chirurgo* would brand it on the upper left arm with an elaborate 'P' for 'Pietà'. This practice was later changed to branding the sole of the foot, and did not die out until the nineteenth century. Baptism followed the next day.

Mortality rates were not good – but the Ospedale della Pietà was better organised and funded than most, had its own bank and bakery and took in food and wine from its own estates in the country. In contrast to other Italian institutions it was not under the control of the Church, being run by a board under the Venetian ruler, the Doge. It had also embarked on a specific income-generating scheme. The boys left at sixteen to be labourers and artisans, heading for the stone-cutting quarries and weaving sheds. However, the girls had three options: become nuns, get married, or stay in the Pietà. The majority opted for the last of these, especially if they had been trained in music, for the Pietà's choir and orchestra had a great reputation and their teacher was Antonio Vivaldi. The system had already been tried in Naples, where the strict monastic-style orphanage of Santa Maria di Loretto had produced several professional musicians, and performances brought in handy funds. The idea spread, and large and fashionable congregations assembled for services to hear the sound of pious children who were to be both pitied and admired.

Vivaldi arrived in 1703 and stayed for nearly forty years, following in the shoes of Scarlatti and Lotti. His charges were the privileged members of the institution – being a musician even got you better rations, more rice and beef and wine! However, the girls had no surnames, being called after their voice part or whichever instrument they were learning: Prudenza dal Contralto and Rosana Organista. Some acquired a surname if they married, and the opportunity increased with public concerts (though the girls were never allowed to perform outside the Ospedale). The institution would provide a small dowry, but contact with the Pietà was severed for ever – you had to be a virgin to remain there.

The standard was exceptional: European royalty and nobility, even Pope Pius IV, headed for Venice and attended special concerts. A distinguished French official remarked that 'They sing like angels, and play violin, flute, organ, hautboy, violincello, bassoon, in short, there is no instrument so large as to frighten them.' The lack of male voices seems to have been overcome by having some of the contraltos trained to sing especially low. The girls knew that their music teacher was far from ordinary: he wrote specific pieces for the talents of individual girls and was very conscious of their beginnings, showing immense sympathy for their having been abandoned. It has even been suggested that he saw his music as a kind of therapy for them. From the Pietà emerged some of his greatest works, including the *Gloria*, probably written for the Feast of the Visitation of the Blessed Virgin, one of the Pietà's most important occasions.

Clearly, for those who survived into adulthood and benefited from the special status of this Venetian institution life was extraordinarily healthy: Vivaldi was conducting violinists who reached their seventies. On his travels the English writer and eccentric William Beckford took note, though perhaps more from the point of view of an eighteenth-century gay man: 'The sight of the orchestra still makes me smile. You know, I suppose, it is entirely of the feminine gender, and that nothing is more common to see a delicate white hand journeying across an enormous double bass, or a pair of roseate cheeks puffing, with all their efforts, at a French horn. Some that are grown old and Amazonian, who have abandoned their fiddles and their lovers, take vigorously to the kettle-drum; and one poor limping lady, who had been crossed in love, now makes an admirable figure on the bassoon.'

A remnant of the Pietà's *scaffetta* lurks today in the corner of a plush hotel dining room. The church which Vivaldi knew is now the Metropole Hotel; its replacement, a handsome landmark on the edge of the Grand Canal, lies across a narrow alley. Thousands of tourists stroll past every day but few of them notice an odd bulge in the wall – a kind of curved wooden doorway. Inside, the hotel waiters stack plates and thick linen napkins in the semicircular alcove while diners feast on seafood and pasta in the former church. The archives are stored in the basement of the newer buildings across the alley: huge leather-bound ledgers list each entry for over two centuries. Most names have an elaborate cross drawn next to them, indicating infant death, usually from consumption or *mal di peto* – chest infection. There are piles of cardboard boxes; open one, and the thick dusty documents can be unfolded – whereupon a sliver of paper usually slips out. Half a picture, cut diagonally, most often of a guardian angel: the token left by a mother over a century ago. An official description of the infant is attached, with the day, hour and minute of its arrival followed by a baptismal name added in different coloured ink.

The Pietà buildings still ring to children's voices. A dozen live here, having been put into care, and it's not unknown today that a woman can be heard asking: 'Is this where you can leave a baby?'

The classical music tradition was one of the few positive achievements of the Foundling Hospitals, and was mainly confined to Italy. However, it was adapted through the years in many orphanages and institutions in Europe to create military-style bands – considered healthy and disciplined exercise for young boys, and often preparing them for adult life as army bandsmen. Generally, there were no great opportunities for foundlings: their education was rarely above the most basic and a very definite stigma attached to their background. Living in closed institutions, they were moulded to obedience and expected to serve society. There was constant fretting that they would 'revert to type' and that 'bad blood will out', as their mothers were regarded as immoral and no better than prostitutes. The difference from the ever-popular fictional fantasy about well-born children being 'mislaid' or 'mistaken' was enormous. In reality, little romance ever attached to the life of a foundling. A pious upbringing with heavy emphasis on religious observance was the norm and there was little chance for a fairytale reunion with a welcoming parent, despite the tokens left with the new-borns. For both sexes the option on leaving was usually service: below stairs for the girls, a cannon fodder for the boys.

And all the while, the actual incidence of abandonment never went away. There is a theory that the Foundling Hospitals actually exacerbated the problem, by offering a refuge for distraught pregnant women and buttressing the belief that such mothers did not deserve to keep their babies. And there was the unforeseen effect of the huge death toll in the Hospitals: disease, neglect and indifference carried off so many that society did not have to worry about what to do with large numbers of unattached children of dubious origin. Halfway through the eighteenth century, abandonment had become epidemic in some of the larger cities of Italy, Spain, Ireland, Poland and Portugal. And the mortality figures matched the rise.

In many countries by this time legitimate children too were being deposited, sometimes for just a few years: the Hospitals were a convenient place to leave surplus or unwanted offspring, who were often reclaimed when they came to a useful working age. Jean-Jacques Rousseau, a philosopher who wrote extensively on the innocence of children and their need to learn by expression rather than repression, did not hang around to see if his own five offspring might benefit from such thoughts. He abandoned them all in a foundling home claiming that he was short of money and would make a bad father – an institution, he thought, would deliver a better upbringing, away from the perils of 'high society': 'This arrangement seemed to me so good, so sensible, so appropriate, that if I did not boast of it publicly it was solely out of regard for their mother. . . . In a word, I made no secret of my action . . . because I saw no wrong in it. All things considered, I chose what was best for my children, or what I thought was best . . .'. At least Rousseau came round to profoundly regretting his actions.

7

Where is your home?

In Britain in 1749 the public was avidly reading Henry Fielding's highly successful novel *Tom Jones – The History of a Foundling*, a jolly tale in which young Tom was found 'wrapt up in some coarse linen, in a sweet and profound sleep' between Squire Allworthy's sheets. Tom was to lead a boisterous and eventually rewarded life, gaining the fair Sophia Western – but this was the world of fiction. In reality, Fielding had taken an interest in a new venture in London in which his friend the artist Thomas Hogarth was involved, and had written about it in the magazine he edited, the *Champion*. This was the Foundling Hospital, the first in England, to which fashionable society was drawn in the same year that *Tom Jones* was published to hear a benefit concert given by George Frederick Handel.

Fielding, Handel and Hogarth – the crème de la crème of London Society. However, the moving force behind the Hospital was a man whose portrait Hogarth had already painted and who didn't see himself as a society peacock: Thomas Coram, an exceptional but distinctly bluff character among these men of art and letters. In his portrait, described by Hogarth as the one which gave him the greatest pleasure, Coram looks every inch a practical, no-nonsense man, rather florid and with his own white hair curling on to the collar of a serviceable heavy coat (no fashionable powdered wig for him), but with a kindly, benevolent face.

He had spent his life as a shipwright, much of it in the new colonies in North America. Unpretentious and not particularly well educated, he had been born in Lyme Regis in 1668 and sent to sea at the age of eleven. There are a few reminders in the local museum of his connections to the Dorset port, a hive of activity in his youth when ships traded with the continent and the colonies of the New World. Curiously, there's an odd link to his later endeavours on a wall plaque in a narrow alley called Long Entry near the seafront, which states: 'Here the novelist Henry Fielding attempted in 1725 to abduct Sarah Andrew.' It's a tale worthy of a novel, in which fifteen-year-old Sarah, a wealthy heiress, lodged with her guardian who had his eye on a match between Sarah and his own son, John Tucker. Young Henry Fielding, fresh from Eton, 'was an occasional visitor at the place, and enraptured with the charms and with the more solid attractions of Miss Andrew . . .'. Some kind of altercation took place between Fielding's servant and a man allegedly hired by Mr Tucker to attack him. For reasons which aren't quite clear, Fielding decided that abduction would be the next best step and lay in wait with his manservant near the church. The Tuckers beat them off. At the subsequent town tribunal Fielding sent his manservant in his stead while he left town, announcing that he would not appear before the 'fat and greasy citizens'. Sarah was married off to 'an eloquent preacher of Bath' but must have remained in Henry Fielding's mind, for there are numerous suggestions that she was the inspiration for Sophia Western.

It's doubtful whether Thomas Coram, trying to make his fortune in the New World in the tough shipbuilding trade, knew anything of this. He was an energetic man who immediately ran into the kind of religious strife that informed most North American ventures at the time: Church of England versus Puritan New Englanders. It took energy and enterprise to thrive in Massachusetts and Coram had both, but he was dogged by financial disputes, tended to speak his mind about his opponents and got involved in the occasional brawl. He returned to England heavily in debt but set to work undaunted, promoting investment in other colonies and settlements in America, gaining a respectable reputation in London society and championing several radical causes.

In his fifties, married but childless and living in the shipyard district of Rotherhithe, he regularly walked to the City of London to conduct his business. On his journey he was struck by the constant sight of abandoned babies, lying often dead or dying in the mud and middens of the narrow streets. However, considering that a large percentage of the poor were sozzled on cheap gin and cluttered up the alleyways insensate, infants among the rubbish were just another public hazard.

Until then, enthusiasm for Foundling Hospitals had not caught on in England. The grand institutions of Florence and Paris had been seen by travellers – who were probably unaware of the mortality rates – but there was no move to take the problem off the streets in London. Illegitimacy was something which the local ratepayers rather than the Church dealt with by means of the poorhouse – a place of grudging accommodation, often starved of parish funds, filthy, verminous and crowded with lunatics and beggars as well as the poor, the blind and unmarried mothers. Infants rarely survived more than a few weeks – there was no one appointed to look after them. Even Christ's Hospital, founded by Edward VI in 1552 for the education of poor children, had specifically excluded illegitimate children since 1676.

And other unpleasant things happened to the unwanted. Surgery was pushing new boundaries in the energetic 1700s, and dissection and anatomy were becoming an essential part of medical knowledge. The indefatigable Hogarth pictured the Company of Surgeons at work in 1751 – an instructive illustration, with the learned surgeons wearing wigs and mortar boards while watching the disembowelling; a dog under the table chews happily on the unfortunate's heart. The corpse would normally have been obtained under licence from the gallows, but there were also alternative means of obtaining the relevant study material: bodies were bought and sold like any other commodity, and supplied by gangs often known as 'Resurrectionists', forerunners of the 'body-snatchers'. They apparently made a comfortable living, helped by the general neglect and overcrowding in graveyards. By the end of the 1700s the 'Lambeth Gang' was reported as selling corpses for '12 guineas and half a crown'. Chillingly, the list of prices also includes children: 'Six shillings for the first foot and nine [pence] per inch for all it measures more in length.'

Life and death were rough and raw for many: and in such a society, the sight of foundlings in the street was not outstandingly shocking – and anyway, they were presumed to be bastards, so didn't have the requisite virtue to merit much charity. Added to this was the resonance of Puritan thinking which was none too keen on the idea of sexual fun, especially among those who were not married. And in an increasingly money-minded society, in-heritance was always an area ripe for dispute: illegitimacy messed it up royally. For the moral-minded *and* the practical, what persisted to thwart any remedy for abandoned children was the view that provision of some kind of refuge would only encourage women to have yet more bastards.

One proposal which surfaced at the court of James II in 1687 was a Scheme for the Foundation of a Royal Hospital, put forward by a midwife, Elizabeth Cellier. There were to be two thousand midwives in London, organised into a Corporation and respon-sible for a dozen 'parish houses' and a 'hospital for the education of foundlings'. The plan might have stood a better chance if Mrs Cellier had had a less colourful life. She was a robust supporter of women's right to practise midwifery, which was traditionally assailed by those who equated it with magic and secret knowledge; but midwives were also recognised as necessary – and could therefore move around the city streets at night without suspicion of prostitution. Mrs Cellier, however, was thought to take advan-tage of this by acting as a messenger for Catholic plotters. Eventually she fell foul of a conspiracy while undertaking charity visits to Newgate Prison. She was tried for treason but acquitted, and immediately published her story in which she alleged that Catholic prisoners were being tortured in Newgate. Tried for libel, this time she was convicted. With more charges added, she was put in the pillory three times, fined, and had her books burned. Seven years later she published her foundling hospital plan – but it sank without trace.

So Thomas Coram walked through streets whose problem was

no secret. Acceptance and indifference were the enemies of his strong personal feelings that something should be done for foundlings. Nevertheless, in 1722 he embarked on a long campaign to win support and stir public interest. Although known for his robust Anglican views, he viewed foundlings in the same light as the journalist Joseph Addison, who saw mothers who abandoned their babies overcome with 'the fear of shame, or their inability to support those whom they give life to.'

Coram was quick to realise that neither the state nor the Church was a likely source of support and funds, so he began to think of a novel way of financing his project: a charity which would be a non-profitmaking joint-stock company. Although he had influential friends – the writer Horace Walpole described him in a letter to his father, the Prime Minister, as 'the honestest, the most disinterested, and the most knowing person about the plantations [American Colonies] I ever talked with' – he was still of modest origins. He needed to enlist some noble clout to appeal for royal approval. His first efforts got nowhere and he testily complained that he could no more persuade a bishop or peer to help him than he could get them to 'putt doun their breeches and present their Backsides to the King and Queen in a full Drawing room such was the unchristian Shyness of all about the Court'.

So he decided to use distaff power, corralling a forceful bunch of upper-class ladies, and set about collecting an impressive list of duchesses, countesses and baronesses. He was helped by the fact that many of the women were related; even today, the family names are familiar – Cavendish, Thynne, Cadogan, Berkeley, Montagu. (It also has to be mentioned that the upper class wasn't particularly exercised by its own by-blows: money and status somehow cancelled out the shame and sin which attached to the lower orders.) To the Lady Petitioners' list were eventually added nobles and gentlemen, JPs and 'Persons of Distinction', but not before years of argument and misgiving among London society along the well-rehearsed lines of encouraging illegitimacy and fooling decent folk into paying for other people's fecklessness: 'I have found Many weak persons, more Ladies than Gentlemen,

say such a foundation will be a promotion of Wickedness,' observed Coram ruefully.

His seventeen years of persistence, letter-writing and tramping
the streets from one noble house to another eventually paid off. In
1739, King George II signed the Charter establishing the Hospital
for the Maintenance and Education of Exposed and Deserted
Young Children. By that time, Coram had found sympathetic ears
among the royal family and was learning that grand aristocrats
were taking to patronage of charitable initiatives because it was
both virtue-enhancing and fashionable. The noble work began,
and the governors – including Thomas Hogarth – convened:
curiously, women were not included, despite the work of the Lady
Petitioners and although the examples of Paris and Amsterdam
suggested that much of the management of such institutions was
thought proper for women. However, it was not an argument over
gender which disrupted the first year of operation: Thomas Coram
fell out spectacularly with his fellow governors, and for his troubles
was ousted from the board. His enthusiasm, plain speaking and
individual mind-set had met the smoother creatures of gentle-
manly administration and he paid the price, being excluded from
all the primary committees planning the new building and its
running. Later, his only contact with the Hospital he had in effect
created was to be godfather to many of the foundlings. He was seen
sometimes on private visits, 'distributing with tears in his Eyes
Gingerbread to the Children'.

The Hospital opened its doors in temporary accommodation in
Hatton Garden. The first day – or rather night – of business was
traumatic. The governors had publicised its opening, giving notice
that '. . . on Wednesday, the 25th March, at 8 o'clock at night, and
from that time till the House shall be full, their House will be
opened for the reception of any person bringing a child, nor shall
any servant of the Hospital presume to discover who such a person
is, on pain of being dismissed'. Secrecy to counter the shame. The
lights in the entrance were also extinguished to enable women to
avoid identification. As a precaution against babies being left in the

street, the governors employed watchmen to patrol outside and the porter was told to stop women leaving their babies if they hadn't been formally admitted.

In an age when literacy was limited, the governors must have wondered if their notice had stirred any interest: ten of them assembled inside at seven o'clock. By midnight they knew, as their committee minutes record:

> About Twelve o'Clock, the House being full the Porter was Order'd to give notice to the Crowd who were without, who thereupon being a little troublesome One of the Govrs. Went out, and told them that as many children were already taken in as Cou'd be made Room for in the House and that Notice Shou'd be given by the Publick Advertisement as soon as any more Could possibly be admitted. And Govrs observing seven or eight women with Children at the Door and more amongst the Crowd desired them that they woul'd not Drop any of their Children in the Streets where they most probably must Perish but to take care of them till they could have an opportunity of putting them into the Hospital which was hoped would be very soon. . . . On this Occasion the Expressions of Grief of the Women whose Children could not be admitted were Scarcely more observable than those of the Women who parted with their Children, so that a more moving Scene can't well be imagined.

Eighteen boys and twelve girls were inside and their condition was carefully noted:

> All the children who were received (except three) were dressed very clean . . . nevertheless many of them appeared as if Stupified with some Opiate, and some of them almost Starved, or as in the agonies of Death thro' want of Food, too weak to Suck, or to receive Nourishment, and notwithstanding the greatest care appeared to be dying when the Govrs. Left the Hospital which was not until they had given proper Orders and seen all necessary Care taken of the children.

Two died before they could be baptised. Affecting and private occasions? Not exactly.

The next day, fashionable London was at the door keen to display its new-found enthusiasm for charity. And so the public face of the Hospital was born, one which continued into the twentieth century, with the children on display on Sundays and the beneficent encouraged to view them and dig deep into their purses. Some of the visitors – 'Persons of Quality and Distinction' – attended the first baptisms and lent their names, a practice which withered when the children grew up and a number of them claimed kinship with their noble namesakes. Heroes from history, writers and poets were employed thereafter.

The original records, housed in the London Metropolitan Archives, contain boxes of faded letters and bound record books which catalogue the daily intake of the Hospital from the first few days. It's extraordinary to unfold these pieces of paper and see line after line of beautiful script describing the infants. The Index for 17 April 1741 is typical:

> A female child two months old. A pair of red and white narrow striped sleeves, white worsted stockings with red cloak, yellow leather shoes quite new, tied with yellow a fringed cap and very neatly dressed. Delivered to nurse Page.
>
> A male child about 2 m. old . . . a printed linen mantle lined with blue check . . . asleep when taken in.
>
> A female child about 2 m. old almost naked a paper with it a pink ribband knot. Delivered to nurse Rayner eleven o'clock.
>
> A male child about two months old with which a letter delivered Sealed, a fine India dimity mantle. White corded dimity sleeves exceedingly neat. Delivered to nurse Wilkinson.
>
> A female child over two months old . . . shift sleeves with cambrick ruffles . . . a wart on the middle of the neck under the chin.
>
> 16 males 14 females for that day.

The early intake appears to have been relatively well dressed, suggesting that illegitimacy among the better-off was as unwelcome as poverty among the poor. However, the majority who were recorded later had a more ragged appearance or were near-naked, so much so that the governors had to warn against 'stripping any such Child or Children of their Clothing'.

The governors' main preoccupation was a fine new building, which arose amid green fields to the north of the city. Today the site would be designated central London, being in the middle of Bloomsbury near Gray's Inn Road. However, in the 1740s it represented fresh air and open space. An imposing but plain design was chosen – there was a feeling that a novel charitable venture should not waste money on extras. It emulated in many ways the grand Hospitals dotted around London which had been developed by both royal and private benefactors – Christ's, for orphaned children, Chelsea for disabled soldiers and St George's for local medical cases. They were imposing, spacious and rather draughty. In the Foundling, girls lived in the East Wing, boys in the West. And the records show that at least the British foundlings – unlike their counterparts in Catholic Europe – were evenly divided between the sexes.

There were some ornate public rooms, for the Hospital had to raise funds and entertain the influential. And Hogarth, as one of the governors, was not slow to realise that there was considerable potential for both increasing finances and trumpeting the Cause of Art. London had artists and sculptors – but nowhere to show their work. Hogarth himself eyed the walls of the new building as a likely display area for his own work – but, a true philanthropist, he donated his pictures – and then got others to follow suit, thus creating a fashionable milieu for exhibitions, drawing in potential patrons of the Hospital and possible further commissions for the artists, among them Gainsborough, Reynolds and the sculptor Rysbrack. It was a hugely successful venture and became the precursor of the Royal Academy.

Meanwhile the elegant chapel in the new building was attracting musicians: Handel saw it just before it was finished, and on 27 May 1749 he 'Generously and Charitably offered a Performance of Vocal and Instrumental Musick' to raise funds to complete it. This concert, the first of many, attracted the Prince and Princess of

Wales. It was a great success: 'There was no collection, but the tickets were at half a guinea, and the audience above a thousand.' Handel became a great benefactor, through both his love of children and his acquaintance with orphanages in his native Germany. He wrote the Foundling Hospital Anthem, subtitled 'Blessed Are They That Consider the Poor' – with a chorus borrowed from the *Messiah*. The oratorio itself became a regular fixture in the Hospital's musical calendar, and on his death he bequeathed it 'a Fair Copy of the Score and all Parts of his Oratorio call'd the Messiah'.

The rich enjoyed the art and music. The charitable felt good. The children looked fine – dressed in their uniforms of brown and scarlet, designed by Hogarth. They led a regimented life, with plain meals, some exercise, and education for the boys, domestic skills for the girls. Discipline was strict – and there was a degree of isolation, apart from the public visitors who came to services on Sundays. There was still a lurking suspicion that such children could 'revert' to their origins. The sins of their mothers reverberated quietly.

What was not so celebrated was, as in all such institutions, the mortality rate. Once received in the Hospital the children were put out to wet-nurses – a system in use for centuries, and not confined to the rich. There were constant problems – not enough dependable healthy women, not enough care in the rudimentary country cottages where many of the infants were sent to nurse, and appalling journeys made by babies to and from the Hospital. Those who remained in London fared even worse: there was little understanding of overcrowding and infection. Of the original thirty children received, twenty-three died in the first five months, though many were clearly very weak when they arrived. Not that this in any way put off new admissions – there were regular rowdy scenes as women fought to get inside the door.

To sort this latter problem out, the governors devised a lottery. Each woman drew a coloured ball from inside a bag or box. A white ball allowed her to leave her baby, after it had been examined for disease; a black ball meant immediate rejection; and a red ball provided a chance for a second shot if any of the 'white ball' babies proved to be unhealthy. Not unnaturally the mothers got into a terrible state, and to add to their emotion – or rather because of it – the general public was permitted to come and watch them, the entire circus becoming a public entertainment. Even so, this system still did not dissuade women from queuing in large numbers on Reception Days: in the five years from 1750, 763 babies were admitted – out of over two and a half thousand brought to the Hospital.

Notes were often left with the children, as were tokens: coins, odd earrings, ribbons and metal tags, sometimes with a name. The Foundling Hospital Museum in London still has many of them, attesting to the forlorn hope of many mothers that they might reclaim their children at a later date, bringing with them a matching half-coin or button as well as the certificate given in exchange for their child. The notes pinned to clothing showed both straggly letters spelling out a name and neatly written poems and messages: 'You have my heart Tho wee must part (Born – 6 Sepr 1759).' The certificate given to the mother was a vital document, even if she could not read. Since 1624, the onus had been on the mother of an illegitimate baby to prove that she had not murdered her child if a corpse was found. She was faced with the uphill task of proving it had died naturally or been still-born. And as bodies were left willy-nilly in the streets, a woman who had just surrendered her baby needed a document to confirm she was not a 'baby-dropper'; otherwise she faced a prison sentence or hanging.

Confronted with a never-ending stream of children and struggling to administer a complicated and expensive wet-nursing service, as well as maintaining a large Hospital, the governors went to the state for help. A government grant was forthcoming – but with strings attached: the Hospital would have to accept *every* child offered to it. This so-called General Reception, which lasted for four years, nearly broke the institution. Fifteen thousand babies arrived. The whole country had got wind of the scheme, and infants were being bundled on to wagons, brought by pedlars and sent from the shires by packhorse; and the parish workhouses spotted a chance to offload some of their inmates. Six new hospitals were set up outside London, including ones at Shrewsbury and Chester, but the damage had been done. Infants had been found by the roads leading to London, discarded by their carriers, and the lengthy journey weakened the new-borns. Out of those fifteen thousand, more than nine thousand perished. The governors were at their wits' end and Parliament was unimpressed: having hoped to have solved the abandonment problem at a stroke, it found itself faced with chaotic scenes and aggrieved moralists banging on about illegitimates and bastards getting more attention than the families of the virtuous poor. The net result was a drastic overhaul of the Foundling Hospital's administration and a government wholly convinced that helping a charity care for children was not a good thing.

Back in control of their business, the governors gradually introduced one major change which altered the entire meaning of the word 'Foundling' in their title. Although babies found in the street were occasionally brought by servants and others to the Hospital, most mothers had had to surrender their children in person – the assumption being that otherwise the child would inevitably become a foundling or perhaps be killed. Over the next thirty years the emphasis swung towards the support of illegitimate children, with the accompanying view that the mothers should be rehabilitated – 'the restoration of the mother to work and a life of virtue'.

The result was a procession of women betrayed – by their babies' fathers. Promises of marriage, desertion, seduced innocents and rape victims – all figured in the pitiful ranks of those who found their way to the Foundling Hospital: the petitions written by the women are a tragic catalogue of the limited options facing the poor when in collision with conventional morality. The governors made great efforts to enquire into each 'case'. As well as the petitions, there were the records of each case hearing – and a list of the twenty-one questions which were to be put to the mother to discover what the Hospital thought pertinent:

'Is this your first child?' (One hopes that the mothers might be aware of this first hurdle before the Foundling Hospital gate – entrance was for first-borns only.)

'In what manner did your acquaintance with the Father commence?

'How soon after acquaintance did he pay you particular attention?

'What led to your seduction?

'Was the criminal intercourse repeated?' (Tricky one, this; the governors were much more sympathetic to one-night stands.)

'When did you first find yourself pregnant?

'What enquiries have you made of the Father?

'Is your Child healthy, is it a Child of Colour or has it any natural marks?'

Then came the moral test: 'Should you be relieved of your Child, what do you intend to do to gain a livelihood?' Anyone falling at this fence by failing to deliver an earnest commitment to a life of hard work, preferably with a prospective employer attached, forfeited the chance of acceptance.

Finally, a question which would not look out of place in the most rampantly market-oriented modern consumer survey: 'When did you first hear of this Hospital?' What the correct answer was is hard to ascertain. But the detailed answers to the rest are faithfully recorded in the case hearings, along with the letters and statements of these anonymous women, known only by initials, under the headings 'Admitted' or 'Rejected'.

1832. D.E.: Admitted –
Aged 19, servant
F [father] also a servant. Mother does not know what had become of him.
Evidence: Became acquainted whilst living in same family. He was the first. A month afterwards he proposed keeping her company. 2 months afterwards seduced her in Housekeeper's Room. Finding herself with child she told him – and he promised Marriage in a month. This he afterwards put off – at length, one of

fellow servants told their master who discharged them both.
Steward's Report: Her mistress has known D and her family
many years. The petitioner's conduct is satisfactory – nearly 3
years' service. F is a married man – and not forthcoming.

Not forthcoming. Covers pretty well everything, but the favourable report from the employer probably clinched the baby's place
in the Hospital. Others were not so lucky:

1835 B.M.: Rejected –
A creole brought to England by her Mistress – who gives her the
highest character.
F a butcher, in the country. Courted and seduced her in Mistress'
house. 2 months pregnant – told him – he bid her be patient and
he would Marry her. F said afterwards he could not support her,
therefore would not marry her.

Clearly a good character recommendation was not enough. Other
rejections were more terse:

A.B: Rejected –
Said she was seduced by a sailor in 1833 aged 22. She is a servant.
F a seaman. She was courted and marriage promised and en-
quired everywhere for F in vain.
Steward's Report: altogether false.

It all reads like a Victorian ballad, baldly stated: a pattern of
betrayal, with the miserable refrain 'Oh, I am undone.' The reality
was not a sentimental situation: these women had little support and
much opprobrium. They were condemned by society for having
believed in love and promises, attention and affection, and their
crime was to have become pregnant.

The Foundling Hospital was by now a respectable nineteenth-
century institution, whose inmates led a regular life – tedious
maybe, but a marvellous alternative to the dreaded workhouse,
and one which not all mothers managed to secure for their
children:

1831 C.P.: Rejected –

Aged 22, not in Service

F: Foreign Officer. Is in France

Evidence: Became acquainted with whilst at present residence kept by a relation. F met and accosted her in the street – followed her to the Home. Waited for her the following evening and frequently afterwards for a month. Then took her to a House which he said belonged to a friend – where he seduced her – previous to which he promised her Marriage. After she found herself with child he gave her altogether £20. Ultimately said he was ordered to his own country by his Government.

Steward's Report: Relation of P gives her a good character and knew of courtship.

F – at Paris

F – a married man.

P confined in Workhouse and will be passed to the Parish.

Passed to the parish workhouse where, since the Middle Ages and until Coram's institution was set up, most foundlings had fetched up – and usually died, very quickly. And as the Foundling Hospital rapidly limited itself to the illegitimate offspring of the repentant, the rejected children and all foundlings were headed for the place which no one in society wished to visit. In my home town of Sunderland it was reported in 1797 that 'There are 176 persons present in the Workhouse. There are 36 children, two thirds of them bastards.'

By the nineteenth century, workhouses were a staple building of all centres of population – the only refuge for those fallen on hard times or unable to support themselves. They were the all-embracing sink of society into which were swept the penniless, the idle, the mad and the helpless. Blind teenagers mingled with lunatics and idiots; the old and the infirm huddled in corners. Beggars and vagrants were set to mind-numbing work: stone-breaking, bone-crushing and oakum-picking (unravelling old rope). And foundlings were deposited on the doorstep, such as Kitty, who in 1815 was left outside the workhouse in London's St Marylebone with a note attached:

I am little Kitty, my parents are poor,
I crave your pity, now I am left at your door.
I do not despair but a hope I do cherish
I shall be taken care of, as I am left to the parish.

Hm. Even allowing for a relatively well-schooled woman with a poetic turn of phrase, a little note of doubt creeps in as to the authenticity of the verse. Nevertheless, a poor mother would be very aware that the workhouse was a heartless place where her infant would be grudgingly regarded and rarely given any attention. Perhaps if she could pull at a heart-string . . . ?

The poorhouses before them, and the workhouses, were the object of irritation to the ratepayers. The game of shunting the unwanted from parish to parish, to avoid having to feed and house them, went on for centuries. Considering that until modern times the majority of the population lived a relatively precarious existence, the resentment of the workhouse is understandable. However, in the early 1800s industrialisation increased the problem, with urban slums housing working people in appalling conditions and attacks on poorhouses in rural areas – those inside were deemed a drain on an already poor parish. The Poor Law Act of 1834 was intended as a major national reform of the parish system and resulted in a large number of new buildings springing up over the length and breadth of the land. It was based on the hallowed view that there existed the deserving poor and the undeserving, and that if anyone was prepared to commit themselves to the care of the austere and unpleasant workhouse then they lacked the moral fibre to survive outside it. The standard of living within these new buildings was intentionally positioned lower than that of the 'independent labourer of the lowest class'. Harsh regimes proliferated, and the workhouse became a place of shame and a form of punishment. For the remainder of the century, most of these institutions were what would now be termed 'Dickensian' – Charles Dickens frequently wrote and campaigned about the squalor and overcrowding which he witnessed at first hand.

A tide of miserable humanity washed into the stark buildings, many of them designed on the same lines as the Victorian prisons and often called 'Bastilles'. The inmates were free to leave at any time, but the stigma of the workhouse made re-entry into the community a difficult task. Unmarried mothers could be housed along with their babies, which meant they did not have to abandon them. A glance at the list of inmates in 1861 in Teesdale gives a snapshot of the social unfortunates, each of whom had been an inmate for at least five years, with the reason given as to why he or she was 'unable to maintain Himself or Herself:

William Allison	10	[years as inmate] Infirm
Thomas Barron	9	Lunatic
Mary Brunskill	7	Having two illegitimate children
George Clayton	8	Idiotic
Phoebe Greenwell	10	Partial Lunatic
Elizabeth Thirkell	6	Having two illegitimate children
Mary Watson	5	Infirm – being deformed
Mary Ann Wright	5	Having two illegitimate children

It was a grim existence, and thousands experienced it. Abandonment was as common as ever. Victorian England made a fetish of the virtuous woman and, though charitable organisations began to flourish, having a child out of wedlock continued to be a barrier to sympathy.

The few remaining workhouses look quite imposing (many were transmuted into hospitals in the twentieth century) and contained huge numbers. The St Marylebone Workhouse in London, near the present Euston Station, held over two thousand people in the 1840s. It was inevitable that foundlings did not thrive. They were not expected to. There was no one to look after them and the overcrowding and filthy conditions usually finished off most babies. If they survived, what followed was only rudimentary education and a modest life of service. Even the word 'workhouse' was a powerful weapon in modest households until well into the twentieth century, calculated to carry a threat in the face of profligacy and idleness.

The St Marylebone Workhouse records are detailed. The names, birthplace, age and occupation of the inmates are inscribed in careful copperplate handwriting: page after page of charwoman, labourer, bathchairman, horse hair curler, mangler, domestic servant, mariner and muck carrier, interspersed with imbecile and lunatic. The parish authorities regularly found little bundles on the doorstep, and in 1815 would have taken in little Kitty with no great sense of charitable enthusiasm. The suspicion that illegitimacy, and therefore sinful behaviour, was the reason for abandonment left a question-mark over the child, which increased as the Victorian age refined its view of morality and propriety. Kitty may have been left to the parish, but the parish guardians merely worked out how much she was going to cost them in food and care. Such babies were not a boon, but a burden. Moreover, pregnant women had been seen as the biggest drain on expenses for a long time, and even the law discriminated against them as inmates, giving them fewer rights than beggars and lunatics.

That Kitty's mother should have written so eloquently might have raised an eyebrow or two. Few 'poor parents' – especially women – had much education, and the ability to write was much less common than that of reading. However, a short distance away lay the Foundling Hospital, and for those who had heard of it, and who were prepared to present themselves with their infant rather than abandoning it, there was always the possibility that a rather better future awaited – cleaner and more orderly than the workhouse, with the opportunity of a basic education. And some of the women who plucked up the courage to face the formidable band of worthies who would decide whether to accept or reject their child were able to write desperate letters, or at least notes, to support their case. Hundreds of these documents, the petitions to the governors and guardians of the Foundling Hospital, survive. Attached to the official printed page which had to be filled in by the mother are letters and notes and scrawled messages – mainly from employers – to sway the mighty decision-makers in the Committee Room.

In 1815, as Kitty was presumably being shunted to a professional wet-nurse (more grumbling from the parish guardians), Rebecca Carter of Hoxton Town was clutching her petition and her daughter and trying her luck at the Foundling Hospital. Her smudged petition, recording that she was twenty-four and unmarried, had been filled in by someone else for an X stands for her 'mark' or signature. In the space for 'father' is the name James Hill. In the space for 'whereabouts', 'gone as a soldier'. Ann Martha Broomfield was next in line, a married nineteen-year-old from Stepney Common whose daughter was not Mr Broomfield's. Instead, Richard Bennet Neal is named, a mariner last seen eight months before the baby arrived and now believed by Martha 'to be in the West Indies'. And all through 1815, the pile of petitions lists deserting plumbers, bakers, smiths, post-chaise drivers and shoemakers, many described as having 'absented himself from residence' or 'no trace to be found'. However, every so often there is a personal note from a mother. Hannah Taylor of Westminster, unmarried and twenty-one, squiggles her answers on to the form: The Father? 'dose not no the name'. Trade? 'a gentleman'. Where met? 'at a dance'. And as for his whereabouts now, 'he dose not no how he made me this.' Attached are notes from her employer describing Hannah as coming from a poor family, her mother being 'a poor Irish woman . . . going out a-charing'. Hannah worked for the public house in Clipstone Street, 'hired to carry out their beer'.

Alas, she and her daughter fared no better than Rebecca and Martha. On the back of their petitions is the word 'Rejected'. One can only conclude that their children stood a high chance of following Kitty to St Marylebone or one of the many other workhouses dotting the city. Another petition from Philadelphia Odell gives a clue to the rejections: an attached note carries the observation that she and the father had 'criminal congress – this was repeated'. The lack of good character, that essential for winning the hearts of the Foundling governors, took precedent over the circumstances. And if there were no endorsements of industrious and penitent behaviour, accompanied by a promise to mend one's ways, then rejection was inevitable and the workhouse beckoned.

Bastardy was beginning to irritate the Victorian mind, too. Until

1834 there had been the reasonable expectation that the father of a child should bear some responsibility – even if he disputed the matter. However, the sheer cheek of getting pregnant annoyed the law-makers. Ignoring the fact that it takes two to tango, they removed all legal responsibility from the father and dumped the problem on mothers, insisting that they alone should provide for their child up to the age of sixteen. The law took the view that women went around having a good time, and should be heartily discouraged. This legislation survived for ten years before being amended to allow mothers to lodge affiliation orders. But the moralising tone did not abate and the general public were not sympathetic. The result was more unmarried mothers crammed into the new workhouses, alongside the hapless indigent, the mad and the lame, the blind, the mute, the deaf and the aged.

The workhouse was institutionalised: men and women were separated on arrival, regardless of marriage or family ties, and were often forbidden to speak to each other. Uniforms were introduced, made of coarse material, characteristically striped, usually blue and white. In some places the ancient custom of yellow for immorality re-emerged, with single mothers forced to wear the colour as an extra symbol of their shame. Food was basic, centred on bread and gruel, and the daily routine monotonous and rigid.

Kitty, if taken in by St Marylebone, would have been spared the later rigours of the Victorian reforms. However, the stigma attached to workhouse life persisted for a century after the Poor Law Act, and in the 1930s women were still loath to enter even though they still had no alternative.

Had Kitty's mother heard of Coram and the Foundling Hospital, and had she been accepted, there would have been a better future for the child, though hardly a soft option. Discipline, respect for rules and a sense of orderliness pervaded every nineteenth-century institution from posh public school to workhouse to prison. Uniforms, military precision, rules, routine, unappetising food, exercise drill, silence when gathered together, a regular dose of Christianity, and an unassailable conviction that all this was Good for You. At least Coram's kindly nature and the strong conviction that the foundlings had a future hovered over the Hospital.

After being put out first to a wet-nurse, and then to a foster-mother, the surviving children came back to the Foundling Hospital when they were five years old. They entered a building vastly different from the tiny cottages where they had spent their infancy. In the heart of London, frequently visited by patrons and society folk, their whole world was contained within the gates. Routine was the backbone of daily life. In the early 1800s, every hour of the day was prescribed:

> They rise at six in the summer and daylight in the winter, part of them being employed before breakfast in dressing the younger children, in cleaning about the house, and the boys in working a forcing pump which supplies all the wards and every part of the Hospital abundantly with water. At half past seven they breakfast and at half after eight into school, where they continue, the boys till twelve, the girls a little later. At one o'clock they dine, and return to school at two, and stay till four in the summer, and in winter till dusk, except on Saturday when they have half-holiday. They are also instructed in singing the Foundling Hymns and anthems, and in their catechism, and are occasionally employed in and about the house during play-hours. At six in the evening they sup, and at eight go to bed.

Sir Bernard Thomas, the Hospital's Treasurer, was describing a regime intended to create a specific product: a dutiful and industrious child who was a hard-working adult in the making. And one who knew his or her status in life. Humility was expected, for after all these children had been plucked from the mud of poverty and shame or perhaps a worse fate. One of the oldest documents – the subscription roll of 1739 – had a headpiece designed by Hogarth, which shows a mother about to murder her infant when Thomas Coram intervenes and saves it (while holding the Hospital's Charter).

Gratitude was demanded, too. All around lay the disorder of the slums, the appalling conditions in which the poor of London struggled to find enough to eat. Let there be thanks for the clean and airy building and for the regular meals, even if they seemed to feature bread and gruel and rice pudding and porridge rather often, though meat did appear three times a week – as ever, the girls and boys dining separately, and usually in silence. The accounts were kept meticulously, for those in charge were always amazed at the amount children can eat, and food took up a large part of the Hospital's budget. Small portions were the order of the day – and just as Dickens' Oliver Twist discovered in the work-house, Asking For More was an unheard-of presumption.

Should a child fall ill he or she went to the infirmary, where the complaint was entered in the Apothecaries' Report Book. In 1835 around a dozen inmates are listed most weeks, reporting the cuts, bruises and 'itch' (scabies) that were to be expected. Fever, abscesses and chickenpox are common, along with 'eruptions' and numerous skin problems under the heading of 'tetta'. Bugs and worms, lice and nits – even the spartan and much-scrubbed Hospital couldn't keep out what the rest of the population was alive with. William Page has the indignity of 'disordered bowels' compounded by the unmentioned whereabouts of 'a very large Wart'. Peter Pole spends three whole months in bed, ill with 'Lepra'. Again, such attention and care would be almost unknown in the families they'd left behind – and utterly absent in the workhouse. So gratitude was expected – and taught.

Nevertheless, there was a tradition of intelligent medical care – the founders had included distinguished physicians – and in the Apothecaries' Book is a carefully hand-copied article from the *Sunday Herald* of 3 May 1835. It reports a debate on the diffi-culties encountered with the cowpox vaccine for smallpox – still a lively issue, and important to the Hospital as it had always endorsed vaccination.

In the schoolrooms the boys received a basic grounding in useful skills – reading and writing, geography and catechism. There was strict discipline, but a much milder set of attitudes to punishment when compared to those in some of the more vigorous public schools. And there are records of small rewards given for excel-lence – perhaps a 'Bible & Prayer Book, better bound than common, with initial Letter of the Boys and Girls Names in Gold Letters'. Children were beaten for misbehaviour rather than ignorance, and appear to have been chastised in a relatively benign fashion in an age when flogging adults nearly to death was still thought a necessary example to unruly society.

Eventually, girls too were taught to write as well as read – a future domestic servant needed to make out a laundry list. Sewing, knitting, darning and even spinning were the practical subjects, and a good appreciation of the catechism rammed home the need for piety and humility. For all of this was preparation for the precise station in life for which the children were intended. 'Notwithstanding the innocence of the Children, yet as they are exposed and abandoned by their Parents, they ought to submit to the lowest stations and should not be educated in such a manner as may put them upon a level with the children of Parents who have the Humanity and Virtue to preserve them, and the Industry to Support them.' So it had been laid down in 1749. The sins of the fathers, or, to be precise, of the mothers – were to be passed on and atoned for by their children. In reality this meant, as the governors put it, 'to undergo with Contentment the most Servile and laborious Offices'.

Already in uniform, trained to be obedient and familiar with military marching though hours of drill in the Hospital grounds, the boys were eagerly accepted by the British army and Royal Navy. An empire was being built, and recruitment wasn't always easy for the government; life in the forces was rough and tough and the taverns and docksides were trawled for likely lads. The Coram boys had no family role models to follow, and were used to communal life. Added to this, they had had some musical training, not only singing in the Sunday services but often playing in the school band. Perhaps Handel has to be thanked for providing an extraordinary supply of military bandsmen right up to World War II. Other boys became apprenticed, often as early as ten, to learn a trade. Butchers, bakers, candlestick-makers, weavers and dyers, shoemakers and cobblers. The Hospital kept a sharp eye on their progress, and intervened when things went wrong. However, in the reports from those who employed the boys the Hospital put good character first and foremost.

It was the same for the girls, who swapped their maid-like school clothes for a very similar outfit below stairs. Their mistresses regularly had to fill in a lengthy questionnaire about their servants' conduct, including an annual form to be completed 'before Young Persons under Age, brought up in this Hospital, can receive the customary Reward for Good Conduct during the year'. There was a list of virtues which had to be ticked on the form: Honest, Sober, Truthful, Obedient, Industrious and Respectful. A tall order for young girls sent out from a large community where they'd been brought up isolated from other children and had known only institutional life.

From all over the country came these sheets of paper, a record of mishaps in parsonages in north Wales, breakages in the pantry in Yorkshire, and quite a lot of cheek in Dorchester. 'Emily Eaton', writes Mrs J. A. Soloman from Putney, 'is not industrious and has not made the improvement she might have done. She is most careless in her work and requires continually reminding of her duties – and has given me a great deal of trouble.' The last sentence heavily underlined as Mrs Soloman's pen sprays indignant blobs over the form. Rose Onslow, a maid in Beverley, is described by Mrs Elizabeth Stevenson as 'thoughtless and helpless', with the added suggestion that she'd be better off in 'a clergyman's family in Norfolk', to which Mrs Stevenson has already packed her off. Sadly, some girls did not prosper at all, with Lucy Varnham's form scrawled across: 'This girl is in Brookwood Asylum insane!'

Sympathy was shown by some employers, such as Mrs Emily Hallett of St Mary Cray in Kent: 'Helen Playford . . . does all she can, but my impression is her natural powers are not good . . .'. And Mrs Annie Seton Adamson of Bow in London, who made a number of complaints about her diminutive maid Sally Drysdale, concludes, '. . . a very bad temper at times, quite forgets herself; I make allowances for her stuntedness.' And there were many kindly households, as typified by Mrs Margaret Roberts of Castelnau

Villas in Barnes. Jane Balden, she writes, 'is very trying and I only feel sorry I cannot heartily give her a good character – but I wish Jane to have the treat this year.' Again, the last sentence is underlined and the impression given that there were few 'treats' that came into the girls' lives. Especially if they behaved like Emma Geldhouse in the Manor House, Great Church Lane in Hammersmith: 'The general conduct of Emma Geldhouse is turbulent and refractory in the extreme,' according to Mr John Macartney, who writes 'No' in large letters next to Truthful, Obedient, Industrious etc. To the question of whether she is sober he appends waspishly, 'No opportunity to be otherwise.'

Nevertheless, the Foundling Hospital children rarely threw over the traces or ended up shaming their governors. They had been brought up to feel grateful and to serve, and it was deeply ingrained in them. And even by the end of the nineteenth century, very little had changed in the Hospital: the uniforms would not have been out of place a century earlier, the ethos had been maintained and the system worked. And outside its railings, genuinely abandoned children were still being sent to the workhouse.

Charlie Chaplin was sent, with his brother, to Lambeth Workhouse in 1896. He had not been abandoned, but his mother had fallen on hard times and didn't have a farthing to her name. He always remembered the shame attached to such a fate, crying when he saw his mother in the workhouse uniform. He had the good fortune – though he wasn't so sure about it himself – to be transferred to Hanwell School, just north of Ealing, one of several erected to house and educate children away from the capital's overcrowded central workhouses. What remains of it – a rather forlorn community centre, but still a handsome building near the A40 in West London – still houses photographs of the hundreds of children who passed through its doors until the 1930s: rows and rows of neatly dressed boys and girls in a huge dining hall, watched over by staff in severe nursing uniforms and starched caps. The well-scrubbed faces represent many of London's foundlings, for whom this was their only home, the place where they would remain until heading for a life in the forces or in maid's uniform, just like their contemporaries at the Foundling Hospital. A life of service – being made to pay for their mothers' mistakes.

8

What schools did you attend?

On a hot summer's day, the school buildings are softened by the huge cedars of Lebanon and the white flowering catalpas. It's like entering a very grand stately home, slightly austere because of its rigid symmetry, but huge and confident. The drive is flanked by lamps on severe Art Deco pedestals; there are ornamental urns perched on rooftops and in front of you is a not-at-all-small chapel. You curve round it, stone colonnades march off to equally imposing wings, and the front door looms, surmounted by stone carving. Fine if you're a visitor snooping around England's heritage. Utterly, utterly dreadful if you're five years old and your mum hasn't told you she's going to leave you there – for the rest of your childhood.

'It was the first day of my life – I was five, and I must have blanked out the years before that. The first day at school is my first-ever memory. I remember this lady – obviously she was my foster-mother – and she took me to the village green, where there were other grown-ups and children. Along came a charabanc, we all got in, picked up others on the way, and I remember being given a banana. The coach went up a countrified road and stopped at very large, locked gates. Later I remember they were always locked.'

Lydia Carmichael is sitting in her Hertfordshire home, while her husband Don is busy watering an impressive display of marigolds and sloshing at the petunias overflowing their hanging baskets. She's lively and outgoing, and there are family photographs everywhere. Lydia was born in 1932 and her first five years are missing, but it's likely that she spent them somewhere in the Home Counties, fostered out with a working-class family, probably in a small village – such was the pattern for Coram children.

The coach waited for the lodge-keeper to come and then trundled slowly down the main drive, skirting the chapel, towards the main building. 'My foster-mother took me to the great big door and a very fierce lady – whom I came to dislike and despise – my foster-mother said to follow this lady.' So I did, and we walked to the concert hall as far as a large stage, and I looked at this lady when she stopped, turned round, and my foster-mother wasn't there. She never said goodbye, good riddance, nothing. I didn't see her again until I was thirteen or fourteen years old. I never got a letter, a card . . . she never came on the "Mums' Day" [the annual visit by foster-mothers] . . .'.

All this is recalled without rancour, but in vivid detail. That first day at Coram was burned into a child's mind for a number of reasons. Most of the children had spent their earliest years in little country cottages, with not an inkling that their rural life – which was recalled by many as carefree though not luxurious – was going to be ended abruptly on their fifth birthday. That they were not as other children was kept from most of them. However, some, like John Caldicott, got a hint of their 'different status'.

'I was off to the school in the village where I was fostered – I was three and a half – and I didn't know that I was fostered. Mummy was mummy, but when I went to that school I was told I should no longer call her mummy. "You can call me Mum," but that was it.' John was born in 1936, so four years after Lydia had stared at the locked gates and huge buildings he too found himself bundled on to a coach, taken over by a nurse and led into the hall. Nothing was explained to him: 'I remember sitting in the hall, the great rows of blue chairs, this nurse coming up to my mum, and taking me, and my mum said, "Oh, by the way, he wets the bed." And the nurse said, "He won't do that any more."'

It has to be admitted that anyone given the dubious privilege of a boarding school education in the first half of the twentieth century could describe a Horrible First Day at School in roughly similar terms. However, Lydia Carmichael's and John Caldicott's situation was different. No school fees had been scraped together by parents. Never mind the lack of fees – they lacked parents.

John's Foundling Hospital qualifications were that he was a first-born child, he was illegitimate, his mother was 'of good character', and she had given him up to the Foundling Hospital three months after he was born. Lydia too was first-born, illegitimate, and her mother had a good character to preserve – she was the first lady film editor for ABC Films at Elstree Studios. Neither child knew any of this when gazing around the hall, from which ran long, wide corridors in all directions. Then the boys were led off to one wing, the girls to the other, where their clothes were stripped off and taken away before a nit inspection and then into a 'gigantic bath' before entering a dormitory with thirty beds. The nurse – not medically trained but more a nursery attendant – ended the frightening day with a demonstration to saucer-eyed children of proper bed-making, 'hospital corners' and all.

At the age of five, in bed in a dormitory with several others very definitely suppressing sobs, and certainly not tucked up with a kindly goodnight kiss, the feelings of bewilderment must have been overpowering. What was happening? The immensely smooth running of a traditional system, in fact.

All through the nineteenth century the Foundling Hospital, no longer among green fields but now surrounded by the streets and squares of ever-encroaching London, had diligently continued Thomas Coram's work: in effect, the rules and regulations laid down by his fellow governors in the 1740s. Thousands of children were inspected by the great and the good who sat on the board – or, rather, their mothers were. If it were deemed that these women could be 'returned to be rehabilitated in respectable society', then their child gained a place in the Hospital. The mother had to sever all contact – and in most instances in the Victorian era, vanished back into the poverty in which she'd already slid to a place on the lowest rung. The child, on the other hand, was guaranteed shelter, food and an education – something to be envied in the nineteenth century, regardless of the price paid, which was the loss of a mother and the acquisition of the stigma of bastardy.

As in Coram's century, those who were rich and respectable supported the Hospital generously with time and money. The practice of public visits on Sundays was well entrenched. In came the benefactors, the governors and the well-meaning bourgeoisie to gaze benignly upon the well-scrubbed and obedient children, singing lustily in the choir and eating silently at the table. Here were the future maids and footmen and soldiers for the empire, dutiful and already well disciplined. By the mid-nineteenth century all the children were taught to read and write, and had lessons in mathematics, English grammar and geography – a useful but rudimentary education. The catechism loomed large – piety and prayers measured the day, leavened only perhaps by the renowned choral singing. The chapel choir attracted large congregations on Sundays, and the collections were destined for the Hospital's coffers.

But all, it was felt, was not perfect. By the beginning of the twentieth century the capital's grime and soot were beginning to perturb the governors – London smog offended their tradition of a healthy environment for the children. Realising they were sitting on an excellent spot of real estate, in 1926 they sold to a property developer and Jacobsen's Georgian building was knocked down. The Hospital decamped temporarily to Redhill in Surrey until they moved into new buildings in Berkhamsted, Hertfordshire, very much on the pattern of the eighteenth-century original: neo-classical, imposing, and supposedly easy for children to find their way around.

As a building, Berkhamsted could hold its own with those expensive establishments to which the fee-paying classes despatched their offspring. It was built to last, and to the highest specifications. The children would walk on parquet flooring past oak-panelled walls with elegantly plastered ceilings above them. There's a sense of gracious space – and a labyrinth of wheezing radiators which are still functioning after eight decades. The staircases, doors and long tables in the dining room are of solid, well-polished oak. The corridors are half-tiled in different pastel colours; the corner room of the girls' wing is in bright yellow, relieved with a scattering of farmyard animal tiles – a Shire horse, ducks, sheep. These tiles, though, are perhaps the only concession in this vast building to the notion that children are its inhabitants.

Considering that, in one form or another, Berkhamsted has been a school for some eighty years, it shows less wear and tear than a three-year-old comprehensive. Stained glass from the original chapel was transplanted and a majestic new one built, with a crypt to house stone and marble tablets recalling the beneficent Georgian and Victorian great and good. In London, Coram's historic interiors – the smart parts of the building which had drawn in the wealthy patrons for art and music – were saved and incorporated into a new headquarters building in the corner of the original site. The Picture Gallery and the Court Room survived, as did the Committee Room where, in 1936, John Caldicott's mother found herself undergoing the traditional interview. Hung, with ornately framed paintings, furnished with a large oak table and elegant chairs, this was a room in which any gentleman would feel at home. The same would probably not be said of the mothers who peered round the door while holding their baby.

Twenty-eight-year-old Daisy Throsell was a laundry worker who'd come up to the London area from Gainsborough in Lincolnshire. Having fifteen siblings, she'd been kicked out of the family home at sixteen to earn a living packing laundry in Luton. She fell in love and became pregnant, but the man disappeared; she was then ridiculed by her fellow workers and thrown out of her digs. The only place she could go to was the workhouse in Luton, where she was offered a place on the understanding that she would stay there until the child was fourteen and work for her keep. Daisy thought this unacceptable – a workhouse upbringing led to imbecility, in her view, since it offered no education whatsoever. Her position in 1936 was no different from that of a woman a century earlier.

Somehow she heard about the Foundling Hospital, and turned up to be interviewed by about a score of men who questioned her about her life and morals. Daisy wasn't one to be bullied – she'd already tried to commit suicide, which was then illegal. Feeling highly emotional, she refused to exhibit the expected contrite and remorseful demeanour. The men were not impressed: women In Trouble were not expected to have attitude. On the point of their refusing her child admission, a vicar intervened to suggest that 'this lady be given a chance'.

However, she and her son had to return to Hendon Hospital, for the baby had been sickly when born. For three months Daisy was not permitted to touch the baby she'd called David Thomas, never mind nurse or cuddle him. Then, one day, he was taken away. She had nowhere to go – so back she went to the workhouse, to be told they didn't want her. All she remembered of the day was leaving the workhouse and standing at a bus-stop.

David Thomas was placed with one of the foster-families supervised by Coram. But he was no longer David: one of the fundamental rules of the institution was the breaking of all ties with the mother, and this always meant a new name. He became John. He also, as several thousand children before him, gained an official number, 24349 M, which he still rattles off with military precision. And the Caldicott? 'My name was just picked from –? Lords and ladies, telephone books, counties, everything. I was actually christened Jack Caldicott, but when I left school – this is the story of my life – the manager at work was called Jack, so I was told, "You'll be John."'

Names had been left behind and the past was a mystery. The Coram children went about their daily routine and were never encouraged to ask questions, with the memory of that first frightening day at school lingering in their minds. Many former pupils remember it as the day they lost their identity – yet again, for they found themselves in a world in which they were no longer individuals. Although most large institutions have some sort of 'unifying' effect, the Foundling Hospital was run on lines which left the children with the sole sense that they were just one of a group. They did everything together: played communal games, slept in dormitories, sat in chapel row by row, marched in lines and paraded en masse for important visitors – 250 girls and 250 boys in the 1930s. 'Like a lot of sheep' is a frequently heard comment.

Boys and girls were, as ever, rigidly segregated – there were two dining halls, side by side, and the meals were staggered so that separation was reinforced. When some of the former pupils return for the annual reunion these days, it's noticeable that they only explore 'their' half of the buildings; some can't even now be persuaded to cross the invisible line into the world which was inhabited by the opposite sex.

This sense of merely being one amongst many was emphasised by their ignorance of their origins. Most playgrounds resound with shouts of 'My dad's a fireman' and 'My mum's prettier than yours'; not the spacious grounds of Berkhamsted. Significantly, there was hardly any conversation about where they'd all come from. There were hints and snippets of information gleaned from the staff that they were 'different', and many children just left it at that.

'The effect of that first day put most of the children into some sort of trauma, as they built up a brick wall against everything that was going on around them, and we gave no thought to what was going on – or what had happened.' John Caldicott can only recall tiny bits of information being filtered through to the effect that they were 'actually motherless – and we used to talk about the possibility of being claimed by your mothers – they were always princesses – somebody well-off and they were going to whisk you away to a life of unknown luxury. . . .' The only information regularly divulged was that they should all be grateful, having been given the chance to be brought up in the Foundling Hospital, and that they should be prepared to serve others.

Lydia Wingate hadn't a clue why she was at Berkhamsted, nor why she was called Lydia Wingate: 'I've no idea at all where I got that name. We used to bandy about lots of ideas – ooh, it was from books . . . no, it's someone very important . . . but the Foundation's secretary once said there was no rhyme or reason as to where they came from, though in olden days they did call us after famous people. . . . I've no idea about mine. . . . And as far as I remember, we knew nothing about why we were there. Obviously we knew we were different and we didn't have a family. We didn't talk *about* ourselves much, just sometimes asked each other if "Mum" was coming up on "Mums' Day". We weren't told anything, except a governor – who'd found me being naughty – once told me we were there to "serve the public . . .". Really, no one ever sat us down and told us why we hadn't got real mummies and daddies.'

John thinks that the reason why they accepted this 'life of service' was 'because there was something shameful. It's really odd, because I can never remember anyone saying to me, "You were born out of wedlock." But it was made very, very clear that our mothers had done something wrong, and that we were also to blame. We were guilty and we *felt* guilty, and the interesting thing is that guilt follows you through life – it doesn't disappear. Even though you know that these days people don't get married any more, live in partnerships, there's still a guilt. And I feel an unfairness – I'm a grown man, but it still goes though my mind, this guilt.' Lydia too carries with her the sound of a governor's voice saying, ' "It's about time you learned, Wingate, you are a very lucky person. If it wasn't for us, where do you think you'd be? . . ." It sticks, it sticks . . . charity, charity.'

All of this was reinforced by the distant relationship between the staff and their charges. Admittedly, in the first half of the twentieth century no posh boarding school was renowned for its caring and affectionate atmosphere, but at least there was a home to go to in the holidays. As Lydia says, 'I know boarding schools have a reputation for being harsh, but, let's be honest, those children had someone to go to, to confide in, or say, "I don't like it there." And no one put their arms round you, asked if you were all right. The only physical touch you got was if you were going to get the ruler or the strap.'

The Coram children were uniquely isolated. They didn't play with children from other schools, never met individuals in local families, and literally dwelt within locked gates. They were just on the edge of Berkhamsted; however, it was regularly remarked by the townspeople that the children were rarely to be seen – even within the grounds, and certainly not outside. When the school was in London, there had been a rule that no child was ever to go within six feet of the school gates lest the public stand and stare at them. Even in the grimmest boarding schools, children usually forge alliances: if you're bullied, you find someone smaller and spottier who's also picked on. If you're lonely, you notice the other child who seems left out and make shy overtures. If you like games, music, stamp collecting, digging up worms in the garden and slicing them in half, or whispering about your revolting teacher who clearly proves that aliens have landed on our planet, you soon find a soulmate who may be rewarded with the important title: My Best Friend. But this didn't happen at the Hospital.

So as well as guilt, what set the place apart was the lack of close friendships – for the children had nothing much to say to each other. Each lived an identical life, every day followed a set pattern, their personal possessions were the same and their knowledge of the outside world was minimal. Excitement, gossip, a new toy, the neighbours, a pet, your family's goings-on – the Coram children were exempt from the ups and downs of childhood. Many eventually found the outside world something of a shock, and John saw one or two children at the school who could not cope with the regime and certainly not with life beyond it.

Though it all had the ring of a prison more than a school, it wasn't an unhappy or violent place; the children just didn't know anything else. Today's young would greet its regime with a long, loud shout of 'BOOOOORING'. However, there were two events to look forward to. 'Mums' Day', when the foster-mothers were invited to see their former charges, was a mixed blessing. Some turned up with whole families in tow, year after year, anxious to see the child who'd lived with them for the first five years of its life. They brought unbelievable goodies: a small toy, a doll – perhaps chocolates. Eyes widened and emotions were mixed: 'Why didn't they take us back home with them?' In reality, the fostering was a contract, and the women who undertook the job were invariably from poor working-class families who needed the money. Even so, there are warm memories of kindly, motherly souls who bothered to come to Berkhamsted and maintain contact with their former foster-child.

Those who didn't have visitors disappeared into the bowels of the building, unwilling to witness reunions and gifts. But they were able to discuss the one treat available to all: summer camp. Every year Berkhamsted High Street got its official sighting of the Institution's inmates, who lived only half a mile away up the hill. The Coram band – army musicians in the making – marched out of the iron gates and headed for the railway station. In step behind them came the whole school, dressed not in their eighteenth-century formal uniforms but in khaki, and bursting with excitement at the prospect of six weeks' relative freedom in tents near Folkestone – games and adventure and the chance to escape the mass organised routine. They felt proud – and the locals turned out in their hundreds and often applauded them. However, John was at the camp in the summer of 1939 when it was cut short. War had been declared and the children were rushed back to Berkhamsted, which they never left for the next six years.

Both John and Lydia talk about school life in detail – and, though they show occasional sadness or regret at what they now know they missed, they don't talk with bitterness. Both have handsome prints of the old London buildings on the wall at home, and Lydia has a tiny doll dressed in the traditional Coram uniform on display. They attend reunions and keep in touch with other pupils. They've come to terms with their time at the Foundling Hospital, and both have much more concern for the moment when they began to learn about their own backgrounds.

John Caldicott left the school in 1951 when he was sixteen, wanting to join the band of the Blues and Royals. However, the school had changed many of its old ways since the end of the war, and he was abruptly informed that 'We don't send boys into the army now.' When he signed on as an apprentice to a radio company in Oxford, he wrote to the Thomas Coram Foundation asking for details of his mother and father. Back came the reply: 'This is not possible'; and it was too expensive for a young apprentice to have them traced. John just accepted the situation, and realises now that he did so because 'one of the things you learned in the Hospital was if you were told something, that was it, you didn't argue'. Later he discovered that he could have had all the information the very next year, for the Foundation had advertised in the *Daily Telegraph* and *Times* for all former pupils to return and find out about their parents – but 'We'd left the Hospital with no qualifications whatsoever – and we were unlikely to read those sort of newspapers!' And even though attitudes were changing, former pupils frequently sensed a certain holding back, a reticence in the Hospital's attitude. In 1952 illegitimacy still wasn't a very public subject.

John married and had three children – and reflects that he had to learn how to live *in* a family. The Hospital had been a place of survival, where trust was missing – your name was taken from you, your parents had gone, even your foster-mother might not return. Finally, decades later, his wife Kaye encouraged him to try again. Yet even in 1981 the Coram Foundation had a particular way of dealing with requests. Mr and Mrs Caldicott were taken to an upstairs room and the door was locked. It was explained that 'in old times children used to just run out when given the information'. The officials told them the story slowly, reading from a sheet of A4 paper numbered 24349 – John's registration number. Then they turned it round and let the Caldicotts see it. It gave the main details of Daisy Throsell's tale of pregnancy, the workhouse and the acceptance of David Thomas into the Hospital.

Within three weeks John had found her. She'd stood at the bus-stop after surrendering him and somehow fetched up getting a job as a housekeeper to an elderly man. Having had a wretched year, she now found she'd encountered a man who, in her own words, 'just wanted to get her into bed'. But she married him – for he gave her to understand that she could then retrieve her baby. The moment she married him, though, he said No to that. However, he died shortly after she'd borne his child eighteen months later. She returned to Lincolnshire but her family refused to take her in, whereupon she had the first piece of luck in her life, meeting a farm labourer who'd been her childhood sweetheart, and they had four children together. John knew her for six years before she died – 'We got on extraordinarily well,' he says. And she always called him David Thomas.

Lydia Wingate had left in the late 1940s and, luckily, avoided going into domestic service; the brighter girls were by now allowed to study a 'commercial' course. She'd been spending the holidays with a new set of foster-parents, yet another 'mum and dad', elderly and rather old-fashioned. When she left the Hospital at fifteen to learn shorthand and typing she never spoke about her upbringing: 'There was this shame within you – we were very innocent. It was the end of the forties, start of the fifties, and my foster-mum said to me, "Lydia, we've got to be very careful you don't follow in your mother's footsteps."'

Like John Caldicott, she'd written to the Thomas Coram Foundation asking about her family; a letter came back saying no one had heard a thing for fifteen years, but if they did they'd let her know. Three years later another letter arrived saying two aunts had come forward and wanted to meet her. 'I had to go up to London, I met the aunties, and they told me my mother had died at the tender age of thirty-four – I'd missed her by three years.' Lydia pauses while telling the story. What about her father? The aunties had replied, 'Your mother died with the secret on her lips.' It's the last line of many a melodrama, but when it's for real, and the woman who wants to know, needs to know, is describing something of utter importance to her own life, it's hard to understand how much it hurts.

However, Lydia has unexpected mementoes of her mother, bringing out carefully preserved programmes for film galas: 'A Film Grand Premiere' on 15 April 1937 at 9 p.m.: the ABC Picture Corporation presents Mary Ellis and Otto Kruger in *Glamorous Night*. It was produced at Elstree Studios and the four most important production staff are credited on the front page: after those responsible for the photography and settings come music and lyrics – Ivor Novello and Christopher Hassall – and the film editor: Flora Newton. Says Lydia proudly: 'Flora was the first female editor for ABC in this country, working with Herbert Willcox, Anna Neagle, Michael Wilding. . . . I've got programmes for the premieres and one of the aunties gave me a glamorous evening bag given to my mother – she said – by Ivor Novello.'

Both Lydia and John have successfully brought up families of their own. They're passionate about their relationships with their children, emphasising the importance of love and security. Their own childhood offered stability, food and clothing – but the Hospital was a loveless place. There's also an understanding that society was very different then, and initial bitterness about a mother giving up her baby has given way to the view that there was no alternative at the time. 'How could our mothers keep us?' asks Lydia. 'There were no benefits, and mine was one of ten. And then there was the shame.

'Do I ever wish that things had been different? Well, I've accepted it, but I do wish it had been different. And my father – he's probably long gone, but if someone turned up on my doorstep saying I know where your father is, I'd be there like a shot. Despite the fact that I've had a good marriage, good family, wonderful friends – I'd be there like a shot. And I still wish I'd known my mother. I remember when I gave birth to my first child – I hadn't even thought about it . . . but after the baby was born, I put my head under the bedclothes and cried and cried, because I wanted my mum, who I never knew.'

Twenty-seven thousand children passed through the Foundling Hospital.

9

Have you any children?

The notion that a mother could give up her child without too much ado if a better future beckoned seemed logical to many in the institutional world. Poverty and misfortune, stigma and society's disapproval: how much better for everyone if the mother was relieved of the burden of the child's upbringing and those with better means could step in to help. If you insisted on keeping a child in circumstances deemed 'undesirable', even in the twentieth century, then you could expect trouble. Take the Schaedler family, with three generations' experience of society's mutterings of Shame.

Life in the Swabian countryside in south-west Germany has much that seems idyllic: dark forests, pure air streaming round pretty mountains, snug villages with romantic castles and not too much violent history thundering through the remote valleys. At the turn of the twentieth century there was also a holiday industry, with spa towns booming, Lake Constance – or the Bodensee, as the Germans know it – offering spectacular views and serene boat trips, and the whole area recommended for its 'health-inducing' properties.

The Schaedlers didn't belong to the leisured classes; someone had to keep the countryside neat, milk the cows, pick the berries, thresh the corn and see to the needs of the travellers. Antonia Schaedler worked on the family smallholding with her son and two daughters. When looking up from the long rural day, there would be few vistas which didn't include one of the white-walled and elegantly domed churches proclaiming the sturdy Catholicism of the region. But it can't have been a consolation for Antonia, who'd had her three children – Anton, Senta and Antonia – out of wedlock. What she faced, and what her own thoughts were about her situation, have not been handed down to her family. Such matters were not spoken of openly, if at all, but there was always a cloud of shame drifting over their situation.

During World War I her young son Anton was threshing corn in the barn; as the hours went by, he needed more light and borrowed an electrical cable from another farmer. Unknown to him it was faulty, and when he plugged it in he was electrocuted. His mother rushed in to find him dead and the sight of the grisly accident gave her a nervous breakdown, which she grimly re-called as going somewhere where 'I was on bread and water for six months.' When she returned, the meagre family fortunes had shrunk to a hand-to-mouth existence for a single mother with two little girls. Fruit-picking, farm labour, selling boot polish door-to-door.

Her daughter Antonia eventually moved north to work in a hotel in Bad Honnef, south of Bonn, starting a long career in cooking and catering. It was now World War II, and there were few pleasures to be had by a country girl on low wages. Along came a young man from Wilhelmshaven, working away from home because of the war. When the young Antonia found she was pregnant, the young man wrote to say that he was married with two sons. She was hard at work until 27 June 1940 when she went into labour and headed for the hospital, only for the hotel to be bombed while she was giving birth to Doris.

Mother and baby spent a fortnight together, before more domestic labour claimed Antonia and Doris began two long years in the care of nuns in a Catholic Home. They didn't look kindly on the sort of children who fetched up with them; after two years of their ministrations, with the baby's mother only able to pop in on the odd day off, Aunt Senta arrived from Swabia, to be hissed at by one of the kitchen staff that 'if you don't get the child away, she'll die of malnutrition'. There was a war on, and the infants got only skimmed milk and jam – but no one denied that the nuns had butter and cream. Antonia senior – hitherto unaware of the baby – was summoned to take her back to Swabia. Antonia junior

123

managed to visit only on the occasional holiday, but finally took off for England when Doris was nine, having nurtured a curious desire to learn to speak English.

While Doris lived a spartan life in post-war Germany in the Black Forest region her mother was in Derbyshire, having taken a post as a cook for Rolls Royce, who kept a grand house at Duffield Bank for visiting VIPs. No expense was spared at this establishment, which boasted a housekeeper, a butler and a parlourmaid. Antonia was well down the pecking order, given her shaky English, and was pointedly told that even the butler's mother wouldn't have her in the house 'because of the war'. But hard work was the only thing she knew, so she stuck it out, managing to visit Germany once a year.

'She was like a stranger, really,' remembers Doris, who by this time had lost her grandmother and was living with Aunt Senta. At school she'd been embarrassed when asked where her father was; she possessed a photograph of him, with his date of birth scribbled on the back – and that was all. Lies were not an option in a small village. Gossip had seen to that. 'I was made to feel guilty. I've always felt picked on – it's been like that throughout my life. I've always felt guilty.'

Doris talks in a soft, gentle voice, and without bitterness, sitting on bright crocheted cushions in her semi-detached house near Dudley in the West Midlands. The room is overflowing with pretty trinkets and china angels, brass Buddhas and quartz crystals on lace cloths and embroidered mats, and there are scented candles lit on the table. More than a touch of the Oberammergau festive decorations, a genuine *Gemütlichkeit*.

After her grandmother died, life followed the family tradition of hard grind. She left school before she was fourteen and followed her mother's example, becoming a cook's assistant in an educational institution run by nuns. More sniffs of disapproval from her new employers. Her aunt got married and Antonia didn't get on with her new Uncle Fritz, whom she felt had taken away the only relative left near her. 'We had a fall-out,' she says, 'and Auntie Senta said, "She'll have to go." ' At fifteen she was job-hunting again, and was apprenticed in a hotel in nearby Konstanz. They treated her like a skivvy: she was up at five every morning, cleaning the floors and then waiting at table. After a year of this she overslept for the first time and was scolded for a few minutes' lateness: 'What time do you call this?'

Taken back in by her aunt, she found that life with a pernickety master tailor and his wife involved more skivvying, also starting at five in the morning, so she took a job at a local inn run by Herr and Frau Kaiser for more domestic work but less domestic strife. Papers arrived from her mother in Derby – Antonia wanted to bring her daughter to England; the Kaisers told Doris to ignore them: 'Not everything that shines is gold in England.' Doris's voice for the first time sounds German, overcoming the light Birmingham accent and perfect English. As the words tumble out cataloguing her life, the names of those who made decisions for her dominate her narrative. She was always told what to do, and did it without question; as a child she says she didn't know there were better times to be had.

There was trouble at the British Consulate in Stuttgart when her mother arrived, followed by a fight with Immigration in Dover. Eventually sixteen-year-old Doris became a Rolls Royce employee, helping her mother in the kitchen and earning a share of the tips. Mother and daughter cycled to Wales in their first summer together, and Doris fell in love with the mountains and forests which reminded her of Swabia; the next summer, it was back to Germany for a holiday. Hans was 'blond, blue-eyed and lovely, everything a girl could wish for'. There's not a trace of irony from Doris as she describes the student who was studying in Konstanz whom she met at a dance and who took her out a few times. When she returned to England, he wrote to say he was married with two boys. Which was a tune her mother had heard eighteen years previously.

The third-generation unmarried mother. Doris sat mutely while her mother 'went berserk, went up the wall, tried everything, gave me hot mustard baths, hot salt baths that scalded me, Beecham's pills and God knows what else – but it didn't work. She threatened to send me back to Germany, and I was bullied every minute of the day because we shared a bedroom. But I didn't argue. I'd vowed never to fall out with my mum, because I'd seen her and her sister argue, with me piggy in the middle. I felt desperate, but I didn't talk back.' Matters were not improved by Rolls Royce deciding on a little 'restructuring' of the Duffield Bank establishment. They thought it was time for the cook's assistant to leave – and the cook as well. The women were left in no doubt that pregnancy didn't go down well in a house entertaining Roller VIPS.

Once again, a Catholic Mother and Baby Home – a polished, bleak establishment in Borrowash presided over by an ancient priest – was the only alternative. After toxaemia complications and a lonely labour, an 8lb 10 oz baby girl arrived. The nuns said not to breast-feed her, and Doris spent weeks of painful misery with dripping nipples swathed in nappies. Cuddling was discouraged. Bernadette Maria was baptised in a Catholic church in Derby. All that remain of this time are two small photographs, the larger showing a rather cross-looking baby, sixteen days old and fast asleep on a crocheted shawl. Doris points out the tiny, V-shaped birthmark on her forehead. Would it have disappeared? Perhaps, and with it one of the clues to Bernadette's whereabouts. For Antonia had written to Doris, finally admitting that *her* mother had written to her in the same circumstances, and with little sympathy: children were hard to bring up, 'so don't expect any support from me'. Two generations passing on what they believed to be the incontrovertible facts of a hard life.

Doris doesn't pass judgement, but suddenly says with intensity: 'The only thing that's kept me going over the years is that I gave her a chance to have a good home – and with people who couldn't have children. I gave her up at nine weeks – it was May. I packed my case, the bus-stop was opposite the Home, and the baby was dressed in new clothes – which were later taken off, because the new parents had brought some clothes. . . . We took them to the Cathedral House in Nottingham – I was with another girl and baby from the Home – and I left my case in the bus station and went across the road and into this room. Every time prospective parents arrived, the priest would come into the room for a baby – we were about five girls in there, all with little babies, and everyone was crying. It was like a bad dream. We never saw the parents. I got the bus back to Derby, then to Worcester, where my mum was working in a big house that had been turned into a hotel. I worked as an assistant cook. I didn't tell anyone – I had to keep it close to my heart, always feeling guilty, mourning the loss of my child. It was horrendous.'

All this is said in a rush, but the details are clearly there, nearly half a century on. So were harsh lessons learned? Doris adds matter-of-factly that she only got a little bit of time off in the new job – the odd trip to Worcester to go shopping. And got pregnant again. However, we're now into the sixties and the country was changing – but social attitudes didn't alter overnight, nor did her mother: 'She hit the wall again,' recalls Doris, after the father had, in time-honoured tradition, enlightened her by letter regarding his lack of obligations. Another Mother and Baby Home beckoned, in Solihull and as chilly as ever, but this time Doris wanted to keep her son – and even her mother agreed, nurturing some long-felt desire which was rooted in the early loss of her brother in the threshing barn decades ago in Germany. The baby had to be fostered, though – four sets of parents in two years, for Doris had to work. Then in 1963, she married.

Doris sits in her front room, her husband quietly getting in the weekend's shopping and providing chocolate biscuits with the coffee. He and Doris have a family of five – plus the son she took back from the foster-parents. Photographs are produced – slim, laughing girls in graduation robes, the son and daughter-in-law off to a new life in New Zealand, the grandchildren who live round the corner. 'I love being a mum,' she says. She's serene. She started to tell her children of her earlier life only a few years back and now says she understands that she was always looking for affection – and a father-figure. She felt she'd been 'got at' by the Catholic Church, and on marriage jettisoned it for the Church of England; she's since joined the Spiritualists – she's President of the Midland Society – and a certificate hangs on the wall to say she's a

Healer member of the National Federation of Spiritual Healers. She treats her patients by touch: 'My hands become red-hot.' And her personality is warm and thoughtful, her heart-shaped amber earrings glinting in rhythm with the twinkling cherubs and potted plants and bunches of silk flowers.

'I tried to find my daughter a few years ago, in the early nineties. I wrote to the Home and they forwarded my letter, but they couldn't give me the date the adoption went through in Stoke-on-Trent. They'd lost the papers – maybe because it was six months before I signed them. I took my time about it until I got such a nasty letter from the priest. . . . They said they couldn't trace without a date.

'I think all this has made me stronger in a way, and I just loved the children when they were little – I didn't go out to work. Maybe I never stood up for myself then – I just went along with what people thought of me and it affected my confidence. And I knew nothing. My own sex education was just a talk with the nuns – I ask you! I feel hard done to by the Church – they made me feel guilty, and it stays with you. I don't know if this happened to my mother or her mother – they didn't talk about it. They just had to work hard.

'I'm a Spiritualist and I had a medium tell me that Bernadette is married with her own children, and that I'll meet her some day; but at the moment she's all angry inside. But I'd love to see her.'

10

Have you brothers or sisters?

'I always thought there was a gap – a space – and there was: it was you.' My elder sister is not given to fantasy, but having never known of my existence until I turned up rather unexpectedly after four-plus decades of absence, this remark carried an odd ring to it.

My mother has four children and I'm number two, but as I arrived illegitimately I was adopted immediately and brought up in the north-east, where I was born. I grew up an only child, unaware that I had half-siblings, but I was one of those children who didn't long for more in the family, perhaps because so many of my friends were also onlies or in very small families. Some had elder brothers or sisters – but as the war had intervened they were often a good six years older, and we post-war children thought them from another era.

There are now many theories and theses about the pecking order in families, but it's odd to find yourself coming in at number 2 in your forties, when all the time you had thought yourself number 1 or an only. And for my sisters and brother, there was a kind of mental shifting along the bench to accommodate this extra number on the team. With great good fortune, none of us seems to have minded. As my elder sister reminds me: 'You never had the childhood arguments about whose turn it was or who borrowed my best pencil case.' We don't know if the odd gap or space which she felt was instinctive or just a natural reaction to being a few years older than the younger two, and always being put in charge of them. We laugh about it and don't indulge in introspective rumination.

The only child is sometimes pitied, thought to be deprived of useful experience such as sharing and making compromises; over-indulged and forever polishing the ego. And brothers and sisters would seem to offer more opportunities for a wider circle of friends, of more stimulation and sympathy. Then you meet siblings who have never spoken to each other for thirty years and don't intend to for the next thirty. It's very difficult for the only child to imagine such a rift: surely you feel something in common, have some kind of bond between you?

If foundlings were fortunate enough to be taken into a family before the twentieth century, they usually joined a large clan: whoever had survived infant mortality among a dozen-plus children. When the state systemised adoption in the 1920s, it became much more common for foundlings to be placed with childless couples. A large number adopted again, often with the unvoiced feeling that the first child had already been 'alone' and was in need of a playmate. Depending on the happiness or otherwise of childhood, and especially where there wasn't a good relationship with adoptive parents, some foundlings can be wistful about possible siblings. However, even more than the adopted child, they feel that finding such relatives is well beyond their reach.

Much more rare are the siblings in search of the foundling. And the motivation cannot be quite the same as that of the child searching for 'family'.

Four sisters sit in a small house stylishly furnished with wooden floors and potted plants, with mounds of sandwiches and coffee on offer. They are a close family – the eldest sister, Judith, was born to her mother, Christine's, first husband, and four more daughters followed in a second marriage. All but the second eldest have gathered to discuss what has been an unexpected conundrum in their lives.

Judith, Vivienne, Christine, Jane and Susan thought they knew their family history, with an array of uncles and aunts and a childhood spent living with their grandmother. They were all born in Wales and have that intimacy of family knowledge that comes with having lived near or next to each other for a long time. The story starts with the eldest, Judith: 'Mum married when she was about nineteen, on 2 November 1940' – and is taken up by Vivienne.

'He was a South African who'd been to university at either Oxford or Cambridge, and he was a pilot officer in the RAF, stationed in Wales – at St Athans. They met at a dance and she went home that night and said to my grandmother, "I've met the man I want to marry." And my mother was called the second most beautiful woman in our town – she was stunning. And the fact that she's . . .'. Vivienne breaks off, because all the family memories have now been changed because of what they've learned.

Judith begins again: 'I was born in November 1941 – on their wedding anniversary – but he'd been killed two months earlier, in September. So, a young widow in the war, she went back to live with her mother and her sister Mona and sister-in-law Frances. She married again when I was four. She'd met her second husband on the way back from South Africa where she'd been to meet her in-laws after their son had been killed – his mother, who was Jewish, wanted to see me – and possibly leave me there. She married in 1945.'

'My father was a merchant seaman,' adds Vivienne, 'and she went to live in Southampton, then had us four girls in the space of six years!' When the eldest was fifteen, their mother died. So their half-sister Judith, who was only nineteen, took them in and looked after them until she herself got married a year later. There was talk of splitting up the four sisters, but once again their grandmother stepped in and they returned to South Wales to live with her and their Aunt Mona. Therefore they were rarely out of touch with close relatives until they themselves left in the sixties to marry, have children, divorce, remarry – 'live regular lives', as they put it, with a great deal of laughter. One of the sisters suddenly adds, 'She died so young – and she was eight and a half months pregnant, and the baby died with her. I think she was secretly hoping for a boy, for I remember her saying if ever she had a boy she'd call him Jonathon.'

Family get-togethers were frequent, and all the girls were back in their home town in 1996 for a celebration, described by Vivienne. 'We came back here, with Aunt Mona, Mum's sister, on the day

Judith's granddaughter was getting christened. It was a lovely day, we had a barbecue, the ceremony was lovely, the weather was gorgeous, it was a perfect day and our aunt decided – she just came out with it: "I want to talk to you girls, quietly." We were all there at the barbecue – it was quite funny really, because there were quite a lot of people milling around and she said, "Come in the shed, I've got something to tell you." So she told Susan first, and then Susan sat on the lawn and said, "It appears we've got a brother."

'We said, "What are you talking about?" '

Judith chimes in: 'As soon as she said it, something clicked with me and it was something I'd heard as a child. When her next daughter – also Christine – was born, somebody came to the house to visit and said, "Oh, *another* girl," and my mother's sister-in law Frances was there and said, "Christine had a boy once" – and then, very quickly, "but she miscarried." I was about eight or nine – and it clicked. To me it was like a bolt coming out of heaven – I mean, looking at this big blue sky that day of the barbecue and thinking that we've got a brother somewhere! And Susan said, "This is a hell of a legacy." But we were *meant* to know . . . however, it took a long time before we were told. I had so many questions. How old was I when this happened? When did it happen? Who is the father? Why haven't we found out before? And she said, "I didn't tell you for all this time: to protect your mum."

All the sisters join in at this point. The moment they were told changed their lives and they have only a few shreds of information to go on. 'It was a long time ago.' 'Judith was about seventeen months old, we think.' 'We think it might be 1943.' 'She went to London – her sister-in-law Frances went with her.'

Vivienne takes up the tale: 'The only thing we were told was that Mum abandoned the baby in London, on a station . . . we don't really know which one . . . and they waited until somebody picked the baby up. They watched and waited, Frances and Mum. I do know that my mum was desperately, desperately upset. We believe Mum had the baby in a London hospital, because our grandmother apparently found a nursing bra and a baby's identity bracelet – and she burned them after Mum came home. Burned them, and said to my aunt, "I think Chris has had a baby." And *nothing* more was said. She didn't approach my mum about it, and when Aunt Mona told us about it that day of the christening it was a case of . . . well. "I was very young myself," she said. "It was one of those cases where you know that you don't talk about it. It's been dealt with. Grandmother didn't ask any questions – she just swept it under the carpet.

Again a chorus of voices: 'Aunt Mona only knew a bit of this.' 'We don't know if she knew at the time that they'd gone to London.' 'We could have found out more if Frances had told *us*.'

Jane: 'I find it difficult to believe that Aunt Mona didn't know more – two sisters who were very close . . . ?'

Judith: 'I felt so emotional about it. Mum was a young widow . . . there has to be a certain time, hasn't there, when . . . anyway, this child was conceived – and not from my father, he was dead by then. I felt that the bottom had dropped out of my world, because Mum died at thirty-eight – I was nineteen – and she'd carried this grief with her, and I'm sure she'd have told us when we were older. She was this wonderful, loving woman . . . but she couldn't keep that baby. Where did she have to go? She didn't have a home – she was living with her mother and sister. She had a young child of seventeen months. What could she do?'

Vivienne: 'My grandmother was really strict – though she was a good woman, a kind woman. But it was the times . . . the stigma of having a bastard, a child without a father . . . and we had to wait fifty years to find out.'

Judith: 'My aunt's sister-in-law Frances had died the year previous to Mona telling us at the barbecue. Frances was very close to Mum, and she knew. We'd met her a few times when she came back from Australia where she lived. She never told us. She never *mentioned* it. She was lovely – *and* she spoke her mind – and my mother confided in her. And she said *nothing*. Aunt Mona's the only one left who knew, and she died of cancer eighteen months after she told us.'

The sisters have started to search; they talk all the time about *him*, not about themselves, as Vivienne says: 'We're very concerned about him. *We* had a shock, and it still remains a shock eight years down the line – but for him to be told that he's got five half-sisters . . . it must be a terrible shock to him. And Mum's not here to speak for herself. Each and every one of us loved her very much and we wouldn't want to hurt her memory in any way.'

Jane adds: 'What would be nice would be for someone in his early sixties just to know that his mother was a wonderful person . . . she was the best. On the other hand, we don't know how it's affected his life. We don't even know at this stage if he realises he's a foundling. Perhaps he does, perhaps he doesn't – we don't know. He might not want to know us . . . we've just got to wait and see. It's a strange feeling and it never goes away – and we won't, until we know one way or the other. If we're lucky enough to meet him it would be wonderful, but what we really would like to know is that he's had a happy life, that what happened hasn't affected him, because we've all brought children up and you do love your kids desperately. We'd like to know that he's had a happy life, really. . . .'

Vivienne is still thinking of her mum: 'The fact that she's got a son somewhere – I find this so sad . . . and that he doesn't know about it.'

And Judith adds: 'And if he looks at all like Mum, even though he's sixty, we'll know him. All we really want to do is to give him a hug.'

And, incredibly, they have. After nine years of searching, just before this book went to press, they have found him with the help of Norcap. The sisters are still getting used to the news, but Vivienne told me he has had a good life and they had just had a magical day together. 'We were all bowled over.' The seemingly impossible has happened.

11

What is your religion?

My home town once had the odd claim to hosting more religious sects and denominations than anywhere else in the country. On inspection, this didn't render Sunderland particularly godly. Methodism ruled the roost, the Church of England was seen as a little flabby and the Catholics were beyond the pale (literally, corralled on the bleak housing estates). Odd little outfits glorifying the Lord up a flight of stairs in a dingy room down by the docks were happily tolerated, and the occasional spring procession of Joyful Witnesses added a touch of colour to the terraced streets. The Salvation Army was reported to be very active round the pubs, but as Sunderland had a pub every ten yards prior to slum clearance the Army had to march round for a whole year with its *War Cry* in order to visit even half of them.

My family appeared to absorb the idea of inter-denominational behaviour by doing a devotional supermarket round. Bits of non-conformism went into the trolley of worship, courtesy of a grandfather's lay-preacher status with an enthusiastic bunch of Bethesda Baptists (brimstone and hellfire mob, but very good at bring-and-buy sales for the poor); Methodism offered a grand church in which I was christened, and a number of chapels and 'missions' built in Victoria's reign near the shipyards in order to save the working class from sin (and Vaux's best bitter).

Early on I was inducted into the main aim of the Methodists, which was to out-sing any other church in the local eisteddfods. The Congregationalists, Unitarians, Independent Methodists, Wesleyan Missioners and other assorted non-cons were a social-minded community, liking nothing better than long evenings in packed churches listening to small choirs murdering

Stainer's *Crucifixion* or Mendelssohn's *Elijah*, followed by tea and buns. I did the rounds, learning to sight-read six-part music in tonic sol-fa and wondering why the Football Club's fans shouted Ha'way rather than hosanna or hallelujah.

Having absorbed the Methodist way of doing things, I found myself being educated in an establishment run by the Church of England Schools Company, a robust organisation which appreciated a Low Church tradition and full-scale annihilation of the local Catholic school's hockey team. The small differences in ritual between the non-conformists now widened into a large gap from the C of E: 'We kneel, Kathryn – we don't crouch.' On the other hand, a girl who'd unwisely spent her early years in High Church surroundings was briskly informed: 'We *incline*, dear. God doesn't like curtseys.'

After moving through the Anglican shelves the Adie trolley suddenly headed for the Presbyterian sector, attracted by a thriving Brownie pack full of Elves and Pixies. Enrolled in the Sunday School, I asked if Elves and Pixies were like Angels and was told that I'd 'learn all about that sort of thing when I was older'. Still waiting.

A holiday visit to relatives in Lancashire resulted in strong condemnation of American-imported holy Special Offers: a cousin had 'gone Billy Graham' but it was thankfully short-lived, failing to live up to its advertised claim to convey grace – and success. Half a mile from us, the only church to be built in a modern style was rising above a respectable part of suburbia: the Church of the Latter-Day Saints. It attracted mild curiosity, mainly because it had money – something a bit new-fangled and foreign to leaky-roofed Anglicans and thrifty Methodists. However, it was not seen as a threat, as the Mormons were a bit too keen on house-to-house proselytising which was regarded as very un-British. Nor was their music up to scratch. Meanwhile, we lived amid lots of Lithuanian Jews, Orthodox in some observance (I switched on next door's lights every Friday evening in winter) but Liberal in their desire to integrate and socialise with the neighbours – and with invitations to bar mitzvahs.

In post-war Britain, our religious life was neither intense nor doctrinally based. The Thirty-Nine Articles were unknown. The Creed was a difficult bit of plainsong, and Communion was on a take-it-or-leave-it basis. Christmas was the Salvation Army on the green with the Jewish families carrying the collecting tins: 'Well, it's your holiday, isn't it?' Easter was the non-conformists' day out with new frocks for the little girls and only the Catholics doing the Stations of the Cross. Religion was, in the main, the stuff of social life, a series of regular musical gatherings and jollies which branched out into social welfare, hospital visiting, charity work and an interest in missionary activity in the far-flung British Empire. If Methodist Communion came in little glasses ('Rather a downmarket drinks party, don't you think?' said the C of E) and the Anglicans had a single large silver chalice ('Heavens, the *germs*,' said the Methodists), no one was going to make a jihad of it.

There was tension in one area: for teenagers, the issue of the RCs and marriage raised its head. The Catholics were seen as a breed apart, and the majority were descended from Irish workers imported into the coal-mines and shipyards in the glory years of Victorian heavy industry. However, there was the odd farming or professional family who – there was no doubt about it – represented 'a problem'. Marrying into such a family would raise the spectre of argument over how the children would be brought up: at that time the Vatican insisted that, in 'mixed' families, Catholicism claimed the children. Whether people were devout or didn't give a fig for belief the actual demand seemed an interference in private matters, and the mention of a new boyfriend occasionally met with the remark, 'They're Catholics – aren't they? Just remember. . . .' There were little prejudices which were gossiped about – that the town council was huffy at the thought of a Catholic councillor, but that was put down to all of them being Masons. And there were sharp glances in the local hospitals when the occasional nun sailed in. Matrons grasped them firmly if they hovered near the beds of those who did not have RC on their form: death-bed conversions were considered unsporting.

In my teens, returning from an exchange visit to France in 1961, all talk of snails and wine and garlic was blown away when it emerged that the family I'd stayed with had taken me to Mass one Sunday morning. It was as if I'd strayed near the jaws of hell and the flames had nearly licked me. I countered that it was all bells and smells, just as was suspected by any good little Methodist, and that the most interesting thing had been that the congregation talked all the way through Communion – except when those at the back of the church lit cigarettes and wreathed a statue of the Virgin in a blue haze. This produced a deep satisfaction that the RCs 'didn't know how to behave'. Years later I saw an Italian TV technician do exactly the same, though this was in St Peter's in Rome and the smoke was within sniffing distance of the Pope.

In 1961, the Catholic Church in Ireland was not the object of the dismissive and patronising remarks that I was used to in England. It was the power in the land and had a grip on everyday life that amounted to near-strangulation of liberal principles. As an ordinary soul, you challenged its authority at your peril. In the smallest of villages the priest was the fount of all knowledge, the source of influence, the judge and jury on behaviour. The busy nuns, who seemed to be more plentiful in Dublin than in the environs of the Vatican, still retained a detachment from society which rendered them remote and untouchable. And the Church still rivalled the state when it came to decisions about family relationships. In 1961 Siobhan Lewis started life with the Church very much in charge: 'I know nothing of how I arrived. Just the date of birth – and in a nursing home.'

Siobhan talks in her large living room in London with three lithe and energetic daughters zooming in and out and a small boy crawling speedily among toys. A dark-haired Irish woman, she laughs readily at some of the gaps in her past but becomes impassioned when she emphasises how much she wants to find out. 'I suppose I'm illegitimate. I've so few clues, but I'm searching. I've very few first memories, but the major one was being told at the age of six that I was adopted, being told you were loved – and your own mother couldn't look after you. I have a birth certificate –

but it has my adopting parents' names on it! And I don't even know if my adoption was legal – I've never asked, and in Ireland one doesn't go into that. There was a priest and a public health nurse involved – that's how it all came about. The authorities weren't involved.'

Siobhan was brought up in Dublin – 'an up-and-down childhood with a few scary nuns along the way' – alongside an older sister, also adopted, but her background was not much mentioned at home. 'To be honest, my adopting parents didn't seem to know anything.' Later 'I remember, after having been told about the adoption, you just didn't say a word at the RC school. What with the nuns and everything and what we were taught about sexual matters – all evil and bad – you didn't dare say too much. When we got to be teenagers as well. But it was always there. Every birthday that comes – 25 December – it's there. Though I'm now no longer sure it *is* my actual date of birth. And as a teenager I questioned a bit – but I was told there was nothing, and there was some resistance to the idea of my asking questions.'

She came to England and married, and the arrival of her children stirred her into action. 'It comes and goes, this feeling of wanting to know, and I look at my children and I'm trying to see myself in them. When my third daughter was born she got viral encephalitis – and she was so sick that I thought something medical might be going on connected with me, and I had no information. All I knew about events in '61 was that I came to the family as a result of "voluntary good works" on behalf of the priest. However, I feel more positive about everything when I'm searching. I found out the name of the nursing home, which apparently was unregistered at the time. I was lucky enough to talk to the daughter of the home's owner on the phone twice, and she checked the books for me. But I'm not on the books. After my fourth child, the pressure increased – after the first two I'd felt very together about it all, then after three and four I said to myself, "The time's come." You can't go through life without knowing. I want to find out for my little family – it'll take them forward. My eldest is coming up to teenage and I want her to have a strong sense of self. My four children – I couldn't dream of giving them away . . . and I keep hoping that I might find her – my mother. I have a great love in my heart for her. I just want to know why I was given away, my past, what's she like. Does she like music . . . ? Just the simple things. . . . The girls are musical, the eldest with the flute – perhaps. . . .

'I've been to Barnardo's, the Irish Adoption Association – there are no records anywhere. And I also phoned up the priest – the one involved in the "voluntary good works". He said, "Oh dear, no, I don't know anything." And that was it. He would say nothing more. And apparently the public health nurse died years ago.' She grips her fingers and seems quite tense. 'I'll still go on looking.'

There's no doubt when she talks about the call to the priest that it was an out-of-the-ordinary brief conversation. And even considering the secrecy and guilt which attended these matters in the early sixties in Ireland, Siobhan's story seems particularly bereft of official existence. She knows that priest is the key to her past – and there's a distinct possibility that she's literally a daughter of the Church. It would be part of a familiar tale in Ireland, which for centuries has blurred the lines between the rights of Church and people and has witnessed some of the grimmest aspects of abuse to be found anywhere in Europe.

Some years before Thomas Coram embarked on his mission to create a Foundling Hospital in London, there was already one in Dublin. It was in a city expanding into a metropolis of elegant buildings but already possessing a reputation for savage poverty, partly because of the tide of desperate poor who headed there from the bleak and unproductive bogland. Abandoned children got scant sympathy: their fate can be read into the statute which appeared in 1707, an 'Act to Prevent the Destroying and Murdering of Bastard Children'. As in England, a woman who hid the death of her illegitimate baby could now be executed if she failed to provide a witness to swear that it had been still-born. Abandonment was an obvious alternative.

Traditionally, the only place to leave a child was at the local church – and even this was a problem, considering that the

Reformation had seen the decline of Catholic church buildings so that many Catholics had no actual place of worship. Nevertheless, some children thus abandoned managed to survive, for there are records of children with names such as Michan (after a Dublin church) and Porch, commemorating the baby's precise location when found. There was, as elsewhere, a distinct reluctance in communities to cough up money to support such children. As with beggars and the homeless, determined efforts were made to move people on to the next parish. The peculiar profession of 'lifter' appeared in Ireland – women who scoured the parish at night for any children lying around, doped them up with diacodium (syrup of poppies) to stop them crying, then scurried off to the next parish to dump them for a second time.

In 1701, a 'House of Industry' was set up in Dublin 'for the employment and maintaining of the poor thereof'; part of it accommodated orphans between five and sixteen. It served to alleviate only a small element of the problem, however, and poverty lapped at the walls of even the grandest buildings, including St Patrick's Cathedral, where the Dean, Jonathan Swift, put pen to paper on the subject. In 1729 the author of *Gulliver's Travels* applied his biting satire to the issue of poor children in one of his most caustic pamphlets, 'A Modest Proposal for Preventing the Children of Poor People in Ireland from being a Burden to the Parent or Country', suggesting that the English rulers should simply eat Irish children: 'I have been assured by a very knowing American of my acquaintance in London, that a young healthy child well nursed is at a year old a most delicious, nourishing, and wholesome food, whether stewed, roasted, baked, or boiled, and I make no doubt that it will equally serve in a fricassee, or a ragout.' Little did he know that his satire would become only marginally less shocking than the reality. By 1730, the House of Industry was enlarged and renamed the Foundling Hospital and Workhouse of the City of Dublin, supposedly an institution of good religious intentions but one which in reality degenerated into a horror story.

The Turning Wheel at its gate had been installed at the behest of Hu Armach, the Primate of All-Ireland, 'that at any time, by day or by night, a child may be layd in it, to be taken in by the officers of the said house'. There was a revolving cradle with a bell attached to it built into the gate, and the porter who turned the wheel could not see who left the child. Within days it was busy. They came in their hundreds from all over the country. Soon there were reports of trips made by women carrying several babies heaped in a basket, and by the end of the century it was an established pattern according to the report of a parliamentary investigation: 'The wretched little ones were sent up from all parts of Ireland, ten or twelve of them thrown together in a kish or basket, forwarded in a low-backed car, and so bruised and crushed and shaken at their journey's end that half of them were taken out dead, and were flung into a dung-heap.'

Both Protestants and Catholics were sent to the Hospital, and often the parents were so poor and desperate that they took little notice of the religious nature of the place: admittedly its first intention was to prevent 'the exposure, death and actual murder of illegitimate children'. However, there was a zealous religious intention as well: 'to educate and rear children taken in charge by the institution in the Reformed or Protestant faith, and thereby to strengthen and promote the Protestant interest in Ireland'. But from the beginning there was a practical obstacle to the proselytising: the Hospital soon ran out of Protestant wet-nurses. With gritted teeth, the governors found themselves having to board out the babies with Catholics. This completely stuffed the conversion process, as was wryly observed by an Irish historian in 1781: 'The children were . . . located with nurses of the Catholic faith, and, gradually imbibing the religious predilections of their foster-mothers, refused when returned to the hospital to adopt the Protestant form of worship, or, if adopting it for a time, speedily relapsed into what the Governors deemed to be religious error . . . thus life was not saved in any degree commensurate with the intentions of the Legislature, nor were there so many accessions to the Protestant interests of the country as had been expected.'

That 'life was not saved' was an understatement. In the 130 years of its existence, it is calculated that no fewer than two hundred thousand passed through the 'cradle at the gate'. A very large proportion died within hours or days of admission. In the early years there was a scandal about the youngest being farmed out to wet-nurses who were paid to look after them until the age of two. Most never made it to their second birthday, the date of payment to the nurses often initiating the infant's murder. To deceive the governors the women sometimes presented their own babies for inspection, leading to the Hospital branding the found-lings on the arm to ensure proper identification – the bodies of thirteen such branded babies were discovered in a sandpit in 1737. In the Hospital the food was literally rotten and bread had a life of its own, being infested with maggots. Overcrowding was auto-matic, clothing ragged and health poor. The infirmary within the building was considered the threshold to the grave.

The Hospital was the subject of numerous reports and parlia-mentary committees: all bemoaned the abuse and neglect and the high number of deaths. Few seem to have made any impact, though one noble lady tried hard to sort out the mess: the energetic Lady Arabella Denny used her own money to improve the build-ings and attempted to run the place on the grounds that it fell within the conventional 'female sphere of observation'. But by the time she arrived, in 1758, children were coming in at the rate of over seven hundred a year, and the best intentions foundered in the face of rows and rows of babies whose fate the general public cared little about. Illegitimacy and poverty were facts of life, but not ones which aroused much sympathy. Poverty was endured by a very large part of the population, and children out of wedlock were the subject of condemnation from the pulpit. After Lady Arabella left, the institution became a killing-ground.

Nevertheless, even though the end of the eighteenth century was hardly a time of soft-heartedness towards society's more unfortu-nate members, politicians were genuinely aghast at the statistics which started to emerge from the Hospital. At a meeting in the Dublin House of Commons in 1790, Members were informed that the previous year had seen 2180 infants received in the Hospital. Of that number, 2087 were now dead or 'unaccounted for'. In the preceding decade 19,367 had been recorded in the books as having passed though the cradle of the Turning Wheel, of whom nearly 17,000 were either dead or missing. In 1797 matters came to a head when a committee was appointed to enquire into the Hospital's management. The previous six years had seen 12,786 children admitted, of whom only 225 survived.

The Irish House of Commons was apprised of the curious habits of the institution, such as 'stripping': those not expected to survive were sent to the infirmary, and any clothes they had been given in the Hospital were exchanged for the rags in which they had originally arrived. Then they were bunched into cradles, five or six squashed together under discarded dirty blankets, with a great deal of vermin for company. There was also the dreaded 'bottle'. The members of the committee sat to hear the testimony – on oath – of the Hospital nurse who described acting on the surgeon's orders when indiscriminately giving the children 'a composing draught'. She hadn't a clue what this medicine actually was, but readily admitted that the children were 'easy for an hour or two after taking it'. The committee took a dim view, with one of them, Sir John Trail, noting that the children he'd seen being put into the Hospital were anything but moribund. Among the 5216 children sent to the infirmary in the previous six years, precisely one had survived. Reform was demanded, and a new set of governors appointed. Nothing much changed – not so much through negligence, but because these children didn't really count. Both Protestants and Catholics were united in the belief that the offspring of immoral mothers carried a sinfulness with them into their own lives – and anyway, meagre rations, dirt and disease were the lot of hundreds of thousands outside the institution.

Thirty-three years later the House of Commons in England (parliamentary union of the two countries had been effected in 1800) was presented with another set of statistics which could be said to represent some sort of improvement on the former regime. Of 52,000 children, only 41,500 had died. This time, they decided to close the place down.

★　　★　　★

With the rise of the workhouse, the nineteenth century saw new efforts to deal with the poor. It became the only support available to the foundling, but there might be a small chance of some rudimentary education and perhaps, later, some work. However, as numbers grew within the walls a system of 'boarding out' was introduced: children were fostered by families who were paid a modest sum. One of the consequences of this, according to the workhouse records, was that the children forgot the surname they'd originally been given – and frequently ended up with no specific name. Foundlings tended not to be taken into the other new institutions which arose in the Victorian era to improve the lot of destitute children, for most were run by religious-based organisations. The foundling was a child of uncertain allegiance in faith, so was unlikely to qualify for a place.

And there was now another way of shifting the poor: emigration. The government realised that there was a dearth of single women in its new colonies, and was anxious to supply willing females for both domestic work and marriage. Poor women sometimes took this option; others were forced by circumstances to board ships for a hard journey to unknown parts because the alternative was starvation. And after the dreadful famine of the 1840s a number of workhouse foundlings found themselves included in the flow, some to America, but mainly to the colonies in Australia, New Zealand and Canada. In forty years nearly sixty thousand women undertook this doubtful adventure.

Some of the earliest who embarked were fifty-nine girls from the Cork Foundling Hospital who were sent as domestic servants to New South Wales in 1831. Four years later, the *Boadicea* left Gravesend in England with twelve 'female orphans' bound for Hobart, Tasmania. They were assessed in the ship's log by the surgeon as being fifteen years of age, but the list supplied by the Hospital describes nearly all as only eleven or twelve. For centuries, parishes had shifted foundlings and orphans over their boundaries to avoid the cost of caring for them. Now the boundaries were extending with the opportunity to send them overseas –

an opportunity seized by workhouse governors with relish and taken advantage of for well over a century.

There were still remarkably large numbers of children in work-houses, institutions and 'industrial schools' in Ireland at the beginning of the twentieth century, a situation that continued for over fifty years due to the inexorable opposition to adoption by the political and religious hierarchy. While countries across Europe altered their opinions about the 'family' and began to explore the idea of legal safeguards for adoption, Ireland remained resolutely apart. Whenever the idea of adoption legislation was raised, the Catholic Church in Ireland used all its clout to block moves which would undermine its position as the sole arbiter of social values and its concept of the 'family' – which meant ties of blood. Thousands of illegitimate children were denied a perma-nent place as a member of a new family because the Church could not countenance the thought that 'the legal parent might be alive', and regarded adoption as an 'artificial substitute' for a 'natural family'. Added to this was a deep conviction that adoption opened up the possibility of 'proselytising' – the chance that the child might slip from the grasp of the Catholic Church and could even become a little Protestant.

The net result was to start up a thriving trade in the illegal export of babies, which was in full swing by the 1940s. The orphanages were bulging, stories of abuse and neglect in them were common-place – and there wasn't enough money to support the children of 'girls who are flocking here daily', for unmarried mothers were considered totally unfit to raise a child. As the law gave inadequate support for those who might want to adopt in Ireland (usually defended with the claim that no one would ever want to take an *illegitimate* child), a solution to overcrowding and cost was spotted across the Atlantic.

The Americans were rich. There was a market. And closer to home, by the 1940s American servicemen stationed in England had discovered that you could hop over to Ireland and pick and choose a baby without any of the complications that arose in Britain. And, most importantly, these Americans were Catholics. It was the latter which allowed the trade to take off. There could be no worries about religious back-sliding, which was a source of quiet comfort to those in authority who knew all about the business – indeed, so much did they care about this that they refused to allow any child to be sent to England, and took special pains to ensure that requests from Northern Ireland were rebuffed.

The Archbishop of Dublin, John Charles McQuaid, a man very conscious of his quasi-political role as the 'ecclesiastical Taoiseach' and devoted to protecting Irish children from non-Catholic influence, was fully aware of the system. He decided how passports could be issued for the exported children and personally frustrated attempts by civil servants to modernise the law, which had parted company with Westminster after the setting up of the Irish Free State in 1921. Then into this cosy arrangement came a bombshell: Jane Russell arrived. *The* Jane Russell, the actress of stupendous bosoms and a string of Hollywood hits to her name.

She wasn't the first to upset the applecart: in 1950 there had been some unpleasant publicity when the *New York Times* published a photograph of six children at Shannon Airport heading for their new adopting families in the United States. This wasn't what the Church wanted at all; the trade was useful and, since it was probably both illegal and unconstitutional, clandestine. Archbishop McQuaid acted swiftly: he got the media banned from Shannon Airport. Then he suspended operations while the fuss about the lack of scrutiny of adopters – other than their faith – quietened down. Such was his power that the news black-out on this and related stories lasted a full two years.

Unfortunately for him, Jane Russell and publicity were synonymous: the woman for whom the aviator and film producer Howard Hughes was said to have designed a cantilevered bra and who was once introduced by the comedian Bob Hope as 'the two and only Jane Russell' loved the press. Not the sort of woman whom you wanted plonk in the middle of an argument about socio-religious behaviour, not to mention murky clerically approved baby-farming. Miss Russell wanted to adopt a second child, heading for Ireland in the autumn of 1951 and telling anyone (i.e. the world's press) who wanted to know that: 'I hoped I would be able to find a boy in Europe, but it seems impossible . . . the British law will not allow me to take a child from England. In Italy I could not get a child because I am under forty; and, anyway, there were difficulties because Italy is a Catholic country and I am a Protestant. Now I have been advised to try Ireland; but I am worried in case the same difficulties would arise there. My husband is Irish, and he would very much like to adopt an Irish baby. If it is possible, I would like to fly to Dublin this week to pick out a child and make all the arrangements for bringing him to America.'

An actress. A Protestant actress. And all over the papers. A quiet word here and there and Miss Russell eventually ended up in London, having spotted an Irish lad living with his parents in England. An Irish passport was issued remarkably promptly, and fifteen-month-old Tommy Kavanagh was ready for life with a movie star. The Irish diplomatic staff, when asked by the media about the passport, delivered a po-faced statement that they believed Miss Russell was taking him 'on holiday'.

Back in Dublin there was much rage, with the Foreign Affairs Department spitting at their colleagues in London – not about the dubious legal situation, but about the nasty spotlight that had been shone on these activities: 'We would be glad if you would refer to the Department any application for a passport made to you by or on behalf of a person of either sex under the age of 18 years . . . the whole business received a great amount of undesirable publicity in the Press (particularly the English Sunday papers of the 11th inst.) and the reason for this instruction is that we wish to ensure that an Irish passport will not again be issued in such circumstances.'

The British media were not impressed and spent a considerable time crawling over this interesting state of affairs in Ireland. But in Dublin, the Archbishop's news black-out on the issue was still being observed. Eventually a German newspaper managed to sting the Irish government with the suggestion that they were auctioning off 'unwanted' children to the highest bidder. *8 Uhr Blatt* alleged that an Irish social worker had told them: 'Our country has today become a sort of hunting ground for foreign millionaires who believe they can acquire children to suit their whims just in the same way as they would get valuable pedigree animals.'

Sheer embarrassment drove the government to act; the instigation of legal adoption was considered, and the lawyers got to work. However, the Archbishop was very much in the driving seat – and it may be noted that the Prime Minister, the Taoiseach, at the time was Eamon de Valera. He was a man from humble origins who eventually rose to be President of his country. And those origins were always the subject of much whispered speculation, for he had been born in the Nursery and Child's Hospital in New York, a place for destitute and abandoned children. . . .

However, the heads of government and Church and their officials couldn't free themselves from traditional habits, framing their adoption legislation in accordance with the Church's priorities: religion was to take preference over any other consideration. Compared to the criteria applied on the introduction of adoption legislation in Britain in 1926, faith loomed much larger than the needs and interests of the children. And with foundlings, there was always a question mark. Who owned their soul as they entered this world?

While Ireland grappled with the new laws, the dodgy overseas adoption system went on functioning for another twenty years. (Miss Russell achieved a much better track record, founding WAIF, the World Adoption International Fund, which placed 51,000 children with adoptive families in the second half of the twentieth century – more than the Irish government, in fact, and free of the religious constraints.)

Another of the features of adoption in Ireland has been the immense difficulty in tracing a mother. The law was written in such a way as to break the link between mother and child – and the government has made it as difficult as possible to access what records there are. Change is under way, but many who were born in the fifties and sixties and are now enquiring about their roots have had a frustrating time.

A few years before the Jane Russell kerfuffle in Ireland, I had been adopted via English law. And there I was in Sunderland, a little

Presbyterian on Sunday, an Anglican Monday to Friday, and with my name on the Methodist Christening Roll – and a great-grand-mother called Susannah who was furtively referred to as 'the one the family nose comes from'. And way back in my own past, though not knowing it then, a little hint that the left-footers had nearly got me when I was temporarily adopted by a Catholic couple. The fact that this happened indicated the obsession with an infant's religion from the moment he or she entered upon this earth – despite the fact that in 1926, while MPs had spoken passionately at Westminster about the importance of religion, they had definitely laid down that it was not to be the most significant factor in adoption.

The law in England may have been framed with other interests paramount, but in practice it frequently went into reverse. Social circumstances, geography, educational levels, lifestyle, all these were subservient to the deep worry that the infant soul would get the wrong signposts on the way to paradise. Efforts to match babies with prospective parents often centred on matching up religion, even though English law imposed none of the heavy-handed religious demands to be found in Ireland. Heaven knows how many women had a moment of blank incomprehension after hours of labour when confronted by someone enquiring about the spiritual guidance of the child they were about to give up. In a large number of cases, the Church of England probably did very well out of the reply which stood for: I don't know, I don't care, I'm not particularly religious and what's the line of least resistance – C of E?

With hindsight, the quirky aspects and social importance of religious life in the north-east seem to me to be just another hang-over from Victorian times in an area which was still clinging to its old-fashioned industrial identity. However, I did wonder about the power it retained: faith-based schools, the rituals of naming, marrying and dying, the inevitable request to state your religion on application forms for myriad activities. But belief was never a decision-maker or a major bar to opportunity in life.

Even if England represented, in general, the more secular

practice and Ireland still had the clergy's hand on the cradle, one place in between presented particular difficulties: Northern Ireland. At about nine o'clock on the evening of 16 January 1962 in an affluent suburb of Belfast Mrs Pullen, a doctor's wife, went out to her car to pick up her shopping. Lying on the front seat was David.

'This was in Dunmurray – near the Conway Road, on the opposite side of the road to the police station.' David McBride is a good-looking man who recounts the details with the serious expertise of the lawyer he now is. Then he smiles: 'I was very well dressed, with quite expensive clothing for the time. Mrs Pullen called a neighbour who then called the police who took me to the City Hospital. There they said I was between ten and fourteen days old and that I had been well cared for.'

His abandonment caused a stir, and his story and photograph appeared not only in the Northern Irish press but also in the national newspapers. 'Perhaps it was unusual in those days – I don't know. But it kept in the news for about a year. Even the day I was taken to court it was in the news. No one came forward, though.' Initially David went from one Babies' Home to another, and then was fostered when he was five months old. He thinks his name came from one of the doctors who saw him when he was first taken to hospital.

'At school I suppose I should have been quite curious, but I wasn't. It's quite strange, having now seen all the notes of the social workers who used to visit on a weekly basis, but I never thought anything about it. Then at school – with the kids saying your mum's not your mum and your dad's not your dad. . . . Finally, my parents sat me down and talked to me. I didn't even know what fostering was. Parents? Fantastic – I couldn't have asked for a better family, and they [the foster-parents] adopted me when I was nine. I was brought up with a brother and two sisters. Mum first worked in a factory. No problems. I made no difference to my family – in fact my mother was more protective towards me because of the way the Social Services acted. They sure kept their tabs on me, through the fostering. Regular visits – and they kept notes saying things like my mother had said she'd like to work a few hours more at a shop, and they'd written that they were going to take Dave back and give him to someone else. I've seen all the notes. Strange people.

'And then there was the way the press went on: sensationalised everything. I mean, I've seen the headlines about me – for *eight months*. Even when I went back to court when I was nearly nine, the whole town of Lisburn knew who I was. Everyone knew I'd "come into" the family. Mind you, they protected me. Even then they used to say – and these were all people who knew – "He's beginning to look like you, Emma!"

'Dad was an aircraft fitter working for the RAF, then he went into the Civil Service. I followed in my father's footsteps and joined the army. Did fifteen years as a sergeant in the Signals, then came out and retrained to be a lawyer.'

When he joined the services, out came the adoption registration card rather than a birth certificate. It says: 'Born on or about. . .' and his birthday had been fixed on the Twelfth Day of Christmas. The army asked no further questions. It's a fact that a considerable number of young men who join up come from difficult and fractured backgrounds. Orphans and foundlings are not uncommon for two obvious reasons. First, the tradition of sending off to the military the young inmates of institutions – workhouses, orphanages, training ships, Children's Homes, Foundling Hospitals – goes back centuries. Used to a regimented life and a structured day, moderately educated, unlikely to be offered enterprising opportunities elsewhere and already living apart from their peers, these lads were always ideal material for the army and navy and helped with the recruiting problem. Second, they also craved a family – and amid the new-found comradeship and hierarchy often found a sense of belonging which had been lacking in their childhood. To this day there are many who discover within the 'family of the services' something which gives them confidence and security which they could not tap into in civvy street. On leaving, they're often doubly discharged: leaving the job and losing the 'family', which contributes far too heavily to the homeless on our streets.

When he was about thirty, David started to search. From childhood he had a few clues. Given all the publicity in the press when he was found, there'd been snippets of information and gossip which reached his foster-parents: 'People who lived in the street at the time all had different stories. That the doctor was my father. Or there'd been a student . . . the doctor had been teaching at Queen's University at the time. Or someone had seen a young girl walking down the street at about eight o'clock. But then some children said they heard a baby crying at six . . . all stories but nothing concrete – and the police didn't do much of an investigation.' There was one other clue, and that lay in the location: at the back of the houses where Mrs Pullen's car was parked stood one of the biggest private Catholic girls' schools in Belfast. And the more David enquired, the more the traditional divisions in Northern Ireland loomed large and the trail seemed to have been scrubbed out in the name of faith.

This was in the 1960s, well before the start of the Troubles which would engulf Northern Ireland for several decades. The rest of Britain took little notice of the religious divide – indeed, was largely ignorant of it. The sectarian attitudes which sliced up residential areas, ensured that certain jobs belonged to one denomination only and produced an education system which rigidly isolated children from 'the others' had no resonance over the water. Ulster traditions and symbols – the world of Orange Lodges and Nationalism, Fenians and Taigs, Apprentice Boys and Altar Boys – were incomprehensible to the rest of Britain. And the fact that religion rooted everyone in their place was something that no one had given much thought to for many a year. Baby David was dropped right on Northern Ireland's fault line.

'Very, very much so,' he says. 'My personal opinion now, having spoken to people from that area, is that they were very, very frightened of me having been placed with a Protestant family – and suddenly my mother turns up? Being a Catholic, they wouldn't have wanted that to happen.' When he began the search and was involved in a television programme which gave his case considerable publicity, details which should have emerged from official sources dried up or appeared not to exist any more.

'I haven't got a birth certificate, only the adoption certificate. And it's a real problem with passports. They ask for the date of birth and I say I haven't got one, and they say *this* is it – pointing to the adoption certificate. I say No – that's just an adoption certificate. And they don't understand. Social Services have insisted that they couldn't trace one. There must be one somewhere. I've tried, my father tried, but all my records – the hospital, the police records – they've all been destroyed. We even wrote to the RUC Chief Constable, and he replied that all records had been destroyed.

'I wrote and wrote to the authorities, and Belfast City eventually gave me my files. That's when I learned that Social Services kept thinking of taking me back. They couldn't take a decision for nearly *nine* years. And there were notes in there saying, when I was four or five years of age, "This baby *cannot* go for adoption. Possibility may still find mother."'

Nine years? What reason could there be for this dithering? David has no doubt: 'Religion. It was only when they'd exhausted every avenue and said, "Well, she's never going to turn up now." . . . And in the notes, all they ever referred to me as was "Baby Blue Eyes". They never referred to me as anything else. All the time. *Nothing* else. But the records of me having been in all the different Homes for nearly six months, *they'd* all been destroyed.

'When we looked at the convent school, we learned that it closed down over Christmas and I could have been concealed. And at that time *they* may well have concealed it through embarrassment – that was the attitude which came through to me when we spoke to the Church. There was one clue: a lady came from the Catholic Church and said that a lady had turned up at one of the Catholic Homes and she left with a baby on 5 January 1962 – but they were unable to trace her. They didn't seem to have been very inquisitive about it. . . . Now they say that they *found* this baby, but I've not seen anything about where they found it or what – and they didn't say they *had* it . . . and that's the nearest clue I've got.

'It's quite strange. When we were doing the research the Catholic Church was only too happy to open up – but they *were* having to be politically correct in their interviews and they were involved at the time with a lot of investigation into children being taken away and sent abroad. The lady who was leading this research did some for me and came up with a couple of names, but they couldn't tie down the dates. The Protestant Church said: "We don't want to help you. It couldn't have been us," and closed up shop right away.

'I've met the nurse who the newspapers dragged in when I was taken to hospital. She was the one who held me for the photographs, and they said that she was the one who was looking after me. But when I met her last year – she was a lovely person, lived most of her life in Africa – she said she was just a trainee nurse then, and the press put me in her arms. She did say, "You were a lovely child" – and she'd kept all the photographs.

'The lady who found me in the car . . . I did meet her and . . . she was very cold, very offish with me. She said that the police visited that night, but that they were only there for about five minutes and they didn't take any statements from anybody in the street. I was in her house, then into a police car in less than ten minutes. Quite extraordinary.

'At some point we were talking about getting DNA testing, and she was opposed to it – but one of her sons was willing, though he was in Australia. And there were no family photographs in the house. She just showed us some very old pictures of her [late] husband. It was very intriguing to see her mannerisms with me, because my parents who saw her later on the TV programme said they thought she knew something. . . . At the present time I just want to get on with my life, but you never forget about it. It's one of those things which go through your mind every day. It's something you have to live with. . . . I could pursue the DNA – without offending her. . . .'

David talks with all the frustration of someone who feels that there's still evidence somewhere of who he is, and that others have already tried to obliterate the tracks that could lead him to his birth

mother. 'I would like to meet my mother. I would have sympathy
for her. But the fact that I was taken very good care of and was in
perfect health – and the fact that I was between ten and fourteen
days – would lead me to think that whoever made this decision had
sat down and had plenty of time to make the decision. I think
desperation comes in when the baby's born. I don't think my
abandonment was desperate. To walk down that street that night
and to pick out a car and open the car and place the baby in the car
and walk away knowing that . . . that. . . . It was nine o'clock at
night and the blinds wouldn't have been drawn and you could look
on to the street and anybody would have seen. And the bus service
between Belfast and Lisburn – to get there that time of night? And
there's loads of places along the road I might have been abandoned. Why pick this place? This is why they pinned it down to the
convent behind the house – or to the fact that at the time, just
across the road, Andersonstown was beginning to be built and a lot
of the Nationalist Catholic community was moving in.'

David has gone through this time and again. He has all the usual
curiosity and looks at his own daughter and wonders where her
looks come from, and the mannerisms. But he also thinks that he's
influenced by his history, despite his happy childhood and loving
adoptive parents: 'The fact that you learn when you're young that
you were abandoned, you build your character around learning
that. I think you tend not to trust people as much as you would if
you were brought up in a close family environment – and knew
they were *your* close family. I've met others who say they had a
fantastic upbringing but they've still got their doubts about people
. . . the people who *aren't* bringing them up.'

There's much laughter as we talk. The shadow of religious
bigotry lies across his origins but hasn't clouded his life. He picks
up his sports bag for a session at the gym, and has a final thought
about the religious tribes of Ulster: 'Quite strange, really – my
parents used to refer to me when I was growing up as "a little
Fenian" because I used to look like a Catholic. But it was all in jest!'

12

What is your ethnic group?

In the 1950s I cannot recall a single black or brown face among a quarter of a million citizens in Sunderland. Even the Chinese had not yet reached our high streets. The shipyards and the coal-pits still regarded the Irish who'd arrived at the end of the previous century as pretty foreign, and the occasional African or Asian was often a visiting missionary or Church member, Sunderland having a vigorous bunch of non-conformist Churches keen on conversion in faraway places. Race, unlike religion, was not an everyday fact of life. The nearest group of non-white faces was in nearby South Shields, where an old-established group of seamen and their families testified to harmonious relations (bar a couple of small riots about poor pay decades ago) between the Yemen and the River Tyne. The novelty of this community of hard-working stokers on tramp steamers led to it being called – without prejudice – Islam on Tyne. The immigrants who headed for the large conurbations in the second half of the twentieth century tended not to reach the north-east. With the major Victorian heavy industries in decline from the Tyne to the Tees, there wasn't much chance of employment.

It would be fair to say that the comments and attitudes from all and sundry about race that I encountered as a child would now be considered prejudiced. However, ill will and dislike were not automatically intended: there was just a reaction to the unfamiliar, along with inherited beliefs about other races. Inter-racial adoption was not publicly debated in the north-east; the idea would have been called 'rather far-fetched'. One belief was that marrying across a racial divide was both unusual and somehow shocking. As a child during Coronation year, 1953, I can remember newspaper pictures of a wedding which elicited tut-tuts and indrawn breath, even though no one in Sunderland knew the couple. Peggy, the daughter of a very prominent politician, Sir Stafford Cripps, was pictured in her finery marrying Joe Appiah, a lawyer and government official in Ghana. The marriage was viewed as sensational, though I could never gather why: just a series of knowing looks and unspoken thoughts, lamely explained by the remark that 'posh people did that sort of thing'.

Into County Durham in 1951 came a lad of mixed race as a foster-son to Violet Masters in the little village of Hett near Spennymoor, a dozen miles from Sunderland. Bruce Oldfield has staying power in the fashion business: honed over thirty years of dressing the elegant, rich and famous, his professional skills had their origin in the front room of Violet's terraced house. We chatted in a room beneath his London showroom, which is completely filled by his desk and his dog, an arrestingly huge and beautiful Rhodesian ridgeback called Babe. We seemed to have skirted each other's lives in the north-east, for I knew several farming families around Hett and we may have chorused 'behind youooo' together at the Sunderland Empire pantomimes ('thrill to the Pantomime Cat *and* the Smith Brothers'). As he's written in his autobiography, Violet was a spinster dressmaker who had taken to fostering well into her forties. She took on Bruce, having grown tired of children leaving her care as they reached earning age, explaining that she'd take on younger children – 'coloureds, whom no one wanted'.

Bruce Oldfield is not a foundling, but belongs to that large number of children who were taken from their parents at a very early age and who often feel that they have been abandoned. In his case, he now understands that his mother was given no choice. The authorities in 1951 took a dim view of women giving birth out of wedlock, and a very definitely dark view of those who had crossed the line with someone who was not white.

'Umm . . . not *exactly* abandoned. I always take a pragmatic view of life and, having looked at the position of my mother at the time, I don't think I'd have done very well if I'd stayed with her. So basically I think the authorities who insisted that I was removed from her were probably right. And there was also the business of her not wanting to have a coloured child in the home. It was the fifties . . . I think it all worked *against* her, but possibly *for* me.'

Betty Lally was married, but had left her husband Lawrence Oldfield and young son. Disapproving noises were already being made by various welfare officials, for that first child, who had been swiftly adopted, was both illegitimate and of mixed race. Even so, while Betty was still living in a Mother and Baby Home in Chalk Farm in north-west London she managed an encounter with a Jamaican boxer 'round the back of the Hammersmith Odeon'. The result was Bruce. As he pointedly writes in his autobiography, adopting Lady Bracknell's stricture in Oscar Wilde's *The Impor-tance of Being Earnest*, 'to have one black illegitimate child might be regarded as a dreadful misfortune; to have two looked like moral turpitude'.

Betty was faced with a situation familiar to thousands of women at that time: stigmatised as a 'fallen woman', her family ashamed of her, no financial resources, no housing except to return to her family, and for her the additional burden of pressure from all sides about race. Betty signed the form handing Bruce over to the care of Dr Barnardo's Homes. Three months later he arrived in Hett, where Violet already had one black foster-son in addition to two white girls. Later, two more half-Jamaican sisters arrived.

'We did stand out a *bit* in Hett. . . . We *did*, but eventually there were three of us boys, and it's quite interesting, because recently I was up in Durham filming a television programme and there was a girl called Shirley Watts – her family worked on market stalls – and she said, "There was no colour problem with you boys . . . or perhaps there was with Barry because he was very dark." And I thought, My God, it's *gradations* in colour. There was no problem really – until later with the mothers, when you wanted to go out with their daughters. I remember a bit of bother at Spennymoor Grammar Technical School when I'd written a letter to someone calling him a bastard because he'd called me a *black* bastard, and

my welfare officer kicked up a big fuss. Eventually she reported
that I "didn't know what the word 'bastard' means".'

He has vivid memories of life in the north-east, first in Hett and
Spennymoor, then at grammar school in Ripon. It was not a life of
ease and comfort, money was always a problem and his foster-
mother and Barnardo's were forever wrangling; but for all that it
was happy and sowed the seeds of his future success: grammar
school education, a growing desire to better himself and a very
early fascination with sewing and style. The young Bruce sat for
hours glued to the mysteries of hemming and embroidery that
attended Violet's work, stating at the age of eight that he wanted to
be a tailor when he grew up so that he could help his foster-mother
earn some money. That this remark has survived is due to the fact
that much about his life was written down – by others. At the time,
he wasn't fully aware of the copious reports made on his progress
through childhood by Barnardo's. However, every incident was
noted down, from comments on his attitude to race, aged eight –
'Does not realise that he is coloured' to teenage pranks and
observations that he is a 'strong reliable honest lad. Strong willed.
Markedly effeminate. Quite a "snob". Good qualities outweigh the
bad ones.' What few scraps of information he was told about his
own background are also in the files – and the occasions when
Barnardo's let him know a little more (such as that his mother was
married when he was born – but omitting to say that it was not to
his father).

Most of us have memories of getting some bad school reports,
but the thick file of personal detail which accumulated over the
years that the welfare officers paid their regular visits and corre-
sponded with a range of adults who had some responsibility for
Bruce's upbringing is a daunting history. It is one, however, which
he wears lightly: 'Life is what you make it, isn't it? I really do
believe that. That's what has carried me through. I was just re-
reading something I wrote a few years ago, and written over it in
red I've found: "New thoughts!" I'm always optimistic. If things
aren't so good, then *do* something about it.' His life is one of hard
work, enterprise and glamour, creating fabulous frocks for royalty

and the famous and seriously fun-loving. Just walking past a single rail of mouth-watering little numbers in the shop produces a squeak of female desire to be very rich and very thin.

Bruce finally got round to searching out his background when he was forty-five, having only occasionally thought about his parents and having gone to Hammersmith Hospital – where he was born – but failing to find the right department. He took part in a TV programme about Barnardo's, of which he is a great supporter, but it wasn't in response to some emotional void, just 'Why not?' – driven by curiosity rather than need. In a single sitting lasting ten hours he read his fat files. At the end of it, having learned of the circumstances of his birth and the attitudes in the 1950s, he had more detail – but no major reaction to what had happened. Eventually he saw his mother's story as typical of the time and felt more sympathetic towards her, having met some of her surviving relatives. Of his father, he now says he has few thoughts.

'It's odd, isn't it? He was reputedly a West Indian boxer. But I don't feel I've followed him in any way! I think I don't even look particularly Jamaican – I think I look Egyptian. And people *will* speak Arabic to me!'

He hasn't forgotten his roots, but he's a creature of aspirations. It worries him not a jot how he arrived on this earth. He's happy in his work and neither confused nor anxious about growing up in foster and residential homes. He's very fulfilled, and dedicated his book *Rootless* to Violet, the dressmaker from Hett.

A decade after Bruce's mother met open disapproval about her partners, the country was beginning to change given the steady increase in non-white immigrants. However, a child of mixed race was still referred to as 'half-caste' and there was little thought as to adoption options; in the years before the contraceptive pill was available, a mixed-race baby was just one of a large number of whatever colour sitting in Children's Homes hoping for a family, rather than a life in an official Home. And race, though an element in one's roots, may not be the dominant question in a foundling's life.

In one sense, a foundling should perhaps celebrate the day they were found – a rite of passage into the life they know about. But the pressure of convention brings the birthday to the fore. Sandie Warren lives with her partner in an airy flat in Glasgow: it's furnished stylishly and ruled over by a mad bundle of a small dog which skids around the polished wooden floors. The kitchen is a modern wonder, and coffee and yummy chocolate biscuits appear.

'It's always there. The milestones were when I was eighteen and twenty-one – and, well, it's a made-up birthday! I was found in Woolworth's in the Holloway Road in Islington in London. It was March 1963, and I was all wrapped up nice and warm and clean, and I looked like I'd been looked after quite well. It was a Saturday, but I don't know what time of day. A woman who was shopping found me. I was left by the check-out. She alerted the staff, who came and got me; then the police came and I was taken to a Children's Home in Highbury. All I know from the case notes is just that I was a healthy baby, but there's no one around to verify this. At the home they counted back seven weeks – that's how old they thought I was, and they gave me my birthday.'

Sandie has given her background some thought but is in no way in thrall to it, even though childhood had its ups and downs: 'The Home in Highbury – it had a big nursery, apparently full of babies. My mum and dad who adopted me already had a daughter, Lesley. But according to my dad, when he came home from work one day Lesley was in the garden playing and my mum was sitting in the kitchen reading a newspaper article and crying. She said, "There's this baby who's been left," and she was all upset and said, "We've got to help that baby – we've got to have that baby." So they tried to do that, but the baby wasn't available – maybe she'd been claimed. So they decided to help another baby and came along to the Children's Home. When she was being shown around, she remembered there were "tons of babies" there, for there was no birth control or things like that then, and she said there were hundreds of us . . . floors of us . . . and they got to me and I was lying there and looking cute and stuff. The assistant with them said, "If someone doesn't come and take her soon, she'll be retarded." They didn't have time to do anything other than bath you, feed you and put you back down, so I'd been lying on my back for nine months and the back of my head had got really quite flat! In fact, it still is a bit . . . but luckily I've got thick hair.

'And Mum said, "We can't have that," and they took me. What was ironic was that I'd been in this clinical environment for nine months, and when my mum and dad took me home they had this nursery which they'd painted in bright colours. I screamed and I howled and they couldn't shut me up until my mum decided to pin a white sheet around my cot – and then I slept. And gradually, as the days went on, they started pinning a bit of it back until I slowly got used to it. Apparently I was quite slow to walk, and it took me ages to talk . . . though when I started, I never shut up.'

Sandie describes her childhood as 'pretty crap', but understands something of the reasons for this. Her mother started off with good intentions – a younger sister had also been born, so there were now three girls; and the early years were happy. Being adopted was not a problem: 'I'd always known I was adopted. For a start, I'm a different colour to my sisters! And my younger sister's six foot one and blonde, and my elder sister's five foot ten and got brown hair, and they both look like my parents. I even remember being adopted and going to St Alban's Crown Court when I was five. In those days, the case stayed open for five years and only after that could you adopt. I remember the judge giving me sweeties and asking me if I wanted to be with them, because I used to joke with my sister and say, "Why did I say Yes?" '

Later Sandie's mother went through a very tough menopause and made life difficult for everybody. Elder sister Lesley had a strong character, taking after her mother, and Sandie was different. She escaped to school and enjoyed it; and being adopted was no big deal – some of her school friends were too. And with her mother becoming less open-minded and more unforgiving, as she grew up she became even more glad that she was adopted and not really related to this increasingly difficult woman. Right through childhood she'd kept in contact with her social worker, Jo, who'd become friendly with her mum before the adoption. And her eighteenth birthday was coming up.

'I'd always thought when I'm eighteen I can go and find out who my real parents are . . . and you have to have that there, telling yourself, "I'll muddle through this, in the knowledge that . . .". And then my mum, who wasn't a very sensitive person, was watching the news on TV and there was something about an abandoned baby. And she shattered my whole dream by saying, "Oh, *you* were abandoned."

'And I said, "What?"

"Oh yeah, yeah, somebody left you."

'And I thought, "You nasty, nasty woman. You've said and done some nasty things, but that's the nastiest thing you've ever made up."

'So I contacted Jo and met her in a pub. And she said, "No, she's right – you were." And then it was like – where do you go from here? And I went out of the pub and never saw Jo again.

'I'd joined a theatre in St Albans called the Abbey when I was still at school, and I wanted to be a stage manager. And I also did a Saturday job in British Home Stores and was lucky to meet the actress Ruth Madoc, who gave me the names of theatre schools you could go to. But it didn't work out – it was all to do with things at home. And then my mum kicked me out. Because I'm gay.

'I went to stay with friends in London. I didn't really know what to do next. One of my mates suggested that I go to where I was left. So this is twenty years on from when I was found, and there was no Woolworth's in the Holloway Road any more – hadn't been for ages. And the Children's Home has gone as well. I went to Islington Library, went through the microfilm and found a picture of me in the papers. All blurry in black and white, with some stuff underneath saying this woman from Devonshire Road in Mill Hill had found me and the police were making enquiries and there'd been lots of people phoning in wanting to look after me. Which was quite nice. I tried to find the woman who'd found me, but she'd moved on. The *Islington Gazette* did an article on me but . . .

'Then I saw a social worker, who got my file. And I sat in a room with this file. It doesn't tell you a lot. Just social workers' diaries for the first four years of my life, but the beginning's, well, all a bit shady. . . . Except, in the case notes it says just that I was a healthy baby when I was found – but there's no one around to verify this. And there's a line to say there had been a note left with me – but nobody kept it. And I was very upset about that. Apparently it just said, "We can't look after this child, please bring her up as your own." Maybe that was the shorter version of what it said – but I don't know.

'I don't think there was a name left on the note – it's a bit confusing. And I think I was named in the Children's Home – Alexandra. And Mum called me Sandra, but as I associate that with childhood I'm always known as Sandie.'

At no point is Sandie sorry for herself. She's taken charge of her own life since she left home, and is confident that you have to steer your own path. She talks about the present and recalls her child-hood in quite emphatic tones, but tempered with insight into her adoptive parents' behaviour. After she'd spent a year or two in London she got herself a steady job in telesales, worked her way up into management and now runs a call centre in Glasgow, a cosmopolitan city with a rich mix of race. She thinks about what happened to her, but doesn't brood.

'I've never blamed my real mum for anything – if there's anyone to blame, it would be my adopted mum, because it's like being rejected twice. The first time you can't take offence, because you can't know the reason. The second time you know the reason, and it's not acceptable.

'Thinking about my real mother, well – I've always thought she was quite young. And I'm obviously of mixed parentage, because I'm a myriad of different colours. So maybe that was it . . . and then there's the nasty things . . . what if she'd been raped. . . . But the bizarre thing was I'd been looked after pretty well for several weeks, so there must have been a bond there. It's not like I was born and then put there by the check-out. I'd been cleaned and fed and kept warm. It was a calculated decision, not a knee-jerk reaction.

'I'd very much like to meet my mother. I've no interest in meeting my real father at all. And I don't know if this was because my adoptive father – although he was a weak, spineless man who should have stood up to my mother – was a brilliant man, and I'd have to go a long way to come up to his standards. He was a plumber, then became an officer for the county [working in local government], and he was a wonderful man with a great sense of humour – and of morality – and a wonderful work ethic. And he always had time for us. So it's never been in my mind who my own father was. I think at the end of the day the father doesn't play that big a part in the child's birth, and they're not around afterwards – they're of no consequence whatsoever.

'If I did find anything out it would be nice. But I'm not a victim. You can go two ways. You can either blame everybody for everything – that would be ridiculous. Or you can just look at what you've got, and go with it. And I've been very lucky. What I've lacked with family, I've made up with friends.

'It's not the be-all and end-all. But it's always there. And I was forty a year ago, and you wonder . . . it's a made-up birthday, so when was I actually forty?'

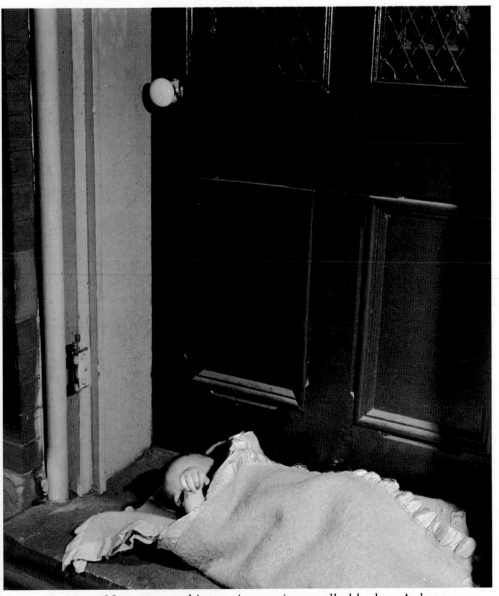

No name, no history, just a nice woolly blanket. A doorstep
foundling in 1955.

Christ in swaddling clothes: one of the many roundels decorating the Ospedale degli Innocenti in Florence.

A painted plaque and an embroidered heart: tokens left by mothers giving up their babies to the Foundling Hospital in London.

Abandoning an infant to the 'turning wheel'.

'Foundling Girls at Prayer in the Chapel'. Foundling Hospital children in their traditional uniforms in 1877.

Thomas Coram, founder of the Foundling Hospital, painted by William Hogarth in 1740.

Foundling Hospital boys being inspected by the Duke of Connaught in 1924.

'Off for the West'. The work of The Children's Aid Society in 19th century America, sending abandoned city children to frontier homes.

With a new doll on the eve of their train journey to a new home. American foundlings about to board one of the 'Orphan Trains' in 1918.

Jane Russell, founder of the World Adoption International Fund and catalyst for change in Ireland's adoption laws.

The Children of Hope Foundation 'Safe Haven' emblem, promoting a safe place for abandoned babies.

New York police burying a newborn foundling in 2003 on behalf of the Children of Hope Foundation.

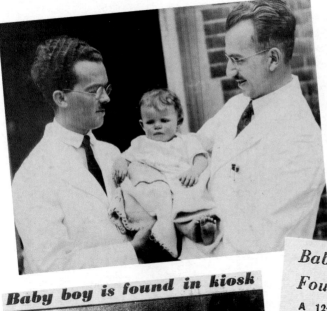

'The Worthing Baby'. Anthea Ring in the *Worthing Herald* in August 1937, after being found on the Downs in a blackberry bush.

Front page news. The *Evening News* story of Christine Simm, found in December 1949.

Baby boy is found in kiosk

Baby in Paper Bag Found on Taxi Seat

A 12-hour-old baby girl who was found in an unattended taxi outside Charing Cross Hospital last night being attended by a nurse in the hospital to-day. The baby was left on the seat of the cab in a brown paper carrier bag.

Ian Palmer, appearing in the *Evening Standard* in November 1963, after his discovery in a phone box in South Kensington.

Abandoned baby found in shopping bag —on front seat of car

David McBride, found tucked into a tartan shopping bag in Dunmurray, Northern Ireland in January 1962.

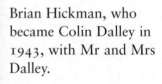

Brian Hickman, who became Colin Dalley in 1943, with Mr and Mrs Dalley.

The homecoming –
Hattie Lighte (left)
feeding her sister, Tillie,
in Hong Kong on the
day they met, 10 April
1999.

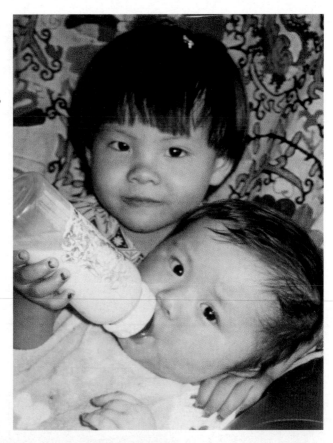

Honey Birch (left)
and her sister Lei Lei
at the Wuhan
Government Offices,
during Lei Lei's
adoption in China,
May 2004.

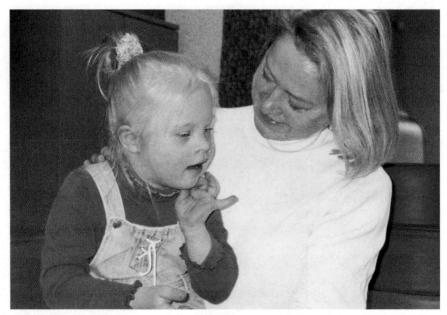

At the Downside Up Centre in Moscow, with one of the children who would otherwise have been abandoned to an institution.

One of Germany's numerous 'baby hatches', demonstrating how a baby can be left, anonymously, in a heated cot in the wall.

13

Do you have any distinguishing marks?

This particular enquiry engenders interesting reactions. When I first encountered it on a passport application I wondered if you were being asked to trumpet some wondrous quality or appendage, like a sixth finger or a very pertly located mole. Or perhaps it was intended as the revelation of a dark secret: lurking beneath your clothes, not on show for the general public, some weird and ultimately shameful Mark (blotch, scar, blemish, disfigurement?) which would be used by those inspecting passports to single you out and subject you to special scrutiny. Wasn't it enough to look like your photograph? Anyway, who did you have to look like?

'Doesn't she look like her mother?' It's one of those remarks which is always addressed across your head as a small child. You, the object of comparison, stand there in a big sulk. For a start, mums are so much older. Also, they wear make-up and have funny hairstyles and you have no intention of growing up like them. The only consolation is that this sort of thing is probably worse for boys.

And if you're adopted, as I am, it's the first hint that adults aren't always right: a useful seed of scepticism is planted in your mind as you mull over their ignorance of the real facts. Nothing resentful or embarrassing, just a private thought that *you* know about yourself, and it's your information to treat as you like. But even when the adults know about the adoption they still make efforts to see similarities – nose, hair, legs, the size of your feet, heaven help you. Wearing your utterly revolting school shoes, you stick one foot behind the other and affect not to be taking part in the conversation. Perhaps it's just the paucity of subjects for a short chat when out shopping; once the weather, the price of sprouts and the rubbish bus service have been exhausted, their gaze falls on you, and off they go. . . .

And it persists through childhood. At least the family doctor doesn't bother to ask about hereditary illnesses. Coming from a middle-class pharmacist's home, I never once went to a doctor's surgery: 'Den of iniquitous contagion, where germs fight for front place in the waiting room, and the people that have them *don't mind* them.' So all consultations took place on Uncle Gerry's kitchen table, just a few doors down the road. I went to school with his daughter and was part of a sizeable group of adopted girls – all of us having appeared in the end-of-the-war period when attitudes to illegitimacy had changed – a little. The novelist Barbara Cartland, who'd worked with the Women's Auxiliary Air Force as a moral adviser, made this observation about husbands who came back from the forces to discover their wife was pregnant: 'At first they swore that as soon as it was born, it would have to be adopted, then sometimes they would say, half-shame-faced at the generosity, "The poor little devil can't help itself, and after all, it's one of hers, isn't it?"' Mind you, a lot of little devils did pop up for adoption.

But it was straightforward. There were myriad adoption societies, many locally based, well versed in discretion. The searching evaluations – influenced by social welfare theory and policy – into the suitability of prospective adopting parents that are now commonplace were not yet developed. And because there were a considerable number of healthy babies available, with no discernible problems, placement was a matter of matching the child to a family similar to its own background – where this was known. The over-riding concern was, of course, religion. Birth mothers were encouraged to stipulate the faith – or, more often, the denomination – in which they'd like the child reared. Somehow, it was considered vital how the little devil prayed. Looks were not a consideration. Anyway, they all looked so cute, just a few days old and ornamented with clean white hand-knitted bootees and bonnets.

And so all kinds of inventive remarks could be heard among

adults peering thoughtfully as the adopted child grew older: 'The carroty hair's a family trait, you know – at least one second cousin's got it.' 'He's merely tall for his age – I'm sure his father was a beanpole when he was a lad.' 'He's very musical – remember, his uncle played the bassoon.' 'She takes after her great-grandmother.'

Most adopted children don't care. To be honest, most children don't care; in fact they fervently hope they won't end up like their Neanderthal granny or spotty half-cousin. It's an adult obsession, rooted in unconscious age-old veneration of legitimacy. If – as was the case with most children formally adopted – you'd known from before you could think that you'd been 'chosen' by your parents, you merely dismissed these remarks as ignorance. You had your private knowledge, and were happy with it. In my own case, I had the good fortune to look a bit like my first cousin. A bit; we were both blonde. This somehow satisfied the adults.

Later, I came to know the fascination with similarity and family features. I have a photograph of the Adie family portrait which hangs on the wall in Voe in Shetland: Victorian worthies all very proper and demure in their over-stuffed living room. When my adopting parents, Wilfrid and Maud, went from north-east England up to the Isles to meet the distant relatives, the resemblance between Wilfrid and his seventh – or was it eighth? – cousin through his great-great-great-great-grandfather John Adie was slightly spooky. However, one of the advantages of having a somewhat obscure surname is that the odds of being related to other Adies are quite high. Not that this implies a simple family tree, or being automatically related. One glance at the copious research into the name reveals an energetic bunch of ancestors who clearly felt the need to populate Shetland, legitimately or not. They were respectable people – John was a surgeon in Nelson's navy – and destined to travel, like so many of the islanders, to the farthest corners of the empire: descendants are scattered to Melbourne in Australia, Vancouver and Guelph in Canada, Buenos Aires in Argentina, and India. However, the continuity of the line seems uninterrupted by references to such as James Mitchell Adie being 'born into uncleanness' in Northvoe in 1833, and Eliza

Adie's indiscreet husband Ninian, who, according to the kirk sessions, had 'several children born in fornication'.

To have a family portrait from the early nineteenth century is something of a rarity, unless you have a string of ancestors glaring down from the walls of a country house or palace. And early sepia-tinted photographs are usually so stern and uncompromising that it's hard to discern a family resemblance: a toothy smile is unusual – considered improper behaviour in front of a camera, coupled with an obvious lack of dental care. Even so, in most homes, there's a fascination with inherited looks.

'You don't look like your mum, do you?' Diana Ross recalls a very happy childhood, but every so often there were these remarks: she has dark brown hair, whereas her mother was quite fair and had a paler complexion. 'The funny thing was, I sounded like my mum. As for looks, a lot of Mum's sisters were dark, and she used to say that her grandfather was Spanish or something.' Diana is in her living room in Hertfordshire, a room stuffed with cuddly toys for which she has a passion: there are heaps of them arranged neatly on chairs and sofa, and lines of multi-hued hedgehogs (a particular favourite) marching over the TV, along the windowsill and across the crowded bookshelves and CD stacks. Married, and with a grown-up son, she talks easily about her background – though trips up immediately when I begin by asking when she was born.

'The first of February 1946 – oh no, me being stupid – that's my *given* date. I don't know. It was assumed that I was about six weeks old when I was found.' She has known that she was adopted since she was seven years old. But it really didn't sink in at the time, though she remembers that she must have also been told that she was found, because she feels she's always known. However, her adoptive parents didn't know any of the details.

'I was found on 13 March 1946 in Golders Green on the back of a delivery lorry – a small open vehicle, with a canvas top. It belonged to Mr George Green who was a grocer, and he'd just parked it outside his house and gone in for his tea. He came out roughly four hours later, and there I was, in the back of the van. I was clothed, and I had a spare bottle of milk and a bit of feed with me. It was a very cold night, and he thought that I was dead. I've read all this since in the papers which carried the story. Anyway, he thought I was dead – then he just saw me move. So he ran round to the local café to call the police and carried me into his house, where his wife held me by the fire to warm me up. After that I was taken to the Chase Farm Home, which is a little cottage hospital in Enfield.

'There was an article about me in the *Ham and High* and another local paper. But having seen them, I now know that no one came forward after they made an appeal. There were no calls.'

Brought up in Palmers Green, north London, as an only child, she'd been adopted by a couple who'd already lost two babies. Her mother, Daisy, worked in a greengrocer's, and her father, after war service on fireboats on the Thames, became a fireman in Hatfield.

As with so many people, the first time the actual details of her birth came to her own notice was when she applied for a passport. She sent in her Adoption Certificate, but got the brusque reply that that was not what was wanted. The Passport Office was insistent that she tell them where she had been born. At the time, Diana hadn't a clue: the back of a grocer's delivery lorry among the tinned food and porridge oats and bags of sugar doesn't seem an appropriate or adequate reply, so Diana said Enfield, where the Children's Home had been.

Getting a passport is often not the moment when you want to embark on a search. It's a long list of questions from unknown officials, and fudging the odd box seems perfectly reasonable, especially as you're planning to go on holiday and don't intend to spend the next few weeks puzzling about where you were umpteen years ago, when you were too young to know anything. And although post-war adoptions were remarkably high in number, it wasn't something you made a fuss about; you just told a few friends and left it at that. When Diana got married and needed to renew her passport for a trip to America she got out all her paperwork – marriage and adoption certificates – and her husband glanced at them and enquired, 'Where were you born, then?' She'd never got round to mentioning it to him. 'I told him I'd wanted to

wait until the right moment . . . I didn't really talk about it much –
so I just said I was adopted and I'd been found. And he said, "Oh."
And that was that, really.'

It wasn't until more than ten years later that the subject came up
again, when she was watching a programme on regional television
about the Foundling Group at Norcap. It struck home, and for the
first time in her life she realised she wasn't on her own. Until then,
she'd never thought that there might be other people who between
them could offer a rich variety of locations where they were first
noticed. She got in touch, realised there were many more like her,
and eventually told her story to a national newspaper – 'Coming
Out', as she puts it. After that she was on the trail: the birth
certificate, with the name Diana Chase, the home where she'd first
been cared for, and the words 'Father Unknown, Mother Unknown'. She saw a social worker, having requested the paperwork
about her birth and adoption. It was a tricky time – an appointment
was made, but the social worker cancelled; then a second appointment, also cancelled. And finally, a tense encounter beginning with
this question from the social worker to Diana.

'Do you know – er – anything – er. . . .'

'I was found in the back of a lorry.'

'Oh. You know. Thank goodness for that. I didn't know how to
tell you.'

She was now eager for more detail. 'I went to the Swiss Cottage
Library and found the right newspaper for the time and area. Then
I got a copy from the Colindale Newspaper Library and saw the
address of where I was found outside. With a friend, I went to the
house to see what it was like – West Heath Drive in Golders Green.
Obviously things had changed – and it was all flats. We went to
look up various electoral registers but there wasn't anyone in that
street, or the next, whom we could find with a memory. There was
a church on the corner, and a man there said there was someone
whose parents had lived there who might remember. But when we
went to see her, her parents had since died – and she'd moved away
before I was born. . . . It's like finding a needle in a haystack.'

Then a woman rang in after Diana was interviewed on television. It was Margaret, the daughter of Mr Crook, the grocer who'd found her. Margaret's grandson had seen the show, told his mum, who told her mum, who arranged to met Diana. She brought a picture of her father – and the lorry! But he'd died in the seventies, before Diana had started to search. Oddly, her son has a shop in Baldock, where Diana lives, and he'd twice been round to her house to repair her washing machine!

'Does it bother me? Yes and no. I know that you had to register a child within six weeks of birth, so whether . . . well, there could have been lots of reasons. She could have been married, or very young. Then again, there's got to be someone else who knows – you don't just have a child one day and not have a child another day. There's got to be a second party, there's got to be. Whether it's the man who got her pregnant – or maybe he didn't know, or maybe a friend – you've got to have a friend, haven't you? I mean, even if you were in a house alone with a child. . . . I mean . . . well, I suppose she *could* have just left me and gone somewhere else. . . . I'd just love to think that I might have half-brothers and sisters somewhere. It would be lovely to find out . . . the best thing. It's just the knowing, it's that little bit of the jigsaw you want to know, that would really complete me.'

The fire of curiosity and longing has been lit – but the trail has gone cold. However, it isn't an all-consuming obsession. She's met other foundlings and is fascinated by their stories, finding that some are very intense about their origins and that others, like her, are what she calls 'realistic' – often sharing stable backgrounds and happy childhoods. She laughs when she recalls telling her son about her background.

'He's all I've got that's my blood – but when I talked to him about it he said to me, "I am *yours*, aren't I?" And I said, "Yes. Yes. YES." '

Diana was found in Golders Green, an area with a large and long-established Jewish community. When she was growing up she was aware that she didn't have the adoptive family likeness. But she could pass for the daughter of any Jewish family in Golders Green.

14

Are you in transit?

In 1859 the *New York Times* published a stirring article about what it memorably termed 'the ulcers of society': orphans. It was the social problem of the day, and the previous year Bayard Taylor, having travelled the globe as a journalist for the *New York Tribune*, had also been much exercised by the state of his own city, a heaving, ever-expanding metropolis whose appalling slums were peppered with abandoned children: 'It is a great mistake to suppose that the moral tone of Society can only be preserved by making desperate outcasts of all who sin . . . at any rate, we can never err by helping those who are in trouble, even though that trouble [may] have come through vice. I have never heard that the Magdalen Societies have increased the number of prostitutes, and I do not believe that a foundling hospital would encourage seduction or adultery.' He'd seen the vast foundling institutions of Russia and been impressed, and had doubtless noticed that his own city had already embarked on an experiment to populate frontier areas by exporting 'surplus' young people; however, he was pessimistic about the 'sanctified prudery' of his fellow Americans in 1858, believing that 'if some benevolent millionaire should propose to build such a foundling hospital in New York, pulpit and press would riddle him with [the] red-hot shot of holy indignation'.

He got it wrong. The American Civil War intervened, resulting in an upsurge of orphans and foundlings – over six hundred thousand men had died of wounds and disease. On 8 October 1869, a crib was placed on the pavement by Sister Mary Irene of St Peter's Convent in New York's Greenwich Village. The next morning, she found an infant in it. The Sisters of Charity had proposed opening a small institution and reckoned it would take them about three months to get things ready for a grand opening on 1 January 1870. By that date, they had already received 123 babies.

An imposing building arose in 1872 on 68th/69th Streets and within a few years most major cities in the Unites States were following suit, with these religious and privately funded institutions taking on the care of foundlings. However, in the capital it took fifteen years to raise the necessary funds, and when the doors opened in 1885 the neighbours took a sniffy attitude – early nimbyism. A letter was penned to the *Washington Post,* in which a Mr Edward Dunkerly sets out his complaints to the 'Commissioners of the District Government' over his family's lack of sleep.

> If you want to see how we suffer through the crying of babies at the Foundling Hospital, come to my house at 1715 Fifteenth Street northwest. We have not had a whole night's rest for over two weeks, and one or more of us have been walking the floor some nights for that length of time, and expect to do so for the next four months at least. I have just spent $20 to keep out the sound of this crying, having closed lots of my windows with four thicknesses, which still fails to keep out the noise. I am afraid I will have to wall them up with brick before the summer is over and how we shall live in the house, I cannot tell. We are now deprived of light and air in these rooms and I assure you they are not fit for a dog.

Nevertheless, it was abundantly clear that the same dreadful mortality rates which had appeared in Europe over a century before were being replicated in the New World. In the *Journal of the American Medical Association,* Professor Edwin Graham pointed out that in Philadelphia in 1871 nearly twice as many foundlings died before the end of their first year compared to other children in hospital. He also recorded that Dr Abraham Jacobi, now regarded by many as the father of American paediatrics, had had the courage to point out the same problem in New York's hospitals the year before and had been asked to resign as a result.

Poverty seemed unavoidable, especially in a society which every year took in thousands of people from Europe who tended to head for already overcrowded communities from their old countries. And although the nineteenth century had nurtured an image of idealised childhood hitherto unknown, with the angelic tot living an innocent existence, this went hand in hand with child labour in factories and little statutory welfare for the vulnerable. It was a situation graphically described by the campaigning Danish American journalist Jacob Riis, who in 1890 published *How the Other Half Lives* and knew the New York Foundling Hospital well.

It stands at the very outset of the waste of life that goes on in a population of nearly two millions of people; powerless to prevent it, though it gather in the outcasts by night and by day. In a score of years an army of twenty-five thousand of these forlorn little waifs have cried out from the streets of New York in arraignment of a Christian civilisation under the blessings of which the instinct of motherhood even was smothered by poverty and want. Only the poor abandon their children. The stories of richly-dressed foundlings that are dished up in the newspapers at intervals are pure fiction. Not one instance of a well-dressed infant having been picked up on the streets is on record. They come in rags, a newspaper often the only wrap, semi-occasionally one in a clean slip with some evidence of loving care; a little slip of paper pinned on, perhaps, with some such message as this I once read, in a woman's trembling hand: 'Take care of Johnny, for God's sake. I cannot.' But even that is the rarest of all happenings.

As at the Foundling Hospital in London, trinkets were sometimes left with the baby – patches of fabric from a dress, a coin, a ribbon from a re-election campaign by Ulysses S. Grant – in the faint hope that the mother might one day be able to reclaim her child. There were also letters:

Dear Sisters
  By the love of God be so kind as to take this poor orphan child in and if she should die, please bury her for me and I will be very happy. You must not think that I have neglected her. I

have worked very hard to pay her board but I can't afford to bury her.

My husband is dead and I have nobody to help me. Be kind to my little lamb. May the great God receive her into Heaven where she will be loved by God.

This two dollars is to have this child christened Willie. Do not be afraid of the sores on its face; it is nothing but ringworm. You'll remember this badge [a cloth badge bearing the slogan 'General Grant our Next President'].

Brooklyn, Nov 23rd 1869

Dear Sister

I now sit down to write to you a few lines but I hardly know what to say, for when I inform you that I am the mother of the child left on Thanksgiving night between the hours of 8 and 9 o'clock without even a slip of paper to tell you the name of the child left in your care, my heart aches so much I cannot tell, but I knew that I was leaving her in good hands.

Although I have been unfortunate, I am neither low nor degraded and am in hopes of one day claiming the child. Her name is Jane . . . born on 5 of October 1869 between the hours of 3 and 4 o'clock in the morning . . . she had a piece of canton-flannel tied around her head and a little blue and white cloud around and little red and white socks on her feet – and if the prayers of an unfortunate creature like myself will do any good, offered to – the mercy of God in heaven – for you know that every night on my bended knees I pray for you.

Other, rather more terse communications also survive:

Dec 10, 1869

Sister M. Irene, Superioress Respected Sister,

You would oblige our R.F. [Reverend Father] Rector Limguber in taking the poor child in the asylum. It has been happily saved from being murdered by his unfortunate mother. She told me she gives up all claims on it. I gave private baptism to the child.

Respectfully yours, Francis Eberhardt, C.S.S.R. [Congregatio Sanctissimi Redemptoris]

May 2 1873

This offspring is the fruit of a brutality on the person of this poor but decent woman and to cover her shame and being too poor to support the children – there are two from her husband – she is obliged to resort to this extreme measure. The child is not yet baptized.

The little baby which was left in the crib last night, if you for the love of God and his holy mother will keep it for me I will give you anything you require. Her father is a wicked Orangeman. I told him it was dead because I want to have her raised a Roman Catholic and have nursed out. I will pay all the expenses.

Will you, dear sisters, remember a kind mother's heart? If I do not see her again I will never do any good on this earth. I work at dressmaking for a living. My husband gives me but a third of his earnings because I am a Roman Catholic. Write to Father Farrell, Barclay Street Church, state circumstances to him. Pray to the Blessed Virgin for me to help me through.

[The first paragraph is a note left with a day-old baby by a Dr J. J. Brennan; the last two paragraphs – all part of the same letter – are a plea from the child's mother.]

Religious faith directed much of the mothers' thinking – and they were probably unaware that it was to be a potent factor in their children's fate.

Jacob Riis was an enlightened man for his time, and may well have inspected some of these letters, yet he had a strong moral code which didn't waver when faced with the mothers' plight.

Few outcast babies survive their desertion long. Murder is the true name of the mother's crime in eight cases out of ten. . . . The wonder is, rather, that any survive. The stormier the night, the more certain is the police nursery to echo with the feeble cries of abandoned babes. Often they come half-dead from exposure.

One live baby came in a little pine coffin which a policeman found an inhuman wretch trying to bury in an up-town lot. But many do not live to be officially registered as a charge upon the country. Seventy-two dead babies were picked up in the streets last year. Some of them were doubtless put out by very poor parents to save funeral expenses. In hard times the number of dead and live foundlings always increases very noticeably. But whether travelling by way of the Morgue or the Infants' Hospital, the little army of waifs meets, reunited soon, in the trench in the Potter's Field where, if no medical student is in need of a subject, they are laid in squads of a dozen.

Echoes of eighteenth-century Europe and the poverty that so many had come to escape – the endless gripe about being 'a charge upon the parish'. And here, too, was the suggestion that medical dissection was a fate awaiting those heading for the Potter's Field – the biblical phrase from St Matthew for the pauper's grave, 'the field to bury strangers in'. (One of the islands off Manhattan still serves this need today, and like its predecessor is known as Potter's Field.)

Though desertion appalled him, Jacob Riis was more exercised by the 'baby farms' which were another consequence of extreme poverty and were frequently prosecuted for being no more than 'starvation houses'. He quotes a charity official describing the farms as 'concerns by means of which persons, usually of disreputable character, eke out a living by taking two, three or four babies to board. They are the charges of outcasts, or illegitimate children. They feed them on sour milk, and give them panegoric to keep them quiet, until they die, when they get some young medical man without experience to sign a certificate to the Board of Health that the child died of inanition [lack of nourishment], and so the matter end.' Panegoric is an echo of the deadly 'bottle' used in the Dublin Foundling Hospital more than a century earlier. Claimed to be something which 'soothes the child', it was a tincture of opium flavoured with aniseed and benzoic acid and could have the strength to floor a horse.

From baby farms it was but a step to baby-trafficking. The New York police kept an eye out for newspaper advertisements offering babies for 'adoption for cash': 'The Society [for the Prevention of Cruelty to Children] has among its records a very recent case of a baby a week old (Baby "Blue Eyes") that was offered for sale – adoption, the dealer called it – in a newspaper. The agent bought it after some haggling for a dollar, and arrested the woman slave-trader; but the law was powerless to punish her for her crime. Twelve unfortunate women awaiting dishonoured motherhood were found in her house.'

Riis was fascinated by the workings of the Foundling Hospital and, though worried about the death rate, approved of the system which was very much based on the notion of 'rehabilitating' the 'wretched mother'.

> Most of the foundlings come from the East Side, where they are left by young mothers without wedding-ring or other name than their own to bestow upon the baby, returning . . . to face an unpitying world with the evidence of their shame . . . no ray of light penetrates the gloom, and no effort is made to probe into the mystery of sin and sorrow. This is the policy pursued in the great Foundling Asylum of the Sisters of Charity in Sixty-eighth Street, known all over the world as Sister Irene's Asylum. Years ago the crib that now stands just inside the street door, under the main portal, was placed outside at night; but it filled up too rapidly. The babies took to coming in little squads instead of in single file, and in self-defence the sisters were forced to take the cradle in. Now the mother must bring her child inside and put it in the crib where she is seen by the sister on guard. No effort is made to question her, or discover the child's antecedents, but she is asked to stay and nurse her own and another baby. If she refuses, she is allowed to depart unhindered. . . . Four hundred and sixty mothers did voluntary penance for their sin in the asylum last year by nursing a strange waif besides their own until both should be strong enough to take their chances in life's battle.

So what happened to the 'little waifs'? Riis mentions in passing that 'at the age of four or five, they are sent to Western homes to be adopted'. And hereby hangs a tale which has only emerged fully in the last few years, and in which both welfare and religion play a role. The urban poor whom Riis was observing were disproportionately foreign-born and Catholic, and Catholic-born children were in the majority in the foundling institutions and orphanages. From the American Civil War onwards their Church made huge efforts to deal with the ravages of city squalor and poverty, alongside its unswerving disapproval of illegitimacy, and a complex and well-developed social welfare system arose: Foundling Hospitals, orphanages, reformatories and foster care programmes dominated the private welfare services until World War II. Entwined in the purpose of caring for its own poor flock was the intention of resisting Protestant and state intrusion into Catholic lives. As so often and in so many places, much of the debate on the welfare of the child began with an argument about its faith – and whether it had been baptised; or, more importantly, which denomination could direct the life and claim the soul.

Foundlings, understandably, came off badly here. In New York, where a law was passed requiring that children be placed in homes or orphanages of their parents' faiths, foundlings ended up in an eeny-meeny-miney-mo raffle in Manhattan and the Bronx. Baby A was baptised Catholic, B became a little Protestant, C a Catholic and so on. And the Catholics resolutely refused to let any newly baptised member of their Church go to an organisation which might just place that baby in a non-Catholic home. So the Catholic Foundling Hospital grew into a mighty institution. And these places were the preferred Catholic solution to the child welfare problem: somewhere run by the religious, where the parents could visit and the children would be taught in the faith. There had always been a strong belief that children who'd had a very unfortunate or 'improper' start in life needed to be in an artificial environment, insulated from outside temptations and the evils of society, if they were to be trained to be decent and devout citizens. Protestants, on the other hand, thought the answer was to remove children from destitute parents, gather up foundlings, and send them all off to foster-families in rural areas and small towns: to fresh air, hard work and a place where most people were Protestant: the West.

Most of us have an image of the American West, probably shaped by Hollywood. How it was populated is usually the stuff of wagon trains and tough frontier families, with the addition of sudden swarms of gold-miners and young men looking to make their fortunes. What is missing from that frontier legend is the arrival of a hundred and fifty thousand children. Or possibly two hundred thousand. Or maybe many more. No one knows the number who rode the Orphan Trains. It was the neat solution to the emptiness of American's interior and the teeming cities in the East: what a new land needed was a fresh young population; what the cities wanted was to be rid of the urban orphans. It all began with the railroads – with the Iron Horse opening up vast tracts of the American Mid-West to easy access and cheap travel.

In New York in 1853 a young Congregationalist minister, the Reverend Charles Brace, observed the city streets teeming with children: some orphans – many the result of horrendous epidemics in the slums, others neglected or thrown out by their parents, and yet more scavenging to survive. In a city of half a million people there were an estimated thirty-four thousand street children by 1854. In the spirit of reform he wanted to improve lives rather than just help the youngsters survive, and founded the Children's Aid Society with the specific intention of having children cared for in families rather than institutions. He came up with the 'family plan' – an idea he'd seen operating in Boston, where 'orphans' from the street were sent 'West' on trains and 'placed out' in families at various stops along the railroad track and 'adopted'. All the terms used by the Reverend Brace bear a little inspection, though there was no intention to deceive. His idea, quite simply, was to replace a dysfunctional life in the stinking stews with the opportunity of a healthy environment and a caring family. 'The great duty', he wrote, 'is to get utterly out of their surroundings and to send them away to kind Christian homes in the country.' And so the Society began a huge social experiment.

It was a very efficient system which functioned for nearly eighty years: fliers were sent to the towns all along the railroad route, and later advertisements such as this in the *Oskaloosa Independent*, 9 December 1910, were placed in the local newspapers:

A circular was sent out from Valley Falls last week as follows:
Wanted! Homes for orphan children.

A company of orphan children under the auspices of the Children's Aid Society of New York will arrive at Valley Falls, Thursday afternoon, December 8th.

These children are bright, intelligent and well disciplined, both boys and girls of various ages. They are placed on trial, and if not satisfactory will be removed. Parties taking them must be well recommended. A local committee of citizens of Valley Falls has been selected to assist the agents in placing the children. Applications must be made to and endorsed by the local committee. Bring your recommendations with you. . . . Distribution will take place at the opera house, on Friday, December 9, at 10 a.m. and 2 p.m.

Come and see the children and hear the address.

The first group of forty-six headed for Dowagiac, Michigan, on 20 September 1854. The previous day the children were told they were going on a train, and that they would get a bath and be given new clean clothing and have their hair washed. Each was then given a Bible. However, they were by no means all 'orphans'. A very large number were – and many were foundlings, for whom this seemed the practical solution for their future as they had no ties to the East Coast cities and no one had a claim on them. But many of the so-called 'orphans' had at least one parent, and had come to the notice of the Society through poverty or homelessness; others had parents who were persuaded that the trains would be a better option than a wretched life in the slums, and handed them over. And yet others appear to have been taken off the streets, some from police cells, with little information about their actual circumstances other than that they were living a grim life. They were commonly referred to – and by Brace himself – as 'street Arabs' and 'the dangerous classes'. Many did not speak English. Many did not possess a birth certificate.

The sheer numbers involved negated the keeping of accurate records, though for the first twenty years at least three thousand children per annum were on the move. One of the Society's agents was always on the train as it headed 'West'; and indeed in other directions, with some heading for the South and others going to Canada – only to be passed by the 'Home Children of Canada' coming the other way, also heading for the American West. Coordination doesn't seem to have been a strong point in the migration business.

The train's arrival at a designated station was a major event: local newspapers carried hundreds of stories over the years of the sight of a carriage full of children peering out at their unknown future. In April 1886 the *Cawker City Ledger* in Kansas devoted a whole page to the story as sixteen boys were paraded in town, supervised by the local committee:

> The Hall was crowded by the curious sight-seers and applicants for boys. The boys were seated on the stage facing the audience and presented altogether a different appearance from the ideas formed of them by some. They were an intelligent lot of little fellows and neatly clad, the most of them having been in the Society's Home four or five years, and have had good training and discipline. All but two can read and write, one of the exceptions being between three and four years old, the ages of the party ranging up to seventeen years. The good humor of the audience was evoked by the chubby baby's comical and pleased expression. This little orphan fell to the lot of Mr and Mrs Chas. D. Brown, and quite a scene was enacted on the stage when their selection was made and the little one threw his arms around the neck of his adopted mother.

'His lines are fallen in pleasant places,' remarked the *Cawker City Ledger* reporter, borrowing from the Bible to describe the child's good fortune. Children were reported to have danced and sung at some of these occasions, not out of joy, but desperate that they should be chosen.

The Reverend Brace took the familiar romantic view of the West as a land of opportunity filled with decent, big-hearted farmers. In many instances, his faith in humanity was rewarded. However, as the children lined up on stages there were others in the audience who were looking for cheap labour. Even so, everything was conducted in the glare of publicity and with the full approval of the local worthies: the *Star-Courier* in Columbus, Kansas waxed eloquent at the sight of eighteen arrivals from New York In June 1894:

> The little ones were as wide awake and bright as if they had not traveled nearly 2000 miles to find homes in the West. At an early hour, many of the kind-hearted citizens of Columbus and Cherokee County, thronged the office and halls of the hotel to see the children and to choose from them such as they desired. Every mother's heart was touched at the sight of the little ones as at nine o'clock they were led onto the stage at the opera house. There was the chubby, dimpled baby, at once 'Monarch of all he surveyed', the little boy still in kilt skirt, his brother in the proud triumphal period of his first pants – all unconscious of how much this occasion meant for them; there were the restless, typical boys of the period, and the older and thoughtful who were evidently pondering these things. It was a beautiful tribute to kindred love when little brothers tenderly said 'goodbye', and two little brothers (mere babies) positively refusing to be separated, one kind-hearted man took them both. One could not look upon scenes like that and not have faith in humanity strengthened. There were more demands for children than the supply.

Not today's view of kind humanity. The separation of siblings was very frequent, with a brother or sister often heading many miles further down the railroad track to their new home.

The Columbus group had the two-year-old 'dimpled baby', a four-year-old and two six-year-olds among them, and all were 'adopted'. Except that they weren't adopted, but indentured – and were given an Indenture Certificate. The terms were used interchangeably for much of the time, with most people seeing no difference between them; however, no indentured child was eligible to inherit, and many suffered discrimination because they still carried the term 'orphan' or 'foundling'. Jessie Teresa Martin of Hays, Kansas, remembered that she was regarded as 'a disgrace to the town. We were told, "No one likes you; your mother didn't." ' In reality, children's experiences varied enormously. Some had love and care lavished on them, while others found themselves as hired hands – although, from what can be gleaned, the majority benefited in some way. The Society kept a paternalistic eye on its placements and intervened when necessary. However, no one addressed the problems of abandonment and separation, or how they came to be on an Orphan Train.

The Reverend Brace was a Congregationalist and just about all of the children he was placing were going to Protestant families. The Catholic Foundling Hospital in New York took note, and in 1875 decided that it would run a similar but much more precise operation: there'd be no sense of 'chance', with children being dumped into remote communities at the end of a railroad line as sometimes happened. Nor would there be the risk of a child falling into non-Catholic hands.

To this end, the Hospital used priests along the train route to tell their congregations that there were foundlings in New York in need of a home – and were there any volunteers to take one? Those who said Yes could specify boy or girl, and preferences for colour of eyes and hair, so that the child would 'fit in'. It seemed to work: one Nebraska newspaper was told by a happy new father that: 'It beats the stork all hollow. I asked for a boy of 18 months with brown hair and blue eyes, and the bill was filled to the last specification. The young rascal even has my name tacked on to him!' The Foundling Hospital booked train space with enthusiasm and began to shift a lot of foundlings, one of its agents, Mr Curran, telling the reporter of the *Dubuque Daily Times* in Iowa in 1888 that the Hospital had placed over eight thousand children:

Handsome Children.
The crowd could scarcely refrain from grabbing the children
and making off with them so eager were the foster parents to get

their chance. 'Aren't they cute?' 'Oh, I want a little fellow with the brown eyes;' these and other expressions were heard on all sides.
. . . A fashionably dressed lady took a fancy to a bright little girl with brown eyes and hair who had been given to a lady at Kings post-office. The lady offered $50 if she would transfer the child to her. The former objected and the fashionable lady increased her efforts to $100 to no avail . . .

All the children on the Orphan Trains were advertised as healthy and well-disciplined. In accordance with conventional thinking, no child labelled in the institutions as 'incorrigible, sickly, physically handicapped or mentally deficient' was selected to travel. Nor were black Americans included, since, at a time when the Civil War was still fresh in the memory, it was thought that there would be a charge of practising slavery. Prejudice also played a part – both in those making the choice in New York, and in those in the Mid-West. Religion and race were both contentious issues – as in the case of Jessie Teresa Martin. She was nine days old when abandoned at the Foundling Hospital by her mother and four years when, as plain Teresa, she boarded an Orphan Train for Kansas. She went to a new home where she was treated well, but never felt loved. In her old age she began searching for her relatives, and through the archives discovered that she'd originally been called Jessie – her foster parents had renamed her Teresa. 'My mother was Jewish. They took all religions [in the Foundling Hospital] but you didn't leave until you were a Catholic.'

Matters came to a rather nasty head in 1904, when the US Supreme Court found itself deliberating on events which outdid any Hollywood Western film in a dusty pair of towns on the Mexican border. Three Sisters of Charity, four nurses and an agent from the Foundling Hospital had set out from New York with forty children aged between two and six. Their destination was the town of Clifton-Morenci – a pair of small mining settlements that had grown into a 'Wild West' boomtown as thousands of Mexican immigrant workers settled next to white frontier families to work underground and in the smelters. It was a noisy place with low pay, hard work and lots of tensions.

The train and its foundlings trundled towards Arizona, with all the children already allotted to families. There was one small fly in the ointment: these were all Irish children and in 1904 the Irish – along with Italians and Jews – were not seen as 'white'. However, the parish priest in Clifton-Morenci had vetted the prospective parents for these Catholic children himself – and all should have gone according to plan for the selected parents were Mexican and therefore no more 'white' than the Irish orphans. The train pulled into Clifton station where the intending parents and a large number of other Mexicans were waiting. Curious onlookers included a number of 'Anglo' women who trotted after the first batch of sixteen orphans as they were taken to the local church to meet their new families. They gawped in disbelief as they saw small blond children being handed over to people whom they deemed inferior – Mexican women who to them were degenerate, uneducated and not fit to care for white children. They decided that, in this instance, the Irish must become honorary whites.

The Anglo ladies stormed home and demanded that their husbands do something. The next morning the train had travelled on to Morenci, where more parents had claimed children, leaving a small number in the town hotel with the nuns. The deputy sheriff arrived from Clifton, prompted by the Anglo ladies' husbands. When he got to the hotel he found a mob outside – armed with tar, feathers and rope. The sheriff demanded that the nuns should go and reclaim the children already allocated. They refused. The crowd indicated that it would do the job for them. The nuns agreed – at gunpoint. The sheriff got up a posse and sent the men off to collect the children. When they returned, they found the crowd still at full throttle and threatening to string up the priest. It took the deputy some time to prevent a lynching. Back in Clifton another posse was rounding up the children delivered the day before, and when they were brought to the town square they were immediately parcelled out among the white townswomen. Outrage was in the air and tempers were up: this time it was hanging for the priest and the Hospital's agent – or burning both at the stake. The sheriff had a busy time reminding everyone that he was in charge.

Next day a judge failed to satisfy anyone, so the agent and the priest were advised to leave town on the next train. The citizens assembled to see them run out of town – then charged back to the hotel and set upon the nuns, calling them 'slave dealers and child sellers'. The sisters had to be defended by an official of the local mining company before they scuttled out of town along with the few remaining children.

The Foundling Hospital went to court in Phoenix, Arizona, alleging that its children had been abducted – and got roundly beaten. The judgement stated that the best interests of the children had been served by their rescue by the Clifton-Morenci 'Americans'. The case went to the US Supreme Court in 1906: same result, the court stating that the Mexican Indians were unfit 'by mode of living, habits and education . . . to have the custody, care and education' of white children.

The trains went on running for another quarter of a century, until both the Depression and more child-oriented law combined with improved foster-care provision saw the last trips West made in 1930. Only a few hundred are now still alive who made that journey, but there are perhaps upwards of two million Americans descended from them.

Once on the train, Bible in hand, nearly all the children thought they were riding the only train ever to take children to the West. It never occurred to any of them – nor was it mentioned to them – that they were part of a massive migration. This is one of the reasons why their story took so long to emerge. In state after state, they grew up thinking that they had had an unusual start in life – and one which was shared by only a few dozen others. That there were thousands and thousands who had had the same experience only began to dawn on the last survivors in the 1980s.

There are mixed views on the 'experiment' now: for foundlings it was a double distancing from their roots. One child wrote from her pleasant new home: 'I would give a hundred worlds like this if I could see my mother.' Charles Brace himself was not unaware of the dilemma: 'When a child of the streets stands before you in rags, with a tear-stained face, you cannot easily forget him. And yet, you are perplexed what to do. The human soul is difficult to interfere with. You hesitate how far you should go.'

15

What is your occupation?

And what do *you* want to be when you grow up? I used to dislike the question. I'd no idea what the choice might be – or even if there was a choice. I didn't hear anyone answer, 'Housewife', yet that – in my generation – was what our mothers were. I remember women occasionally filling in forms and being mildly indignant at the line which read: 'Occupation'. They didn't have one, their husbands did; and they left the form blank. As a child I watched the routine of cooking, washing, cleaning, dusting and polishing, and failed to find the slightest alluring glimmer among the tins of Vim and Mansion polish. Scrubbing and mopping were undertaken by a series of dailies called Mrs Fish, Mrs Haddock and Mrs Roach. I wondered if they were specially bred or just attracted by buckets of water. Of course they worked, but they didn't call it an occupation, just 'Helping out with the money, pet.'

An occupation is sometimes a vocation or a calling, sometimes an ambition, perhaps a chance and very often something that just happens. And for those whose roots don't go back very far there's no opportunity of a family tradition to carry on, or a sense that you are 'in a long line of . . .' Did I have dreams? The usual stuff of little girls' fantasies. Ballet dancer? Until the teacher looked at my feet and actually shrieked at the sight of my cute little bunions. Pianist? Bored by practice. Equestrian star? Not the number of times *I* fell off. Testy grown-ups wanted sensible answers, and the Church High School in Sunderland offered a limited range of options thought suitable for 'naice gels'. How about teaching? One glance at the staff room yielded a repository of unclaimed treasures who wore a lot of their own knitting and appeared not to acknowledge the existence of the opposite sex. Shorthand typist? What was the point? It was a chore to sit though dictation lessons at school, so why do it in a dingy office? Nurse? I'd seen a good few interesting cases collapse through the door of the Adie pharmacy – which backed on to a shipyard – and by my teens was already familiar with gangrene ('Have you something stronger than aspirin, Mr Adie – it won't clear up') and unexpected childbirth ('I *have* put on a bit of weight lately, mind you'). However, I fancied that getting to grips with the mess was more appealing than hovering with a tray of bandages and antiseptic, and such a medical career was only for science whizzes at school – which counted me out. Not that the word 'career' figured much in our education.

What the school traditionally liked to produce were young ladies of virtuous but determined disposition who'd head for the colonies and help those 'more unfortunate than ourselves, girls'. Robust missionary misses, with a spark of leadership to keep the lambs from straying into local ways. Every so often, an earnest bishop turned up to exhort us to higher things in life in a far-flung land, involving dug-out canoes and mosquitoes, with mildewed hymn-books optional. Not only did this calling fail to attract, but in the early 1960s the colonised pink bits on the globe were disappearing. Altogether, none of us was sure where we were headed, or what we wanted to do.

I was singularly unready for a career, and never paused to think if there was some kind of influence deep within me which might point the way to useful employment. Young women of my generation were rarely presented with a range of options as we gained the sixth form. Work was a pie presented to men; women were either the decorative crust or busy washing up the plate. That we were moving into a time when your occupation defines you – both men and women – was not obvious. And certainly lying in ditches being shot at was not on the agenda.

Looking back on several decades in the media, I admit it would be difficult to find suitable training for the tasks which have come my way. Digging latrines, levering bullets out of armoured car doors, midwifing a couple of Bosnian babies by candlelight, milking goats, wiggling out of a police-cell window, impersonating

Princess Anne (*somebody* had to inspect the Guard of Honour and she was several hundred miles away) – there's no obvious course which equips you for this sort of thing. The satisfying aspect is that, training or not, you meet a lot of people in the latrines, hospital and police cells who are equally nonplussed as to how they came to be there, but have an interesting tale to tell. So I have no regrets that I come from a time when role models, career planning and high salaries were absent from any thoughts about the future.

Nevertheless, employment now is different, with much more emphasis on success and achievement and certainly little of the former embarrassment in talking about pay. (I recall that my first interview with the BBC included a mutter from the lordly Corporation beings ranged in front of me about 'modest emolument'. I didn't recognise the word, but rightly suspected that it might mean money and that discussing it would be vulgar – and jeopardise the chance of a job.)

I've lost count of the number of forms on which I've lied about my occupation. Many countries see journalists in the same category as the plague. Entry visas, exit visas, accreditation to all kinds of armies and military units, even press passes – tell the truth and you won't get the right bit of paper enabling you to do your job. So it's bizarrely noticeable how many 'tourists', 'businessmen and women', 'travel writers' and 'charity workers' turn up at press conferences, battles and assassinations yelping, 'I've got a deadline.'

The skills needed in this trade or profession – agreement has not yet been reached on this – are rather vague. For thirty-odd years I've been ignorant of shorthand, nor do I fully grasp how a television actually works. But I am interested in people, having started by staring round in church while listening to interminable services as a child and wondering what made adults turn up of their own free will, what made them wear awful hats, why some sang beautifully and others croaked, why some faces radiated warmth and friendliness and why others were pinched and grey. I wanted to know more about them, but was a curiously shy child and couldn't voice the questions. Becoming a journalist was a liberation, the permission granted to enquire and indulge curiosity, to importune – to poke a professional aardvark's nose into conversations and meetings, and snatch acquaintance with people in the most unlikely settings.

Meeting people in interesting circumstances doesn't always afford a detailed exchange of information. Driving down a bumpy road through the Rwandan jungle, while there are still momentous events in progress following a huge tribal massacre, you keep your eyes on the track and stay alert for inevitable obstacles: large animals you can't identify, men with machetes and bad tempers, monkeys who want to ride your vehicle and pee on the windscreen, burned-out trucks lurking round corners, and the inmates of one of the capital's mental asylums fleeing the chaos along with several hundred thousand other refugees. In 1994, Rwanda saw appalling violence between rival ethnic groups, the Tutsis and the Hutus, with much of the population on the move in fear of vengeance. The scenes were biblical, with towns overwhelmed by tides of humanity and everywhere evidence of dreadful murder. The airport runway had turned into a shanty town despite the number of planes bearing aid swishing in to land on any vacant blob of tarmac. Health, hunger and sanitation were a nightmare, and I recall setting up camp in the pleasant grass courtyard of a mission station only to discover that the reason we had managed to commandeer such space was courtesy of the mission having become a killing-ground: its interior walls were beyond description. We dug a latrine in the avocado orchard, only to realise that ripe avocado windfalls beat a banana skin by a mile when it comes to accidents.

No one seemed to be in charge. Of anything. The refugees spilled over into the neighbouring Democratic Republic of Congo, which appeared to have less working infrastructure than a cat's cradle. More armed men and more confrontation. The French Foreign Legion arrived and took charge of the border, mainly by throwing grenades at those who thought they'd nip across at night by canoe. One day I believe we met part of the government-inexile, or at least men who claimed to be the government, but as we'd just nearly been mown down by a machine-gun party belonging to an impressively violent warlord our minds were not on the minutiae of political manoeuvre.

Aid agencies set up headquarters all over the place, and for some the possibility of being unable to cope became a reality. The numbers, the violence, the incomprehensible behaviour, the overwhelming needs. . . . Médecins Sans Frontières, consisting of some of the toughest and most realistic operators in war and disaster areas, finally met their match. They'd set up a small specialised dysentery clinic in tents outside the local hospital (the hospital itself was a no-go area due to a hysterical fracas involving machetes). A hastily dug ditch round the tents was filled with disinfectant to provide a sterile area and the critically ill lay inside on stretchers. MSF was mightily puzzled to find that their patients didn't look the same the next morning. Not due to a miraculous cure, but because they actually were different people. During the night the militia had substituted their own wounded for the civilian patients, heaving their fighters through the disinfectant and dumping the patients with dysentery on the roadside. MSF upped sticks and went to find other patients who might actually be allowed to stay and be treated.

At one camp set up by the fleeing Hutus near the border elderly sick people were being laid out in front of the gate, along with some of the recently deceased. The Hutus were making the case for food and medical aid in the most dramatic way possible. Here are our dead: where is the food? But the Red Cross were standing opposite with their white vehicles and quietly stating their rules: no aid to people wearing uniforms. The Hutu militiamen screamed in desperation, and the elderly waved limp arms. The Red Cross was unmoved. The young fighters still wore their camouflage jackets and refused to discard them. The white trucks left. The militia shrugged and walked back into the camp, leaving the elderly and the corpses lying in the dust.

The small Irish charity Goal abandoned any sophisticated aid distribution and set about the most basic of tasks: no able-bodied local fighter would bury the dead, so the Irish rounded up a sizeable working party by calling on the Boy Scouts among the refugees. In a clearing near to the enormous funeral pyre which arose we found over seven hundred children sitting in neat lines and circles listening to a handful of adults: the contents of Rwanda's orphanages in the capital, most having lost their parents to Aids and dutifully repeating their lessons by rote. The teachers were polite and thoughtful, having brought these children 'to yet another home, I am sure,' said one. 'We will always manage to make a home for them.'

An entire society in turmoil is a disturbing sight. There are moments when nothing seems to make sense or have a future, only for very definite rays of hope to squirt through the gloom. Reporting on such events is a challenge, because there's so much emotion thrashing about and it's hard to see the priorities. However, it never fails to be fascinating, and you meet all sorts especially when driving like mad and having to brake and skid because several blokes leap out of the jungle carrying rifles and not looking at all like Rwandan militiamen but more like – well, the British army. We shouldn't have been surprised. The Canadians had arrived, the South Africans were flying planes in, the French were on the border, and there were assorted bits of the UN.

A few moments later I was looking at a British officer with cropped hair and a rifle in his hand. A small bell rang. . . .

'Have we met? Didn't we meet behind a sofa during a bit of shelling in Bosnia? Aren't you a psychiatrist?'

'Yes, it's me, Ian.'

'What are you doing here?'

'Obstetrics.'

Psychiatry seemed out of the question in a country going mad, so Dr Ian Palmer was busy being useful and helping a few children into the world. Our respective occupations had taken us more than once to the same uncomfortable locations.

I'd first met him one Sunday afternoon in 1992 in Gornji Vakuf, one of the many divided villages in Bosnia which frequently had its inhabitants at each other's throats. I'd scuttled for cover into the British army's base which, as ever in the Balkans, was an inhospitable cement factory. The afternoon of the day of rest was being spent by some off-duty soldiers watching a *Rambo* video, played at the highest volume. As I went into the 'recreation' room – all trashed furniture and cigarette smoke – I realised that Sylvester Stallone's heroics on the television were being complemented by real bangs and explosions around the cement factory. A window went. The lads shifted along the sofa and one sat on the floor, staring intently at the mayhem on screen. A loud crump juddered the building. A soldier slid forward and tried to see if the volume button would go louder. I crawled behind the sofa and assumed the foetal position, to find a man squatting casually next to me reading a book. We had a conversation interrupted by mortar rounds and quite a lot of small arms fire, though it was hard to distinguish the local war from the video battle, which the lads were enjoying in a full-blooded way.

Somewhere in the chat I gathered that Ian was a doctor and a psychiatrist, was in the SAS, and was quite interested in a psychiatrist-sort-of-way in the fact that the soldiers were concentrating on a fantasy video rather than on the frenzy outside. I think he even explained it, but I wasn't taking much notice, having tried at one point actually to get under the sofa when I heard something whoosh past.

We'd also just missed each other at an earlier event in which our respective occupations had been involved.

'Hi-jack' is one of those words which causes accountants in news organisations to shudder and reach for a small dry sherry. Before the newshounds have scrambled out of the building the accountant has nightmares of a large team deployed round the clock somewhere exotic and obscure, costing a small fortune in air fares and claiming obscure expenses 'for hire of tent at end of runway' or 'for purchase of binoculars in order to see plane at end of runway'. Fortunately, the British method of dealing with a hi-jack which intrudes into our airspace is to guide the plane to none-too-distant and non-exotic Stansted Airport. And despite all the ruses of the authorities involved to isolate the aircraft, the hacks normally get to see the marooned beast by doing nothing more expensive than driving up the M11.

The Air Tanzania 737 arrived at Stansted on 27 February 1982 with ninety-nine passengers and four hi-jackers on board. *Kilimanjaro*, as it was named, had had an eventful journey, with the short domestic flight to Dar-es-Salaam evolving into an unpleasant bounce round airports in Kenya, Saudi Arabia and Greece before landing in the UK. Having had twenty-four hours' warning Stansted was waiting, and what must have appeared to those on the plane to be a runway surrounded by quiet Essex fields was actually a cauldron of anti-terrorist preparations, involving the deployment of specialist police teams and hordes of press amid rather disgruntled package tourists.

Reporting a hi-jack is no picnic. You are guaranteed that the five-minute loo/coffee/food break you finally allow yourself in ten hours of staring at a distant plane will be the very moment something happens. Facts are hard to come by, speculation is dangerous, and there's hardly anyone to interview. Various alarums and excursions are inexplicable at the time – *Kilimanjaro* went for a scary trundle round the tarmac at one point, scattering the vehicles parked near the terminal building. Demands and ultimatums are filtered through the official system and generally mangled in a web of gossip among the media. At least in the early 1980s twenty-four-hour news was only on the horizon – updating a hijack is a thankless task, normally beginning with the words 'Not a *great* deal has happened since you last. . . .' Eventually, after a somewhat fraught night, the hostages were released at intervals the next day without further harm being done. The police held a press conference and the media circus packed up and moved on. And so did the SAS – who'd been lying in wait, keen as mustard to put into practice what they'd been training hard for.

After more than a decade of IRA activity the then Prime Minister, Margaret Thatcher, had increased the resources available to security forces, her determination strengthened by the

Iranian Embassy siege in London in 1980, in which the SAS staged a spectacular assault to rescue hostages. Subsequently, the Regiment was strengthened and given a wider brief before the Stansted events. Luckily I didn't have to spend hours hanging around the tarmac as I was despatched to stalk the politicians involved – not difficult, for no one in government would argue with Mrs T's line on terrorists – and so I hung around the Home Office instead, waiting to be trumpeted at by the avuncular Home Secretary, William Whitelaw. But Ian Palmer was in the grass with the rest of them, watching his colleagues as they anticipated every eventuality, including storming the plane a short notice. He found it interesting.

'They were raring to go. This was the first time we'd had a chance to put into practice all we'd done since the Iranian Embassy siege.' Ian seems a rather unlikely sort of man to be crawling about with a bunch of trained killers. He's softly spoken and endearing, and he laughs a lot with not a hint of the braggadocio that one might naturally associate with this kind of work. In fact, he's relentlessly unassuming and you have to listen hard to his easy conversation to pick up the casual references to gruelling and dangerous experiences. He left the army only recently, ending up a colonel and the first Professor of Army Psychiatry (and probably the last, he adds, knowing the military mind . . .). His career has been varied and unconventional, a mildly disruptive tour through those most conventional of worlds, the medical and the military. He's always questioned, wondered what lies behind the obvious, what makes people tick. And he questions himself as to whether this comes from a difficult childhood – or knowing that he started life being found in a telephone box early one morning in November 1953.

'I always knew that I had been found – I can't remember not knowing. And initially my parents said: "We chose you. You were very special."' Mr and Mrs Palmer looked the ideal couple – indeed, Ian describes them as 'a beautiful pair'. They seemed to outsiders to be all that prospective parents should be: comfortable middle-class, intending to send their two adopted children (Ian has

a younger sister) to private schools. They were a busy, entrepreneurial couple, his father having been an RAF pilot in World War
II who then founded his own aviation business.

Ian went to a local prep school in Ringwood in Hampshire, his
early years – aged five, to be precise – distinguished by having tried
to set fire to the place with a group of friends. At eleven he switched
to the local state grammar school in Brockenhurst, one of the
outward signs that things weren't going so well at home. His
father's business interests were turbulent and he was going through
bankruptcies: Ian believes his father never paid tax in his life.
Finance was central to family conversation at the dinner table and
Mr Palmer 'took great pleasure at every mealtime in saying, "We
haven't got any money."' He was a self-made man who'd pulled
himself up from London's East End, had many remarkable flying
adventures and was proud of his achievements. The children
began to realise that *they* would never bring to the table anything
which their father recognised as a success.

But there was more. His father was termed 'irascible and
difficult', home was 'emotionally a bit of a mess' and Ian bore
the brunt of his father's displeasure, though there were other kindly
relatives around – an aunt who loved him perhaps even more than
his mother, and a gentle grandfather, veteran of the World War I
trenches. Before the adoptions, his mother had had several miscarriages and eventually given birth to a still-born baby. Ian was
the substitute for baby 'George'. As ever in the 1950s, these
matters were not talked about, the force of respectability and
fraught family relationships meaning that the issues surrounding
adoption were never aired. So great had been the shock of the still-
birth that, towards the end of her life, Ian's mother took to saying
that 'she'd never had a child, she *didn't* have a child'.

Few children understand the dynamics of family troubles, and
perhaps many never look into them, leaving it all behind and
closing the door. Ian chose a pragmatic route out, based on his
desire never to be beholden to his father for money. He went to
medical school and in the third year of the course joined the army
on a cadetship. A military career beckoned, and he automatically

thought he should join the RAF because, through his father's business, he'd done a lot of flying. Things went a bit pear-shaped in the interviews.

'I went along to some total RAF arsehole, an alcoholic air vice-marshal, and he was late, and when he arrived he was pissed. He said, "Why are you here?" He was completely horrible and all he eventually said was, "Oh, we've got chaps who ski for England." We didn't hit it off . . . I'm so eternally grateful to him.' Ian delivers a wicked grin and I recognise the traditional noises which emanate from the army about the chaps in light blue. The Royal Navy was next on the list: 'I had a look at the navy, then got drunk myself and was sick all over the wardroom – well, I was a medical student – it's what we do . . . so I got told off. That was that. Then round to the army and in a funny sort of way thought, "I like this." It's out of doors, it was doing something different, and it was being part of a group. It's a belonging. Life can sometimes be quite awful, but all of you are together in it – in a way it's a bit like a family, a structure. And I managed to fit in quite well.'

He wanted to join the 3rd Battalion the Parachute Regiment and be among soldiers but, this being the army, was sent off to work in a hospital in Cyprus full of soldiers' wives and families. He enjoyed it and branched out with his own programme on the local radio station. But he wanted soldiering, so he got an interview with the boss of the SAS and went to their HQ in Hereford, transferring in 1980, the year of the Iranian Embassy siege.

I wondered if he'd 'done Selection', in which men are put through a gruelling series of tests, most of which seem to involve mud, pain, exhaustion and threat. One of my friends technically died during Selection, was revived and lived to tell the tale with a shrug of the shoulders and great pride that he passed: dying didn't earn you Brownie points and he was relieved it hadn't counted against him. Apparently Ian tried to do Selection, but work kept getting in the way: 'I'd been there for about ten days and ended up in the Middle East doing something and sort of missed it. And sitting with the boys round the camp fire, inevitably they asked, "When are you doing Selection?" and I said, "Like now." After a

bit they said, "Why? Why? Don't do it for *us*. You're the *doctor*."
Self-evident truth: they did the SAS bit, I did the medical stuff.' So
Ian was spared yomping over most of the Black Mountains in
Wales in the rain, though you get the impression that much of the
job was not behind a desk writing prescriptions.

'It was an intense time, with the formation of the counter-
terrorist teams. We had to train up all the police forces and no
one had written any integral medical plan into these sort of things.
And as one of the team is permanently on a twenty minutes' Notice
to Move, and there was only one doctor at that time, I was
incredibly busy. I created the SAS's own medical support unit.'
He loved it: travel, tension, comradeship, outings to Stansted and
definitely more exotic hot-spots, and a very interesting group of
people to observe in the most extreme circumstances. After a
couple of years he'd used up much of his energy and decided to
leave the army 'and become a proper doctor in the NHS. I did a
year's anaesthetics, a year's emergency medicine, a year's obstet-
gynae, a year's psychiatry, and spent a year with the Sultan of
Oman's Special Forces – and *surprisingly* every time I was listed as
a GP people said, "Hmm . . . a bit odd . . . ."' Ian dissolves in
laughter. Eventually he returned to the SAS in Hereford as one of
three Senior Medical Officers. Realising that you can't do that sort
of thing for ever, he went into psychiatry. And his own life began to
shift into perspective and into place.

'It was a good move, really. From then on things became a lot
clearer – you have to do a lot of reading, and you have to look at
yourself. And it was a total revelation when I turned a page to see
my father described as "a major personality disorder". I suddenly
realised it wasn't *me* where the problems lay. He'd been paranoid.
He took pleasure in destroying the family, splitting us against each
other. I already knew that my mother had buried her problem with
the still-birth. She'd nearly bitten my head off when I told her that I
was counselling women when I was doing obstetrics – abortions,
infertility and so on. "Counselling? *I* had a still-birth – no one ever
counselled me or said anything to me. . . ." And it became clear to
me that I was George, their child who'd died – and I was in for a

hiding in some sort of way, for I could never be that child. And added to those words that "I had been chosen" there was the feeling that I could be sent back. But if things got really awful, you could always think, "I'm not really theirs – I'm a royal bastard really – one of the Queen's . . . a Fitzpalmer, really." '

With his childhood coming into clearer outline, there was the question of his origins. A few years earlier, Ian had wanted to know a bit more: 'I was working in London in the eighties, and on your birthday you think, "It would be nice to know." Just occasionally you get these thoughts – perhaps there's another family, perhaps better, with brothers and sisters? And I was married then and had two children, and you wonder what you're passing on to them. But I just knew that I couldn't find out. Also, you know that it would upset the family; you know you're going to have to do it on your own. And I think my childhood inhibited me. I went to St Catherine's House and along came a lady who said, "You have to have some counselling." And she was very sweet, and got some details for me. But when you see your certificate which says, "Father unknown . . . mother unknown . . . place of birth unknown", you think . . . oh shit . . . .

'I was found by an underground driver who was coming off his night shift at about six in the morning. I was in a telephone box just off Bolton Gardens in Earls Court. I've no idea of my date of birth – I was maybe three to six days old. My mother decided that my birthday should be 16 November – but it could have been anywhere between the 11th and the 16th. I've never seen my original birth certificate. I was wrapped in a blanket and in reasonable nick, I believe – I found this out later for myself, though I remember my parents had cuttings from the *Daily Sketch* and *Evening Standard* with the headlines: "Baby Found in Telephone Box". But they didn't talk about it: it was "What happened, happened" – there was never any prospect with them of doing anything about it. My birth wasn't registered – that's one bar to anyone coming forward. The law's been broken; and also, abandonment is still a crime. And each year that passes, the chances get less.

'Very oddly, when I was working in London I went running one night and I was paged – and I ran into that phone box, it's very odd really . . .

'Being a foundling? It does set you aside. I've loved what I've done – but is it my childhood, or being found? I'm a GP now and I love the patients, love being with them – and that's what my father gave me: an immense ability to be intuitive about how people feel. Nor am I scared of anyone. But I also question a lot of things. I don't conform, I loathe the conformity of medical thinking – *people* aren't like that. I see things my own way.

'But if I can be just dumped somewhere, what actually does that say about life in general? What does it mean? Does it mean anything?

'What I'd really like to know . . .? Well, I accept that if you're going to find something out that it may be good, it may be bad. You do survive, though. Life goes on. But it *would* be nice if someone read this and said, "I know him" and came forward.'

16

What is your father's occupation?

One of the more curious aspects of Swedish society is to be found in its graveyards. Having wriggled into university by means of a not over-subscribed course in Scandinavian Studies, I had a thoroughly enjoyable, if tough, year in Sweden teaching English to children whose only interest in England was *Beatlarna* – and who were disgusted to find that I didn't hail from Liverpool.

The Swedes in the sixties were a revelation to me. They'd avoided the war, and their cities had none of the down-at-heel bomb-damaged buildings I was used to. The University of Uppsala where I first studied boasted an elegant campus, where students lived in real housing. Students in Newcastle lived in squalor, wrestling with damp, dangerous gas boilers and outside loos. Uppsala undergraduates were in cosy apartments full of potted plants and chic lighting. They were also determinedly democratic. They might have a king (referred to with warmth as 'nice old king') and a crown prince (sympathetically known as 'poor little thing'), but that was it, as far as social niceties went. Equality was king.

In order to achieve equality, you needed copious amounts of education and qualifications. When I returned to work as a language assistant in the far north, just below the Arctic Circle, the local school board spent a good deal of time and energy checking my credentials. They offered me lots of special courses and fussed about my lack of paperwork.

'*Har du inskrivit dig?*' they asked.

I stared back at the posse of education officials, and wondered why they were asking if I'd enlisted in the army. I wondered if we'd lost something in translation. I was aware that the Swedes were keen on pacifism and the doctrine of non-alignment, but I thought the question a bit much.

They looked impatient. 'Have you matriculated?' they said, very precisely.

I still felt rather adrift, remembering only some incomprehensible ceremony in the university's main hall when some bloke dressed rather like Merlin insisted on shaking hands with new students. But I decided to say Yes, and was thus permitted to be let loose on very recalcitrant nine-year-olds. As I flailed my way on skis between the various schools in the town, I became very aware that I was the only one in the education system with no title. Everyone was formally addressed with their degree qualifications, the equivalent of saying 'Good Morning MA Cantab Mrs Smith'. People cared passionately about acquiring new skills – and letters before and after their names. 'Attending a course' was *de rigueur* during the holidays. Every teacher was in keen pursuit of a pile of certificates, and with good reason. Swedish teachers got more money for every additional skill. There was no pussy-footing around about teaching being a vocation. You learned some more – you got a bit more. You took on extra foreign language teaching – the pay cheque increased. You took on playground supervision, sports refereeing, lunch duty – you upped your earnings. As a result, all the young teachers went in for everything and had handsome salaries with extras. All the older ones had already made a fair bit, and had no intention of spending their lunch break supervising ten-year-olds throwing soused herring at each other.

However, all was not lost, as my first monthly pay cheque arrived in an envelope addressed to 'Filosofiekandidat Adie'. I'd become a proper person, though I rather doubted it would cut much ice back in Newcastle where my professor regarded me as a party animal and full-time member of the Gilbert and Sullivan Society rather than a Philosophy Candidate. And the obsession with working status in Sweden wasn't just in life. In the local graveyards of the mostly agnostic or atheist Swedes there were handsome headstones in granite, on which the most prominent detail was The Profession. A walk round the immaculate grounds would yield row upon row of Engineer Svenssons and Headpostman Pettersons. When I raised this with colleagues in school, they replied that surely it was the most memorable point about someone's life.

I noticed that almost the first piece of information about newly introduced people was 'his father was Chief Carpenter at the Steel Works' or 'her father was the Assistant Town Clerk'. The Social Democratic Swedes thought our British hierarchy truly odd, with mention of public schools and where you were born, and the obsession with accent. They didn't seem to have noticed that they'd constructed their own Who's Who at Work.

In Britain, the occupation of fathers is introduced casually in conversation – or left out for fear of claiming in the wrong company either middle-class respectability or working-class credentials. It is, of course, an essential tool of placement and recognition in biography. A great deal is inferred from the father's work – is it that of a qualified, educated man, or is it a badge of the craftsman, or the unskilled labourer? There's a wealth of suggestion as to family background, all lodged in a single job description. And there's the hint that sons will follow their fathers. There are still many jobs today filled by the nth generation of a family – from the army to undertaking. And sons in particular often feel that their dad is there as the ultimate role model in the area of employment. So what happens when fathers turn out not to be what you thought?

'My father was a mathematician before the Second World War started, and then he joined the Royal Navy, possibly as a lieutenant-commander. That's what I'd been told. When I finally saw my birth certificate, where it said "Father" and "Occupation" there was just a straight line.'

Colin Dalley is sitting in the garden of his cottage in Somerset. It's an idyllic English setting, sheep bleating in the distance, the odd tractor rumbling by, a summer haze over the gentle, rounded hills. He's a tall, well-built man and he's had an energetic and fulfilling life, living many years in India, returning frequently, and now with a son and daughter and three grandchildren. He laughs a lot when talking about his past.

'I'm very, very grateful for my life. I've had a fascinating time. I started off working as a tobacco farmer and blender in India. I started in Bombay, then went to Andhra Pradesh – out in the fields – where I was responsible for the quality of the tobacco leaf for Philip Morris in India. Thirty-five years ago I decided there wasn't much future in smoking, so I switched to trading in seafoods.

'I was adopted and I've always known that I was adopted, as long as I can remember. Growing up, I was always told I was a chosen baby – and I had a wonderful childhood, I couldn't have wished for a better.

'I was born during the war, in 1943, and my date of birth – well, I assume that the one my parents told me was the actual date. My mother couldn't have children and so she went and chose me. And I felt proud of that. I was told that I was born in Maidenhead, and I was brought up in Thames Ditton in Surrey. My father was Assistant Tobacco Controller at the Board of Trade.'

So Colin followed his adoptive father into his trade, with the lasting legacy that he still rolls his own cigarettes, a habit he picked up in India and refuses to relinquish. A few questions about his origins arose when he got married – the usual requests for birth certificates and the curiosity of others about circumstances. His wife thought he should try to find out something more, but his adoptive parents were still alive and he felt he should perhaps leave things as they were.

'But when I was forty – well, I felt pushed . . . And when I started to do the research I went to an interview with the local council in Wiltshire, and they'd sent off for my records and thought I ought to be "counselled". And the interview turned out to be with a student just out of college with a degree in sociology who had bugger-all experience . . . so I didn't really get very far! My attitude's always been a bit light-hearted, I suppose – I'm very proud of being what I am, very grateful for my life, but I look on the humorous side. I've always thought I was the product of a rather good time in a haystack somewhere – and so I said so. And this girl said: "No, no, no. You shouldn't take this attitude."

'Then she said, "You were born Brian Hickman. Your mother's name was Betty Frances Hickman. Your father's name we don't know."

'Later I got the right to apply for my original birth certificate. It stated that I was born in Romford in Essex on 9 June 1943 – and this was totally contrary to what my mother had told me. And she honestly wasn't given to lying. She wouldn't have said anything if it wasn't the truth. She wasn't even prone to mild fibbing or exaggeration. And I felt very confused. Instead of having a naval officer for a father, I had a mother who was an auxiliary nurse in Essex – in Leytonstone – and the father's name was just a straight line.

'So I said to myself, and to others, "OK, I'm a bastard, and I've got a certificate to prove it." But then I decided to try and do some tracing, and it's because I've had a wonderful life, and I'm happy to be alive – I wouldn't like to think of my birth mother suffering anywhere. And even if I couldn't do anything directly, perhaps I could do something indirectly to help her. I went to Somerset House and I couldn't find any record for my birth mother's name. I searched records of women aged from fourteen through to seventy, and there was no Betty Frances Hickman born, married or died. Someone then told me it was possible that, as it was during the war, when she'd got pregnant she'd used a false name. And that was my brick wall.

'Even so, in July 1984 a chap I used to work with was listening to BBC *Woman's Hour*. And there was an item about a Canadian man who'd come over during the war and he'd had an affair with a girl. He'd been in love with her, and in 1942 she got pregnant and his commanding officer refused him permission to marry. He got shipped back off to Canada and he heard that he had a son born in 1943 – in June. So I got in touch with the BBC and I got a letter back saying, "No, you're not the man." All my life I've waited for the knock on the door with an old lawyer standing there saying,

"Been trying to trace you for donkey's years – you're the natural Duke of Westminster actually. . . ."' A great deal of laughter follows, with Colin saying, 'At least adopted people can have these dreams . . . .'

However, he hadn't given up: 'I had yet another attempt, though if it was a false name that my mother had given in the hospital what can you do? My adopting mother had told me that the adoption had been arranged by the Church of England Adoption Society, but they told me they had no record of it. I have an Adoption Certificate – so I was legally adopted at Kingston Petty Sessions. But, but . . . I now have a feeling at the back of my mind that there's something covered up in *my* family.'

Time has now intervened and Colin is no longer in touch with any relatives of his adoptive parents. Nor, as with many of his generation, was the whole issue something that could have been raised with those parents. On the other hand, he's convinced that his mother would never lie to him. He's still curious, wondering if DNA testing could help, wondering if his mild diabetes has a family history: 'Just the Where, Who and When. I'm not paranoid about it. Even in the war there was abortion – and this lady chose to carry me . . . 1943, an auxiliary nurse, pregnant, such a disgrace at that time . . .'

We looked again at his birth certificate, stating that he'd been born in the Woodside Nursing Home in Woodford, to Betty Frances Hickman of 33 Rhodesia Road, Leytonstone. If the name was false, I said, then I supposed the address was as well.

'Oh no,' said Colin. 'I've been there.'

'What did you find?' I wanted to know.

'No, you don't understand. It was my maiden great-aunt's home . . . .'

We talked about this. And as a little piece of the jigsaw dropped into place, it may seem odd that it hadn't been noticed before. However, this is often the case when you're dealing with your own background: a familiar address appears on a piece of paper relating to you – so that's natural, isn't it? Its very familiarity knocks it out of the context of significant information.

What is your father's occupation?

Colin had had a subconscious thought about it, he recalls – but immediately dismissed it when the next thought was his great-aunt who'd been well into her eighties when he visited her as a ten-year-old . . .

He's now on the trail again, with hints that a Canadian cousin may have spent some of the war in Leytonstone. And there was a nurse around, too.

'Whatever . . .' he says. 'I'm very grateful for my life.'

17

What is your mother's occupation?

I don't think I killed anyone when I helped out in my adoptive father's pharmacy, but at a rather tender age I was measuring out some lethal stuff and putting the odd pinch of diamorphine into the home-made cough mixtures. The shop was blatantly old-fashioned, not through any marketing wheeze to lure discerning customers into Ye Olde Apothecary's Shoppe but because no one had thought to change a thing for nearly a century. Wilfrid Adie had inherited it from an uncle who'd had it passed on by his father. I expected some days to see a ghostly Victorian gent emerge from one of the dimmer corners and add a jar of leeches to the prescription requests. The cash register was a glorious machine with sliding brass buttons instead of keys. The racks of wooden drawers were a work of art, even if they contained powders which no one could quite identify, except that 'that yellow stuff's good for constipation'. Tiny scales with feathery metal weights sat next to racks of spatulas and hefty pestles and mortars. There were rows of blue-glass syrup jars, pink ointment containers and green ribbed poison bottles, all now coveted by antique hunters. But the trophies were the carboys: those large pear-shaped glass containers filled with red or blue or green liquids, somehow concocted from the odder powders in the wooden drawers. I inherited a couple: the only symbol now of a working life, something which links me to that curious-smelling pharmacy and those who worked there.

Fathers, so identified with the world of work, have often passed down tools of the trade or symbols of their profession. And there are few women who don't have something special with which they remember their mothers. An inherited engagement ring, something special for a wedding day, a christening robe, a favourite piece of jewellery, a piece of furniture, a special photograph – or, as a friend of mine proudly displays, an impossibly huge boiling pan for which she's still looking for a 'proper' use (for now, the potted plants live in it). But until a few years ago, there would have been few women passing on something which reminded you of a working life.

We all value such mementoes and cling on to objects of which no one else can understand the significance. Even children collect all kinds of weird keepsakes, from dried slugs to old ballet shoes. Interfere with a precious childhood hoard at your peril.

Generations in the twentieth century, assailed by the casualties of war on a massive scale, set great store by letters from the front, formal studio portraits of a handsome young man in uniform, and medals. In the aftermath of bombing raids, my parents told me, human moles would dig urgently into the mountainous piles of smashed houses, looking not for the few 'valuables' – the silver-plated cruet set, the rather creepy-looking fox fur – but for a particularly cheap plate that had stood on the mantelpiece and been the only thing that Grandma had left from her first holiday in Blackpool. Such gifts and inherited bits and bobs provide a link. And in the Foundling Museum, one of the most affecting displays is of the tokens left with a child by the mothers relinquishing their babies into the care of the Foundling Hospital – a shell, a ring, even a beer bottle label.

Tokens, keepsakes, souvenirs, mementoes – not so far removed from charms and talismans. Less a nod to the spiritual, more a traditional link between life and wishes, death and fears. The poor in the eighteenth century could only produce a shell or a ribbon – but it linked the baby to its future, the adult to her past.

We all have early intimations that there are things we know nothing of in our past – initially, they're nearly all embarrassing digs from grown-ups about when we were very small. Those remarks by parents: 'Oh, you always did that when you were a baby' or 'I remember the first time you said that – don't you remember?' And it's always something cringe-making, which you wish had flown into the mists of time, never ever to be recalled: you fell in the goldfish pond, you forgot to go to the loo, you were sick at the birthday party . . . the list is endless. It's not meant unkindly – it's the prickly bits of memory which stick around longest.

But there are a different set of references for those who didn't have the conventional background and whose history, reaching back, stops short. In these instances, a single droplet of information excites and thrills and frightens those who know very little of where they came from. The dredged-up memory, the casual remembrance – its actual content need not be earth-shaking – mean much more: the recognition that someone knew something about you. It's a contact with a hidden history, the extraordinary moment when a real link in the chain to the past is hammered – a resounding clang which says: 'You did not begin in nothingness. You have roots, you are attached to a family tree of people – and you are their heir and successor, however humble.'

Remarks such as: 'I once met your father . . . .' 'You were found on that street – it's called . . . .' 'You had on a beautiful pair of knitted bootees . . . .' 'A woman with blonde hair was said to have been seen running away, not looking back . . ..' This is the stuff of cheap novels, of contrived tales, except when it's told to a foundling in all good faith. Even casually, as a suddenly recalled moment, it's like a cast-iron link to the present: you have come from somewhere. You are part of the massive skein of family histories which make up the tangle of society around you now.

It makes you different from those with conventional backgrounds. No one can ever understand the breathless moment when a commonplace remark – 'She had red hair' or 'You smiled at everyone' – means so much more than trivial observation. These are the straws – golden straws – which abandoned children grasp at, right through their lives. That's why it's so important to value these remarks, to understand their significant hinge with the past.

A note pinned to a blanket, a distant relative's foggy memory of an illegitimate birth, a passing acquaintance with the people who gave you life – such tokens and token remarks must never be underestimated. They don't differ in their trivia or crassness, and are in accord with those clomping remarks about 'how you crawled for months and refused to walk' and 'when you burped all over Auntie Hilda'. But they differ in their significance. They are the links in the chain that – whether you like it or not – you instinctively need to forge between your own existence and the flow of genes and emotion and acts which brought you into this world.

In the twenty-first century, every foundling I met produced evidence of that link. The material tokens – a dress, a pair of bootees, a hand-written note, or a newspaper cutting. The symbolic tokens – a photograph of the finding-place, a much-repeated quote from someone who'd looked after the abandoned baby, or a meeting with someone who'd actually made the discovery.

Whatever the success of a subsequent adoption or fostering, there's a need to reach back that one stop further to the period before the 'officially documented' life began. Not just out of curiosity, but from a more deeply driven desire to establish that whatever did happen, whatever has happened since, there was a little space of time when the baby emerged into this world and was a person in his or her own right – regardless of fate.

'There's me' – a foundling adult jabs a finger eagerly at the faded picture, a puzzled, nose-wrinkling bundle taking an obvious dislike to the snapper from the local rag. 'That's me when I – well, that's me how I was.'

'My trousers' – a nine-year-old possessively pats a pair of faded cotton trews split at the crotch, and clearly worn in the orphanage by many before her.

'I've my box of bits' – a successful businessman leafs carefully through old-fashioned certificates and thin sheets of typed officialdom as if they were precious medieval manuscripts.

The journeys made to dull housing estates, the search for long-demolished greengrocers' shops, the need to know exactly where the branch of Woolworth's stood before it was demolished – all to the place where you were first spotted on your own. There's a need to push back through that official line which has been drawn to start the new life. To establish that you survived – on your own. It puts down a marker. You didn't pop up out of nowhere. And regardless of the person who left you, you perhaps cried or howled or just caught the eye. You made it, however you came to be there.

'Dear Mrs Ingram . . . .' The letter is on a very small square of paper, from a standard writing pad of more than half a century ago. The type-face is rather spidery, from an old-fashioned machine which has nearly punched holes where the full stops are. The bundle of faded buff leaves, carefully held together with large elastic bands, has been brought out by Mrs Ingram's adopted daughter, who now calls herself Marion though she grew up as Pauline. She decided she didn't like Pauline, but goes into no detail . . . . She grows intense when looking at the letters, because they are her only link to her past, to that time before she was adopted.

'I was told when I was seven that I was adopted and I grew up thinking my name was Pauline Austen. All I remember from school about it was the nurse conducting the medical. She had a lot of questions about medical history, and my parents said, "We don't know." I knew I'd been in a Children's Home. We'd go visiting to have tea with the matron. I was brought up by the Ingrams after they adopted me from the home when I was about eighteen months old. It was a happy childhood even if my parents were a little old-fashioned, both being at the top end of the adopting age – forty-eight and forty. Only once I was fully grown up did I find out that my birthday was not my birthday, and my name was not my name.

'At twenty-seven, when I had my younger daughter, I was on the phone to my mother talking about naming her Joanne, saying, "I'm going to call her Joanne Elizabeth Pauline, after me." And she said, 'Well, you do realise your name's not Pauline? It's not your original name.' Then she added, 'And you ended up with your birthday because the court gave it to you: March 21st – I asked the judge if I could give you my sister's birthday.'

'I hadn't twigged at all. I was a bit devastated. She said, "You did realise?" and I said Yes, but then I just left it at that. I was a bit shocked by it all, and I kicked myself for months after that, not having seen the coincidence of having Auntie Elsie's birthday. All I now know is that I was born sometime in March. But she didn't actually say at that point that I was a foundling.

'I started making enquiries in 1988, and saw a social worker in Worthing. She suggested I should apply for my own birth certificate, but I saw no point then. It was having a daughter of my own that prompted me – I wanted to know the circumstances of my birth, why it happened, but I didn't want to be judgemental. I got my *short* birth certificate, but it only had the name given to me when I was adopted.

'I'd been told that I'd been left outside a shop in 1948 "in the Dartford area". No more than that. Apparently the police reckoned that my mother had left London and gone down to Kent to have me, and that she'd possibly paid someone to take me in – who then left me . . .. It all seems a bit fishy.'

She fingers the packet of letters which prove she was in the Children's Home. A tangible piece of evidence that is important to her, all headed County of Kent, Beltinge Nursery Home, Reculver, Kent. On 13 July 1948, the matron writes:

Dear Mrs Ingram
Pauline, I think, must now definitely be counted as an abandoned child as the Police can find no trace of her mother.
Pauline is well and happy and is growing into quite a bonny baby. I am so glad you and your husband enjoyed your visit to the Nursery – we always try to do our best and make up for the things they normally miss.
With kind regards to yourself and your husband
Matron L.E. Huggett

All the letters are very brief and to the point, a contrast to today's lengthy official communications and social work waffle. Efficiency laced with humanity shines through:

10th February 1948

Dear Mrs Ingram
I will certainly do all I possibly can to help you adopt a little child, if you desire, and will be only too pleased to pop along and discuss things with you.

The matron, whom Pauline remembers from the later visits to the nursery, was known to her as 'Huggy' and it can only be assumed that a friendship of some sort had grown up between her parents and Miss Huggett. And she knows that she was called Pauline after the matron's mother. However, when she tried to pick up this link with her past she had no luck: 'I wrote to the matron of the children's nursery before she died. I remember from those visits that she'd said, "When you were small, you'd only let *me* deal with you." But she wrote back saying, "I can't place who you were."'

'I've thought about hunting for my story in the newspaper – but it's a matter of getting to the Newspaper Library in London and I haven't really got round to it. It doesn't bother me . . . but it does leave lots of questions. I've often said that I wouldn't necessarily want to meet her – my mother – but I'd like to know the circumstances. We miss out, we foundlings, and people should think about that – even when people abandon their babies these days. They're not thinking about the future, are they? I have two daughters and two grandchildren and you wonder if they take after someone . . . one of my daughters is quite olive-coloured . . .'. She sounds tentative about the matter and carefully folds up the letters and replaces them in the bundle. 'My first husband was keen on genealogy and did the family tree. But on my side of the family, it stops at me.'

At least she managed to keep the letters, even though there's no explanation as to why the matron's memory failed so completely. Other foundlings talk of papers mislaid, and in particular of notes pinned to clothing which somehow disappeared in the official processing of an abandoned child. For them it's not enough that the name or words on the note were copied into an official record book, or passed on to adopting parents. They want the note itself, to look at the writing, to have something their mother once handled.

In Marion's case, there's not a single indication of what her mother was like. It's true that the circumstances under which babies were abandoned in the first half of the twentieth century tend to have common themes of illegitimacy, rather than the dire poverty which drove thousands of women to relinquish yet another addition to a huge brood in former times. However, it's fruitless to speculate on the social standing and education of women like Marion's mother. Contraception and abortion were not generally available – and in many cases not even known about. Social stigma attached perhaps more to the middle classes, but young working-class women had no welfare systems to support them. Shame and secrecy were two driving factors, and in very few cases was there any attempt to pass on useful information of any sort for the child's future. Not surprising, when these women were committing a crime and could fear prosecution on top of social disgrace if found out.

So the odd little token is about all that represents the link between mother and child. Margaret Kent had one once – but no longer, and she wonders about it and her sister's attachment to it. Sitting in her house with glorious views of the Peak District, her grey horse munching in the nearby field, two happy, boisterous dogs and two hefty cats, she's matter-of-fact and unperturbed about her own origins.

'I've never been bothered at all about being a foundling. It was a nuisance when I was about to get married – I had to sign a deed poll to change my name once, and then marry and get another name! My children and grandchildren know – and it's not bothered them.' Margaret too was found in Kent, but thirteen years before Marion, on the steps of a police station in Farnborough, near Orpington, on 14 July 1935.

'I don't know who found me – perhaps it was a nurse at the hospital opposite the police station. I have been back there, but unfortunately it's no longer a police station. I was aged about three weeks – that's what it says on my birth certificate, so I was given the birthday of 23 June – I've no idea who gave me it. I was taken across the road to the Farnborough Hospital and stayed there until I was eight months old. I don't know if there was anything about me in the local newspaper. I was found in a basket, wrapped in a shawl with the name Sheila pinned on it – I was very definitely meant to be found. The shawl was good-quality – we had it in the family for some time.

'I was adopted by Alfred and Mabel Pickrell – but not legally, and I don't know how that happened. As far as I know, we moved house the same day they adopted me! And I was never told I was adopted.

'My parents came from Brockley [South London] and were visiting the hospital to see my mother's sister who was having a minor operation. The story was that my aunt said, "You'll never guess, they've got this lovely little baby girl in here – like a pet!" And my mother saw, fell in love and adopted me . . . that was what I was told, and I never followed it up until it was far too late to do anything about it.

'I was brought up in Dartford – the place they moved to the day they took me. I think they didn't want anyone to know the circumstances, other than immediate family members. I've spoken to some cousins and they know nothing at all. My elder sister Joyce was thirteen years older than me. It was she who kept the shawl for a very long time . . . she wouldn't part with it. But it disappeared.'

At this point I must have been arching my eyebrows and doing some journalistic calculation. An informal adoption, a flit to another town on the day it happens, an elder sister hanging on to the shawl. Margaret catches my eye and has clearly considered the options: 'I think it's highly unlikely. In 1935? And she was just thirteen.

'I had a happy childhood despite the fact that I was brought up during the war, my father's business failed and my mother died when I was nine. And I thought my sister was my sister – she took on my mother's role when she died. Still, I had a lovely childhood. I think this is why I've never tried to find out. What did it matter?

'I was about fourteen and we were studying genetics at school. And you know when you're a child, you see things, you hear things – and eventually it all makes a picture and comes together. It was something to do with eye colour, and there was no way with my eye colour that I could be their child. So I suddenly guessed. And I was reading a book called *Doubting Thomasina*, about a girl who was adopted, and being that sort of age I thought Whoopee – this is me!

'And I was so angry – I asked my father straightaway. He was standing with his back to the window when I came home from school and he said, "Hello, Margaret," and I said, "I'm adopted, aren't I?" And he sort of blustered and I said, "Well, tell me. Am I or not?" And he said, "Well . . . yes, but who told you?" And I said that nobody had told me, I'd guessed. I can remember exploding, saying, "How dare you not tell me!" – and he crumpled. He said, "We never wanted you to know – you were our lovely little girl." And once I grew up and became a mother myself I understood why they didn't tell me, but it was a long time before I came to that.

'And after that I never thought about it at all until I came to get married and needed a birth certificate. So I asked Joyce if there was one and she hummed and hawed and fussed around and it still didn't dawn on me. So my fiancé Trevor said he'd go to Somerset House and look. I felt sorry for him when he came back that night because he said, "You don't exist. You're not in Somerset House." He'd been looking under the name I was known by, Margaret Ellen Pickrell. I had a Christening Certificate and an Identity Card (I was a wartime child, I can remember the number to this day: DHGR/19/4 – and 4 meant that I was the fourth member of that family, so they'd registered me, but I had no legal identification). When you went to grammar school at eleven you were supposed to take your birth certificate – so I asked my parents, who said, "Don't worry, we'll sort it out." They must have quietly gone to school later.

'I now have a birth certificate. I'm Sheila Elizabeth Ward. And you can guess where that came from – the hospital.

'I later became a teacher and had four children. I had twinges of doubt when I was pregnant with my first: what am I passing on to this child? Supposing it's black! Because that's how things were in those days. And then all those thoughts went away and she was born big, white and beautiful.

'At sixty, when I had a riding accident, I became aware of my own mortality and suddenly wanted to know. I contacted Norcap and I enjoyed meeting other foundlings – like Joan, who'd been found in a litter bin. She'd had five children, so what you never had. . . . But I became aware of the deficiencies in the story I'd been told. And the significance of the shawl. So just about four years ago, I went back to the hospital and went to the home of the nurse who'd registered me. Because I did wonder if I was a nurse's child – because they kept me in hospital for so long. I'd asked my father why they'd kept me all that time – was there something wrong with me? And he said, "No, you just stayed there." And I had accepted all this. I wish now that I had asked a lot earlier. The only thing that I regret is – though my mother's probably dead – I would have liked her to have known that everything was all right.

'I suspect . . . that I'm Irish' – there's a glance at the grey trotting nimbly off down the field. 'My mother an Irish nurse . . . I have dark hair and the pale skin . . . and the eyes – and I think I belonged to one of the nurses. . . . Mind you, I never wanted to be called Sheila.'

18

Have you any disease or disability?

You should never judge a country by its railway stations – though it's tempting. An hour spent on the platform of Paveletskaya Station in Moscow gives a fractured insight into the tempo and trials of a country in transition from Communism to – well, to something different. They've finally installed rather modern-looking three-pronged turnstiles so that arriving passengers can insert their tickets and gain automatic exit from the platforms. However, the turnstile barrier is patrolled by a bunch of females straight out of Commie Central Casting – women with frizzy dyed hair, built like battle tanks, whose military-style jackets leave a ten-inch gap for bolster-sized bosoms. If size betokens strength, then these ladies are essential to the smooth running of the station. As the passengers canter off the trains, in their nostrils the smell of a market-driven economy emanating from the neon-garish casinos and twinkly designer shops of central Moscow, their rush is halted every few minutes by a large heap of clothing jammed in the turnstiles. Yet another country babushka has failed to negotiate the metal prongs – or is trying carefully to retrieve the ticket from the nasty greedy machine while trapped in its embrace. Extricating a swearing granny wearing layers of cardigans, coat and shawl entwined with numerous plastic bags and cardboard boxes takes determination and the ham-like forearms of the turnstile patrol. While these noisy incidents draw the attention of frustrated travellers, small, slight figures scoot from the shadows and dive like seals under the barrier – in both directions. The railway station children have their own business of survival to attend to.

That people should live in a railway station had never occurred to me until I travelled to Moscow in a party of students in the

1960s. Our parents thought we'd end up being sent to Siberia. The USSR was a big ugly bear engaged in the Cold War, and few tourists were keen to sample a country rumoured to live solely on beetroot soup (false) and harbour not a single bath-plug (true) or a pair of jeans (not only true but demonstrated by the number of people in Moscow who put fingers on our thighs and turned out to be prospective Levi buyers rather than Communist sex-fiends). Only dim trade union leaders took up the Soviet offer of a free week on the crowded beaches of the Black Sea, oblivious that their fellow holidaymakers had had to earn their place in the sun through good behaviour and devotion to the Party.

We were part of a rather odd experiment by an off-shoot of the official Intourist travel company to entice a younger set to the delights of the People's Republics. Whatever our politics – and our group included four Americans, three French, two Belgians and a New Zealander – Intourist seemed to have been unaware that we were the protesting generation. On the long ride from Ostend through Warsaw to the USSR border (minus the two Americans who'd got off in Brussels to play frisbee on the platform, unaware that trains are not like taxis and feel no obligation to wait for fare-paying folk) we got out the guitars and wondered if we'd see any tanks and missiles in Red Square. We were, we hoped, relatively open-minded. We knew their system was different, but weren't sure quite how. The station at Brest-Litovsk was a good introduction.

As we left our skinny Western-gauge train to look for the broad beast that would take us in five-foot style to Moscow, we were assailed by a demented girl yelling, 'You are late.'

'We aren't late,' we replied. 'It's half past two and the Moscow train leaves at four.'

'*Da. Da.* Yes. Yes. It leaves at four. Yesterday.'

Our tour guide was a delightful student, but one wholly unable to face up to, never mind explain to us, the lunacies of Soviet bureaucracy. We trooped into a large hall in which the guardians of life in the USSR were lined up behind large desks. It became clear that a massive sense of humour failure provided the most effective chasm between East and West. Passports were pored over, fingers licked and pages turned noisily. As a multi-national student group with a penchant for cheap train travel across Europe, we clearly represented an infectious plague that had been allowed to roam recklessly across frontiers and meet far too many strangers. I got involved in a confusing dispute about why I'd been to Finland. 'I went to sing,' I said helpfully, thinking it too much information to describe why I'd joined a Swedish chamber choir in Lapland.

'Zink?'

A hopeless muddle ensued, clouded with suspicions that I was some sort of Western torpedo. Next to me, the New Zealander was trying to explain why it was necessary to travel through a lot of countries to get to Ostend – mainly by train – from Wellington, NZ.

Our inquisitions were interrupted by a bellow from behind the customs desk as a plump and meek-faced Belgian was emptying his rucksack. Old sandwiches went flying, as if they constituted a threat to Soviet food hygiene. An orange was brandished by a uniformed arm. Other uniforms started to take an interest and began hectoring him. The Belgian smiled shyly, dug in the bag and proffered another orange. Being a laid-back guy who wished to emulate Bob Dylan, he rather revelled in being shouted at by incomprehensible people in badly fitting uniforms while humming a little peace song and ignoring them. We all began to enjoy the spectacle, as more uneaten remains emerged from the rucksack, until our student guide appeared. She was clearly frightened.

'Why have you oranges?' she demanded in a whisper.

A number of cute answers came to mind, but her face showed that we'd strayed into something rather serious.

Earnestly she hissed: 'Oranges are all sick, diseased this year. In all the world. No one can get oranges.'

We never got to the bottom of the rotten orange epidemic, being told later that the Soviet government was protecting its citizens from some filthy foreign fruit malady – thus explaining the complete dearth of oranges in the USSR that year. It took time to work out that this kind of ruse to cover up incompetence in the farming and distribution systems was commonplace – and believed by almost all.

The station was the first face we met of the Soviet Empire. Its classical columns and large halls should have impressed. Instead, we were conscious of a large tide of people washed up against those walls, most of whom appeared to have been camping there for a considerable time. It didn't take expert analysis to realise that our little timetable hiccup was symptomatic of a wider problem. The timetable was complex and packed with promise of a veritable horde of iron horses steaming to fetch us. The departures board was crammed with exotic names, with only a few minutes to choose between leaping on board the Leningrad Express or some Long-Distance Siberian Special. The reality was empty tracks and a constant swirl of rumours that a train might have been sighted. Having negotiated the border formalities, been stripped of oranges, old paste sandwiches and several copies of the newly trendy *Cosmopolitan* magazine (tsk,tsk, *nyet, nyet,* much finger wagging as *Cosmo* was perused minutely while being held upside down by the customs ladies), we wondered if we should try to bag a comfy corner until the right train arrived.

The tour guides were having none of this, herding us on to a platform while showing a peculiar mixture of nervous desperation mixed with confident assertions that 'Everything is in order. Please not to make problems. A train we have.' Dumpy figures passed us trailing witches' broomsticks and buckets and set about burnishing years of grime welded to the tatty seats and sticky railings. The towering image of an empire poised to wreak instant havoc across the known world took a bit of a dent.

The Belgian gestured grandly at the empty tracks and said, inevitably, 'A train we not have.' This provoked an eruption which we were to witness time and again in the next few weeks: a burst of frustration quickly disguised as a personal shortcoming. Instead of cursing the railway system, the officials or the government – all of which seemed reasonable, and which we were expecting – there was a volcanic noise followed by a sheepish shrug and 'Maybe I have time wrong.' Welcome to the People's Soviet Republic, where natural reactions were subject to government interference. Acknowledging that a train was missing was an affront to the state; all that was to be done was to be embarrassed and suggest that you personally were responsible for buggering up the entire transport system, perhaps due to a lack of devotion to Marxist principles.

That a state can get under the skin of its people is both fascinating and horrible. We had a marvellous tour, punctuated by bouts of disgraceful drunkenness as we fell victim to very good vodka. Our hosts, a carefully picked group of model students, soon turned out to be hugely human, despite a hard carapace of Soviet belief. We went on boat trips and picnics, taught the Russians lots of protest songs, got scolded for taking a very cursory interest in dismal exhibitions of industrial things, loved the palaces, gawped at the Hermitage Museum and argued about history. Politics was avoided because we could find no point of contact: we assumed that they'd all go to Siberia; they kept asking us what it was like to live 'like Dickens tells us'. But everywhere there was this gap between the system and reality. Buses never arrived. A student hostel in Kiev which was completely empty turned us all away with the explanation: 'Rooms exist not'; when the reservation was pointed to in the receptionist's book there was the usual small outburst, followed by the embarrassed shrug: 'I write in wrong names, so no rooms.' We spent one afternoon sunning ourselves in a cornfield in the Ukraine being shrieked at by the guides: 'Get back on train – it will leave.' We pointed out that the engine had been uncoupled and had chugged off into the distance an hour earlier. More outbursts, more embarrassment: 'Train has other business.'

We had seen incompetence and inefficiency, but the world of the gulags and the ruthless behaviour of the state was not on show for us. And though the official statistics which were regularly shovelled at us were too ludicrous to believe, there were no beggars on the street and no newspaper articles exposing social ills. It was another world, and much of it has shrivelled to a faint memory as glasnost, perestroika and the fall of the Berlin Wall have intervened. But the roots of some behaviour go deep – especially regarding the dark side of society.

Standing on Paveletskaya Station nearly thirty-five years later, watching the officials shrug sourly as ticket evaders leaped over old ladies jammed in the barriers, other signs of a country not in charge of itself were evident. A cleaner swished her brush round a huddle of young teenagers, who suddenly dashed away at the sight of a policeman. They split up and vanished into the dark recesses which all stations afford. I asked about the children. 'There are no children. Why should there be children? Children do not work on the railway.' A teenager slid out from behind a kiosk stuffed with a brewery's worth of alcohol, and legged it past Platform Number 1 which was swarming with cops. The train to Groszny had just pulled in, and anyone remotely Chechen-looking was being given a hard time.

Children do not work on the railway. But they live on the stations. The Russian state is affronted that they exist – and it's a hard battle to get it to acknowledge their existence. They are called 'social orphans' – though they invariably have a parent. It's just that their parents have been broken by modern poverty and the state has only one answer – catch the elusive creatures and consign them to a Home. That the people who pester the authorities to address the problem are funded by money from abroad gives even more cause for irritation.

Médecins Sans Frontières brings the skills it has gained over the years in disasters and battlefields to the streets of Moscow. They arrived in the Soviet Union during the earthquake in Armenia in 1988, which is where I saw them hard at work as the crumbling empire pretended that it could cope. The great Red Army would come to the rescue – literally – of thousands of homeless people in shock. That was the official line. As we drove into Armenia, much of the great Red Army was busy driving over the edge of ravines, its conscripts totally unfamiliar with the territory, and with many at the wheel who'd never had a driving lesson in their life. We saw one truck after another up-ended or crumpled. Since the soldiers were in battalions recruited from the Asiatic states the Armenians, even in their hour of need, were displaying a good deal of racial dislike – and anyway, the lads from the East didn't appear to have a grasp of either Russian or Armenian. Again, the suggestion that the state couldn't cope with such a disaster was an affront. Officials lied to us about statistics and talked about the ability of the state to respond to the people's needs: we listened as the people burrowed under mountains of collapsed brick and plaster, scrabbling for survivors. Bulldozers, cranes, sniffer dogs, listening devices – somehow the state had mislaid them; bit of an embarrassment, but not one to be mentioned.

The resulting chaos in the towns of Spitak and Leninakhan, where a conservative unofficial estimate put the death toll at well over twenty thousand, was a hymn to Soviet centralised incompetence. For several days, the main roads into the area were blocked by military traffic that had no idea where to go – or what to do. In the centre of Spitak the football field was literally covered with bodies, laid out head-to-toe, with no one responsible for their fate and a pack of dogs circling. Some days after the first tremor, realisation dawned that several hundred children were missing. Only then was attention focussed on one of the schools: it had effectively been compressed and and there was no machinery to bore into it. At the airport, not one but three grim accidents on the runway sabotaged relief efforts. And in the capital's main hospital, the medical director surveyed the aid beginning to arrive from abroad and fretted that much of it would be stolen. He stored it in the main assembly hall under a large padlock and key – to which he affixed a seal, using a lump of wax melted with his cigarette lighter.

Into this medieval mess came a horde of foreign aid organisations – the first time many of them had ever managed to operate in the USSR. MSF found conditions akin to those in a war zone, with no one in charge and almost no local resources to be called on.

A couple of years later they arrived in Moscow to tackle what they perceived to be another disaster – homelessness. Head buried in the sand, embroiled in massive economic and political change, the Russian state was taking a traditional Communist position when faced with an embarrassing problem: it doesn't exist; the state takes care of everything; so it's the fault of those who don't have a home to go to. MSF set about embarrassing the state as much as possible, towing round the streets of central Moscow a large poster which recorded the number of people found dead in the street that winter – a number in the hundreds after a few weeks. The mayor of Moscow was reported as loathing the charity – 'too active and noisy'. However, a decade of lobbying and shaming the officials into action by opening a charity-run shelter produced results. And there are now hundreds of beds available in state-run shelters. But it was the adults who used these centres – and MSF had noticed that none of the children sleeping rough had come forward.

By the late eighties, the number of children roaming Russian cities was growing phenomenally. The consequences of the end of the Soviet Empire are still being felt internationally, but the resultant internal disruption went straight to the heart of ordinary lives. The job-for-life pattern disappeared. Outdated industrial plants were uncompetitive in the new world market. Unattractive household goods paled next to the newly imported products of Western consumer society. Who'd buy a fridge that looked like a safe and sounded like a tractor? Bureaucrats and administrators saw their organisations suddenly declared redundant. Parents, driven by poverty or fuelled by rampant alcoholism, abandoned their children to the streets; and foundlings began appearing on doorsteps.

'We have whole villages around the country where everyone's a drunk,' says the director of the Assistance to Russian Orphans programme. 'And people are migrating from the towns – selling up their property and heading for the villages, getting a poor roof over their heads and using the money for drink.' The programme looks for a stalwart local inhabitant to work with, and finds there's no one capable. And in the last decade there's been a lessening of tolerance, she says, of children who are 'seen as a problem', never mind disabled children who are 'seen as a curse'.

The social welfare system, the all-embracing, let-the-state-look-

after-you system, has found itself penniless in a brave new pri-
vatising world. Orphanages, asylums, Children's Homes – all have
found their centralised funds drying up. The result has been an
unexpected crisis – unexpected because there is still so much faith
in the state, and because Russia has a long tradition of dealing with
orphaned, illegitimate and abandoned children through large
residential institutions rather than supporting individual families.
Tidying away the unwanted, relieving families of a 'burden', is an
ingrained habit, expressed in a resigned little Russian saying: 'No
children, no problems.'

Traditionally, mothers of illegitimate Russian babies had two
options, and in this were no different from their counterparts in
most European countries: either abandon the child in a place
where it wouldn't be found, or leave it near the house of a rich,
and preferably childless, family. And abandonment had many
causes – religious disapproval of unmarried mothers, poverty,
and an unhealthy dose of folk-superstition if the baby appeared
'different'. 'God punishes a sinner,' would be muttered in the
villages.

In the eighteenth century, the nation's tough rulers decided to
bring about some order to deal with the problem of illegitimacy,
and women were encouraged to hand in their unwanted children
through church windows. Peter the Great decreed that orphanages
be built at monasteries and nunneries, staffed by women paid for
by both the government and private donations. In 1763 an
enormous building arose in Moscow, commissioned by Catherine
the Great in response to reports of Foundling Hospitals in western
Europe. St Petersburg got a similar grand institution a few years
later, though, as was so often the tale, neither got a grip initially on
how to care for those entrusted to them – in the first four years of
operation, more than 80 per cent of the children died. Nevertheless
the idea took off: the state will provide; and by the start of the next
century Russia led the world in sheer numbers abandoned to
official institutions. The statistics were frightening: when an
American writer passed through Moscow in 1858, he was both

impressed by the grandeur of the Moscow Foundling Hospital and somewhat mesmerised by the flow of infants.

Bayard Taylor, the globe-trotting journalist from the *New York Tribune*, thought the architecture terrific: 'On our way to the Hospital proper, we passed through the church, which is as cheerful and beautiful a place of devotion as I had seen since leaving the Parthenon. The walls are of scagliola [plasterwork], peach-blossom color, brightened, but not over-loaded with golden ornaments. . . .' By this time, he had imbibed the spirit of the place:

> The original design appears to have been to furnish an asylum for illegitimate children and destitute orphans. The plan, however, was soon enlarged so as to embrace all children who might be offered, without question or stipulation, the parents, naturally, giving up their offspring to the service of the Government who had reared them. Russia offers herself as midwife, wet-nurse, mother, and teacher, to every new soul for whom there is no place among the homes of her people, and nobly and conscientiously does she discharge her self-imposed duty.

An interesting thought, for the idea that the infants who had arrived in 1857, the year before his visit, were being 'nobly and conscientiously' cared for is somewhat staggering: all fourteen thousand of them? Unfazed, Mr Taylor added that he'd learned that since the beginning of the year '6,036 had arrived'. Thoughtfully, he totted up the historical total: 'The entire number received in ninety-six years is 330,000, to which may be added 60,000 more, born in the lying-in hospital during the same period – making 390,000 in all. The Petersburg branch affords still larger returns, so that at present 30,000 children are annually given to the care of the Government.' The transatlantic traveller was keen to see for himself how the system functioned in 'this stupendous institution'.

> All parts of the vast building are most substantially and carefully constructed. The walls are of brick or stone, the floors of marble

or glazed tiles in the corridors, and the stair-cases are of iron. The courts enclose garden-plots, radiant with flowers. The arrangements for heating and ventilation are admirable. With such care, one would think that a naturally healthy child would be as sure to live as a sound egg to be hatched in the Egyptian ovens. . . . Of the babies we saw, seven had been brought in on the day of our visit, up to the time of our arrival, and fourteen the previous day. The nurses were stout, healthy, ugly women, varying from twenty to forty years of age. They all wore national costume – a dress bordered with scarlet, white apron, and a large, fan-shaped head-dress of white and red. In every hall there was a lady-like, intelligent overseeress. In spite of the multitude of babies, there was very little noise, and the most nervous old bachelor might have gone the round without once having his teeth set on edge.

We passed through hall after hall, filled with rows of little white cots, beside each of which stood a nurse, either watching her sleeping charge, or gently rocking it in her arms. Twelve hundred nurses and twelve hundred babies! This is homoculture on a large scale.

On reading Mr Taylor's descriptions, a sneaking suspicion creeps in that the nineteenth-century version of a 'photo-opportunity' may have been taking place. This was a country still largely unbothered by serfdom, where the peasants lived in poverty and the climate ruthlessly claimed the weaker souls. Perhaps it's the image of all those 'stout ugly women' in elaborate national costume that gives the game away. . . . To give him his due he does comment on survival rates, keen on his image of 'homoculture'.

'Not all the plants would thrive; some helpless little ones would perhaps that day give up the unequal struggle, and, before men and women are produced from the crop there sown, the number will be diminished by one-third.

'When we consider, however, that the deaths, both in Moscow and St Petersburg, annually exceed the births, it is evident that the Government takes better care of its children than do the parents themselves.' When, in the twentieth century, the Communist Party wanted to spread its message that the state knows better than the individual, they were planting in fertile ground.

A few years after Bayard Taylor's visit, the number of children abandoned to the care of the government rose to an all-time high – seventeen thousand a year. And contrary to the American's claim that the state knew best, the actual mortality rates in the official homes were three times higher than in the rest of the population. Nevertheless, the practice of institutionalising children had taken firm root.

By the beginning of the twentieth century the Moscow Foundling Hospital was still taking in thirteen thousand a year, as was its sister institution in St Petersburg. And in the last years of tsarist rule, the Turning Wheel was as busy as ever. 'A bell is rung', wrote another American traveller, John L. Stoddard, 'and the door turns upon a pivot so as to present to the applicant a little table. Upon this the infant is laid. The door then continues its revolution, and the child is wheeled gently within the walls of the hospital never again, perhaps, to be seen by its parents. . . .' But the conditions within gained his approval: 'The simple arts of washing and dressing babies are here brought as near to perfection as it is possible for me, at least, to imagine. Suffice it to say, the little foundlings are bathed in copper tubs lined with thick flannel, and then are dressed on soft pillows, instead of on bony knees or sharp crinoline of the nurses.'

Trying to achieve a modern-day comparison with the experience of Mr Taylor and Mr Stoddart had pretty well the same outcome for me. Moscow has a couple of dozen Baby Homes, and Dom Rebyonka No. 17 was the only one on offer to a visitor. Trying to discover the whereabouts of other Homes was fraught with difficulty – decades of 'not asking too many questions' has left a population still happy to be ignorant of what goes on next door. 'Being refurbished', 'temporarily closed', 'not possible – babies only temporarily present' were the official reasons for lack of access, though there was the distinct impression that visiting wasn't something to be encouraged. Russia has had over a decade of noses being poked into what was formerly exclusive state business, in prisons, asylums, hospitals and so on, and has yet to become used to unauthorised criticism, especially as there's much more awareness that other countries can do things differently – and often better.

Smelling of clean laundry, with brightly painted rooms, No. 17 was an oasis of warmth and welcome amid the columns of decrepit high-rise apartments which now boast formidable and disfiguring iron front doors welded into the mildewed concrete – the result of present-day fears about terrorism. Inside I was shown into a reception room, only to find I'd barged straight into a maelstrom of emotion: a young woman was kneeling on the floor, arms outstretched, cooing at a toddler. Standing behind her, hands clasped theatrically but in reality suppressing heaven knows what feelings, was a serious-looking husband. The little boy was taking very tentative steps towards them, and deciding whether to gurgle with glee or yell with ire. He gurgled loudly, and the couple inched towards him making incomprehensible noises: Estelle and Laurent Cano had just arrived from Marseilles. For four years they'd been in negotiations with the Russian adoption system, and this was the moment they'd dreamed of. Igor, two years old, was taking his time deciding what to make of this. Two years in the Baby Home would not have given him deep experience of cuddles and love. A camera was produced by Estelle, and the actual moment of contact recorded. A stream of French curled round Igor's ears, but he was far more interested in the lovely fluffy toy on offer.

Igor is a foundling, discovered near a block of flats by a neighbour and taken to the Children's Hospital. It's not a crime to abandon in Russia, and some kind of effort is put into trying to find the mother before she's officially classified as 'disappeared'. There was no information about him at all. To the Canos, this was no deterrent to taking him. As we left the room, they were thrilled and wholly absorbed in his every movement.

Igor had been living with seventy-five other children and the nursery was full of large cots made up with fresh bedlinen, twinkly mobiles above them. There was music on the radio and toys everywhere. That this should be a matter for note is because the Baby Homes have a none-too-good reputation. Over the past few years some have been discovered to be hell-holes of neglect and dirt, bordering on waste-bins for the unwanted. However, this one is run by a relatively open-minded director who's more than willing to accept help from foreign aid organisations: the mini-bus outside is from Germany, the books (in Russian) are from the Lions' Club of Sweden, and a host of international groups send money. There's even a 'sensory room' with a squashy floor, flickering lights, revolving glitter ball and a bouncy ball bath – all from donors. The state pays salaries and funds clothes and food – and that's it. The Home also boasts a newly installed chapel where a priest comes to baptise the children. An old store room, it is now crammed with red velvet, inlaid furniture and icons.

Grisha rolls over to stare at the visitors. He's five months old or thereabouts – it's not clear how long his mother kept him before leaving him on a bench in Ismailovsky Park. He spent his first month in the Home which specialises in foundlings and street children – which isn't open to visitors – before coming to No. 17. (The Aids Baby Home is similarly off-limits.) He looks lively and healthy, but the staff, who know every child by name and are genuinely affectionate, give a little shrug when asked what his future will be. 'He's from the south,' they say, and leave it at that. It's a phrase which occurs time and again.

It's the same with Ruslan, who's two and even managed to tell them his name when he was found in a playground. A woman took him to a police station, saying she didn't know where he came from – though he's obviously, say the staff, 'from out-of-town – the south'. They turn up in parks and playgrounds, often in hospitals and sometimes at the railway stations or airports, and they make up about 10 per cent of the admissions. The staff make an assessment of their health and development – which is not quite the benign routine it sounds, for a well-entrenched system is at work which will classify these children, possibly for life. And the reason is in the next nursery.

Lots more cots, but the blinds are part-closed and there's no music. Four of the babies have Down's Syndrome; others are mentally disabled – the Home doesn't accept the severely physically disabled because it doesn't have a lift for its three storeys. A baby girl lies quietly on her quilt. The carer explains that her mother can't stand to see her: 'She's almost mentally ill because of having had her.' I wondered if she'd been abandoned. 'Oh, no. It's just that – well – the parents both desperately wanted a child – and then this.' Implicit in the words is the core of Russia's problem: no one wants a less-than-perfect child. It's deeply ingrained in society, having been reinforced throughout the twentieth century with full government approval.

World War I, the Revolution, the Civil War – by the beginning of the 1920s there was a belief that as many as seven million homeless children were on the streets of the new Soviet Union. The response reflected the state's new significance in people's lives: 'Our [state institutions of guardianship] . . . must show parents that social care of children gives far better results than the private, individual, inexpert and irrational care by individual parents who are "loving", but in the matter of bringing up children, ignorant.' Collectivisation, which was to be pushed through in industry and agriculture, was also applied to social work. Homes, institutions, camps, nurseries – the state would run them all and emphasise the virtue in having these children gathered together, away from parents who were 'loving but ignorant'. The actual conditions within the Homes were not a subject of criticism: this was the state at work, and therefore beyond reproach.

World War II piled on the problems, following the famines caused by Josef Stalin's collectivisation of farming. With tens of millions dead, population policies included a ban on abortion and a boost to the practice of committing children to state care: it was easy to give a child up – and it bolstered the image of the state as the great mother of the country. In the 1950s, with the population no longer in decline, abortion was permitted – but the demands of industry began to affect the family. President Nikita Khrushchev wanted working women, so day-care nurseries, boarding schools and kindergartens were expanded. There was even a prediction that by the 1980s all the children in the Soviet Union would be educated in boarding schools.

Almost every twist of history seems to have resulted in children being seen less as part of the family, and more as candidates for Soviet citizenship under the state's guidance. You were a Young Pioneer first, and someone's son or daughter second. And these were the ordinary kids, whole and healthy. There was another group which had a much worse time.

The pursuit of the perfect Communist could not cope with those who fell short of the ideal. Adults with 'unsound', 'reactionary' or 'bourgeois' tendencies were separated from the common herd and often treated brutally. The ruthlessness of the regime was never in doubt on the matter – and known well beyond the country's borders. But the attitude towards those who didn't fit the great image dominating the squares and parks was equally determined. The strong couples with bulging biceps who strode towards a glorious Soviet future on countless posters and plinths and murals were not just a figment of imagination: they were a template – and those who were deemed unlikely to measure up paid the price. The USSR developed a useful science to deal with such matters: defectology. It was invented in the 1920s and it's still the undercurrent which flows in today's Russia.

The child was looked at as a potentially productive unit, someone who could contribute to the greater good of society rather than flower into an individual. Any disability whatsoever was defined as a disease – a disease which needed to be diagnosed and the defect corrected. For this to happen, the child must be isolated from the rest of society. 'Diagnosis' today occurs at about four years of age – and it's particularly tough on those children whose only problem is that they've been stuck in a Baby Home since they were born, deprived of individual care and cuddles and inevitably institutionalised. Several of the carers in No. 17 were horribly conscious that some of their charges would fail to make the grade at the dreaded 'diagnosis'. They pointed to three-year-old Sasha, a bright lad full of curiosity: 'There's nothing wrong with his brain,' they said. 'He's just got a little weakness in the legs.' However, the system looks not at the child's potential, only at its failings. Sasha, they said, was likely to be sent to a residential institution where he'd get next to no education and no chance of escape. As for the Down's Syndrome children – not a hope.

Down's comes well within the old Soviet diagnosis category of *imbetsil* or *idiot*. These are permanent labels at the age of four – and if there's any doubt about a child's abilities the authorities have always erred on the side of caution, filling the institutions and asylums with the unfortunate. A hare-lip, a cleft palate, cross eyes, epilepsy – all children suffering from these are quite likely to be classified as 'idiots'. Only ten years ago it was estimated that almost half of those judged 'mentally handicapped' and stuck in the closed system were of average intelligence.

It's grim, wretched and rigid. And it's still going on. That it still operates is due to the deep perception in parents that the child won't be accepted in society. He or she will have a rotten time, scorned and laughed at, despised as useless and qualifying for little if no support from the state. How much better if they disappear out of sight, out of mind, away from hurtful and unsympathetic eyes. That this is still the case is driven home by the experience of Downside Up, the only charity in Russia that advises and supports families with Down's children.

When a small group of their families took a first-ever foreign holiday, the parents' desired destination was Disneyland in France. On arrival they were immensely nervous, peering at the crowds heading for the fantasy and fun rides, clutching their children to them and telling them to behave. Then, suddenly, one of the mothers spotted something and turned – aghast – to her friends. She'd seen a couple of children – in wheelchairs.

'Do they allow them out?' she asked.

The Russians stood in silence as it was explained that this was perfectly normal behaviour, and what was so odd about it?

'This is France – the West,' was all they could manage, eventually trying to explain that they'd expected a rich, successful country wouldn't allow such children to be seen in public. Even though their own children weren't accepted easily in Russia, at least they weren't *imbetsil* in wheelchairs.

Back in the Baby Home, the director was sparing time from filling in endless forms about security. The ferocious attack on the Beslan school in Chechnya resulted in a raft of new rules and restrictions on all institutions dealing with children: gates to the Baby Homes have to be locked at all times and visitors are limited. However, she and her staff were keen to stress that the outside world holds one solution to the never-ending stream of abandoned children: foreigners are keen to adopt. The French couple had just left, clutching Igor like the crown jewels. The Russians loved their attitude: 'Foreigners are so much more open to the idea of adoption – and they're less concerned about appearance.' The director sat staring at the photographs of previous successful adoptions, and added wistfully: 'They look on a child as "their own". It's not our way – our prospective parents want something to show off. . . .' It seemed a harsh judgement on her fellow Russians. Economic woes, middle-class unemployment, tiny flats with shared bathrooms and kitchens, and pitifully small financial support from the state conspire to prevent many from contemplating taking a child. And it's only just over a decade since the mountain of paperwork which used to defeat most prospective adopters in the USSR has been simplified.

However, there's also the stigma which attaches to all the children waiting in the cots – not only the disabled, but those 'from the south'. As she hefted a large pile of files aside on the desk, the director addressed the issue of 'out-of-towners' briefly: 'Oh, the men from the Caucasus – the street vendors – women come from far away to work for them. It's a bit like prostitution . . .' The subject is uncomfortable. Terrorism, racism, the oblique references to being able to tell at a glance if a two-day-old baby was 'from the south'. Conflict in Chechnya, the ancient dislike of those who live in the 'non-European' part of the old Soviet Union, and the feeling that present ills can be blamed on 'Asiatics' all combine to fill the Baby Homes with children who will never be adopted by a Russian family.

The staff marvel at the way foreigners are prepared to confront what they themselves deem 'insuperable' problems. Out come more photographs – 'The American couple who took the boy with cerebral palsy – amazing, isn't it?' Then another Igor, 'Gone to USA – but he has practically no retardation, so he'll be all right.' Then a whole set of snaps of the Home's first foreign adoption in the mid-nineties: a plump child overwhelmed by toys and clothes and hugs and surrounded by wide-eyed staff. Not surprising, for the mother had left her with the words, 'I don't want this disfigured child', who was then described by the staff as 'pretty ugly'. It turns out that the plump girl was deaf.

Officially, the policy is to allow foreigners to adopt only disabled children – or children who've been repeatedly rejected by Russians. This first adoption was a gamble for the director – foreigners were only just beginning to come to Moscow looking for a child, and the Home had been absolutely sure that no one would ever want a child with a problem, in this instance a girl with a particular type of the ear condition called otitis. A couple arrived from New York – the husband a grandson of Russian immigrants and working as a consultant on the construction of the heart-stoppingly grandiose Cathedral of Christ the Saviour, all gold-leaf, Carrara marble and religious reassertion near the Kremlin.

'What a handsome couple!' The staff were goggling over a letter and photograph sent from New York recently: a glowing, prosperous family stand in front of a marble fireplace; their daughter is at ballet school – and her hearing is now normal after treatment. It's still a cause for talk amongst the staff: 'Who'd have thought anyone would take her – such a risk – we were so worried.' Questions of cultural difference or family suitability are pushed aside as the dark cloud of disability is pondered. And there's genuine amazement that three-year-old Victor, who's quietly having lunch in the nursery, is the object of interest to another American couple: 'Victor's got Down's – we've never ever had one of those taken before!'

I asked if any Russians were coming forward, to be told that the number was rising but was still outstripped by those from abroad.

And anyway, so many of the children were, er – well – not *normal*.
For in addition to the disabled and the 'southerners', there are the
dozens of children who are referred to as 'social orphans'. As in
most countries, families who are unable to cope with their children
for a whole range of reasons can expect help from the state. But in
modern Russia, that help does not extend into the community
through supporting the parents; it means centralised support – the
Homes and institutions. There are signs that attitudes are changing
– but the state will be the last to cotton on. To put it bluntly, said
one official, 'The state still doesn't approve of the disabled',
adding, ' "Normal" parents shouldn't produce such children.'
And by 'normal' you can include just about anyone who can't
cope with the chaotic state of Russia's welfare and social systems.
The country's in transition – and a lot of people slip through the
cracks, usually on a tide of drink. As the emphasis slowly swings
towards getting families to take responsibility for their own future,
many are in no position – or condition – to do so.

As I walked from Red Square through the fashionable shops in
the evening rush hour I saw many smartly dressed men clutching
briefcases and getting an eyeful of the West's consumer goodies.
Every so often they'd raise their right hand and swig from a beer
bottle. Further on, near the Tretyakov Art Gallery, hordes of
teenagers gathered in the dusk to hang out after school – fourteen-
year-olds in trendy clothes and bright back-packs. All downing
bottle after bottle sold from the kiosks which display every kind of
drink. Russia's average life expectancy is on the slide, and drink is
a major factor. As a result, as the Baby Home staff put it:
'Sometimes children are just mislaid.'

And given the tradition that the state knows best, they end up
being consigned to institutions. The process begins in the hospital:
most women give birth in hospital because it's free and there's little
prejudice against single mothers. If there are problems with drink,
extreme poverty, disability or sheer inability to cope, then the state
arrives at the bedside pronto. 'Give it to us! You can't cope. It'll
have a terrible life. It's got no future. So easy – just sign.' And it *is*
easy. The system's been going for decades, and the philosophy

behind it is used in all its strength to encourage women to agree that the state knows best. In the lobby of Downside Up's head-quarters in Moscow, I bumped into a young girl with a large blue scarf slung round her. Nestled against the cold, a very small baby was curled inside. 'Sweet,' I said. 'Well, yes,' she replied in good English, 'but Down's – and I was told not to keep it. They nagged and nagged in the hospital: "It'll be a burden, there's no money, you'll get no help, what'll the neighbours think?"'

This kind of onslaught is commonplace. The state knows best and doesn't brook much argument against it. It's almost your duty as a good citizen to tidy away the problem and deliver it to an institution. A veritable stream of advice on these lines will emanate from the midwife, the doctor, the nurse and any passing cleaner. Never mind your own family.

Lena, Marina and Nastya were sharing their experiences in one of Downside Up's playrooms. Each had a Down's child in hospital, and each faced a veritable procession of professionals advising that there was no alternative to surrendering the baby to the state. Nastya, with blonde hair and carefully painted silver nails, recalls every moment after she'd had her daughter, Dasha: 'The doctor arrived a couple of hours later and said, "It's got some genetic problems . . . you're very young. Imagine the situation if you buy a poor toy in a shop – you get the chance to take it back. And you're very young."' The penny didn't drop and Nastya just stared at him. She'd never heard of Down's. Then the midwives, the nurses and the neuropsychologist trooped up to her bed. 'Give her up,' they said. 'Leave her here.' Her husband arrived and signed the baby over.

Dasha went straight to a Baby Home – which worried Nastya, who'd heard from other mothers that some of them were horrible. However, she found her daughter in a well-run place – but the carers immediately looked glum and told her that such babies all died in a few months, and would certainly never walk. Nastya thought differently – she went on visiting Dasha and noticed that she was beginning to develop quite positively. But over the year that she was there she didn't recognise her mother, mainly because the staff refused ever to introduce her as a relation. . . . Then Nastya decided to take her to Grandma's for a month. And that was that. 'I loved walking with her in the street – I'm so proud of my daughter now.' Not so her husband, who found his mother ranting with anger at the thought of 'such a thing' coming into the family. He issued an ultimatum: 'I go or it goes.' Nastya divorced him, and when things were at their lowest ebb, heard about Downside Up at a parents' group. For the first time ever, there was advice and support. Her husband reappeared following his mother's death, but 'he's still a bit scared to hold his daughter'.

Lena's husband still doesn't know about his daughter's condition. She was thirty-eight when her Nastya arrived to add to the three older children. 'Give it up,' said the doctor. 'The child will be a heavy load on your shoulders all your life.' Lena is a strained-looking woman in a brown pullover who works as a cleaner, but she got encouragement from her eldest daughter who belongs to the new generation and is keen on taking matters into her own hands. So Nastya is now at home and, though there's support from Downside Up, 'The neighbours suspect something – though they never mention it. . . .'

Marina is made of feistier stuff. A stout, energetic woman, she runs a transport company and exudes confidence. She snorts as she recalls the scene in the hospital when they decided on a blood test at thirty-six weeks: 'There was a huge intake of breath among the doctors: "Down's!"' Their reaction so shocked Marina that Nadezdha made her way into the world a few hours later.

There followed the usual offer from the staff, and Marina raises her voice to the level which is probably used to sort the transport employees: 'Won't walk, won't speak, will never recognise you. And your other daughters are unlikely to get husbands when people know. . . .' However, she was lucky, as a geneticist took an interest in her child and arranged a minor operation on an abdominal blockage – usually, Down's babies are routinely denied treatment. With determination, Marina searched the internet for information, for nothing was forthcoming in the hospital – and found Downside Up. Having decided to look after her child, and partly to recover from the shock, she bought a mini-bus and set off for Europe with her two teenage daughters. In Scandinavia, she was bowled over by the attitude to children with disabilities. Fancy children with cerebral palsy being taken to the park! She determined to show her Nadezdha in public as much as possible – and get round to telling the rest of her relatives, something she hadn't been able to face. In London she met the leader of a Down's parents' group and realised that Russia had more problems than most – though she appreciated the amount of devotion needed in all circumstances. Back home she acquired another unwanted Down's baby boy, and is now something of a campaigner for a change in attitudes: 'Life's tough, but nothing can compare to a human life – not a car, not a flat.' The comparisons are those she hears time and again from disapproving colleagues.

That these children will be growing up outside the usual system is more than a challenge. At every turn they'll be looking for an alteration in attitudes, an improvement in facilities and a change of heart. And they'll be growing up next to thousands of children who are still stuck in the system – for life.

I went to see a *dyetskii dom* – Children's Home – and it was almost too good to be true. About sixty miles south of Moscow, in a historic town now dominated by a lusciously restored church next to an ancient fortress, 126 mentally disabled children live behind a locked gate and a high wall painted with cartoon animals. The youngest were five and the oldest – none of whom was on parade for us – were eighteen. There were houseplants and nice rugs, clean-swept floors and neat rows of beds with identical coverlets. The young teenagers were under a teacher's gaze in a classroom notable for enormous stuffed toys. These were placed around the room rather decoratively, and showed not a trace of wear and tear. The plastic building blocks were in pyramids, pristine and shiny. A dark brown hamster snoozed in an elaborate cage at the back of the class. The children were frowning over a task involving different shapes and counting; it was Sunday but 'they need to be organised.' The next room had the youngest – who ran towards us, shouting.

'They call you "Mother",' said the teacher. 'They call every visitor "Mother",' added the deputy director. ' "Mother" has no sense for them.'

'We never tell them they've been abandoned. We say their parents are dead or not in the country. We don't want them to try and escape – so if we tell them their mother is "far away" they'll be less likely to head for the streets and end up in trouble. Anyway, if they're going to be adopted it's important that the child knows he doesn't have parents.' How often does that happen, I wanted to know. There was a lot of discussion among the staff. 'Not in the last five years – definitely. Um . . . not really sure we've ever had a child adopted from here . . . .'

The children went back to a counting lesson, with a long description from the teacher as to the intensity of their education. They were very, very quiet for six-year-olds, and something caught my eye. When we'd come in, there'd been movement in the far corner of the room. A boy with a scarf round his head was lying face-down, banging his head on the floor. No one drew attention to him and everyone appeared to be ignoring him, ushering us away. When I turned round a couple of minutes later, a door was closing on a small boy clasped almost upside-down by a plump white arm. The picture was clearly meant to be of con- tented, usefully occupied children.

We were shown the dining room, the training workshops (wood- work and sewing) and the farm. In the pouring rain I went for a poke round the outbuildings – and came across roomy loose- boxes. 'Hippo-therapy,' announced the deputy director with pride and wandered off, confident that I understood riding for the disabled. Well, I know a little about it, and the joy it brings to a child to feel he is up high and there is a great gentle creature beneath him which he can guide. I opened the first stable door and a large, elegant hunter thrust his head out, all snorts and whinnies and full of beans. Um, not what I'd expected. I looked next door: a big mare stood over her foal and gave me a white eye. Banging came from the next stall. A muscular beast was thwacking the door with his hoof and clearly longing for a gallop. I think I counted fifteen – and all could have done duty in the toughest hunting-field. Wondering how the children might be involved with these beefy mounts, I asked the stable-lad who came from the Home. 'Ah,' he said. 'Not boys. Men. They come every week. Pay good money. Ride fast.'

It's an open secret that in a troubled economy, where the state's money can inexplicably dry up and salaries and pensions can be left unpaid, there's nothing wrong with some entrepreneurial activity to generate income. Whether it's entirely devoted to the welfare of the neediest is a hard nut to crack. At least it's some sort of contact with the outside world. For all the claims made by the staff that the locals were involved with the children, bringing clothes and so on, eventually I heard the admission that they weren't so much sympathetic as 'full of pity' for the inmates.

Our tour over, the officials sat down round a table laden with pastries and biscuits and tea in dainty cups on crocheted mats. Poverty and alcoholism were the main reasons for the huge numbers of unwanted children, they insisted – especially since the end of the Soviet Empire. Reforms, the influx of foreign capital, the new marketplace – they meant little. Absolutely nothing had changed in the numbers of children abandoned – or given up. The head of education was dubious about new ideas: she'd already referred to 'Down's *Disease*' and now insisted that 'all children with problems' were 'better off in Homes'.

When the disabled children in the *dyetskii dom* reach eighteen they go to asylums for the rest of their lives. They'll be regimented, institutionalised and isolated. Those who are 'social orphans' rather than disabled get a rudimentary education and are out on the streets at eighteen. Not surprisingly, more than a third end up in criminal gangs and in gaol. Their papers are marked with the initials of the institutions they've been in, and this makes them almost unemployable. And the Homes in and around Moscow are widely believed to be the *best* in the country by a long way. Horror stories circulate about deprivation and death rates in the provinces.

The statistics are reckoned in hundreds of thousands. Adoption by foreigners is a drop in the ocean – though even this can run into difficulties. The director of the Baby Home had fallen silent when I mentioned the high-profile arrivals of the actress Angelina Jolie and the German Chancellor Gerhard Schröder. Although they may well gain publicity in the West, Angelina with a little boy from Moscow, and the Chancellor with his new three-year-old from St Petersburg, it caused embarrassment. President Putin had intervened in the Schröder adoption process on a personal basis – but the Russian journalists who wanted to cover the story were firmly prevented from getting anywhere near the Children's Home. There was hardly any coverage in the local media, with one editor saying, 'We have a feeling that this is a story we should not touch.' No historically proud country wants to hear a German saying, 'There are loads of children who can be offered a better future than the one they have.'

What makes Russia stand out in today's Europe is not the number of foundlings and abandoned children but the attitude to them. Human Rights Watch recorded a letter from the mother of a Down's baby which appeared in 1993 in a leading Russian weekly magazine and was republished in a Moscow newspaper. The letter, entitled 'Why Coddle Such Freaks?', read: 'I am asking the doctor to put my child to sleep. I am told we have humaneness in our country. We have humaneness – so we let them live?' That feeling of resignation which sometimes pervades the country was expressed by one of the helpers at Downside Up: 'It's been one war after another in our country – and everything else. And so the feeling of grieving, of loss, is permanently there. And repressing the grief is a habit – so you can give up the child . . .'

On the platform of the railway station the children crept back to hang around the kiosks, joined by a little group just flushed out from the warmer environs of the Metro. At the approach of another cop, they fled again. He's the state, the man with the key to all those homes and asylums. The shivering children have been rounded up before and, having tasted the system, have no desire to go there again. The alternative is drink, drugs and sleeping rough. It's a measure of the state system that these children prefer street life.

19

What is your nationality?

Li Cunxin is a lucky man. He was born in China in 1961 as the country was reeling from Chairman Mao's Great Leap Forward – a policy which saw cannibalism and corpses by the roadside, as the forced collectivisation of agriculture delivered horrendous famine. Between thirty and forty million people died; Li's family just survived, but his childhood was one of extreme privation where the state meddled in the poorest peasant's life and protest was pointless. At least he wasn't a girl – which added to his chance of survival.

He's had an extraordinary life. He's now a stockbroker in Australia, having retired a few years ago from an outstanding career as a ballet dancer. He wrote a successful book describing his childhood in a commune near Qingdao on the north-east coast of China, from where he was unceremoniously plucked by Chairman Mao's wife to become a pupil at the Beijing Dance Academy. Madame Mao was rounding up ten-year-olds in the fervent belief that Chinese ballet was far too bourgeois and what it needed was more soldiers, workers and peasants in tights. Neither Li nor his family, nor anyone else in his dirt-poor village, had ever heard of ballet. Nevertheless, in 1971 Li was prodded and tweaked in his schoolroom by a bunch of officials and pronounced favourable material for the barre. After a tough teenage training under the eye of dour Communist teachers he eventually ended up with the Houston Ballet in Texas, having accomplished a heart-stopping defection involving one of the company's patrons, Barbara Bush, wife of the then Vice President George Bush Snr. He danced worldwide before joining the Australian Ballet.

When I met him at a festival in Perth in Western Australia he talked about his family, in which he was the sixth of seven sons. Such a brood is now almost unknown – about the most politically incorrect state of affairs a Chinese official could imagine. Li's mother and father belonged to the generation which was allowed to reproduce without the state snuffling round the bedrolls on the low brick stove, the *kang*, counting. At home there was never enough food – a boiled cabbage leaf represented a meal, clothes lasted until they dropped off and education was a diet of Chairman Mao's sayings. We talked about children in China, for his family would now be considered illegal under the country's One-Child Policy. However, his family was 'lucky' – seven *sons*. I asked him if his commune ever came across foundlings, but he wasn't familiar with the word. 'Abandoned children,' I explained.

'Oh, the dying hill children,' he said.

It was my turn to misunderstand, because I thought he was referring to a television documentary about neglect in Chinese orphanages made in 1995 by Channel 4. Called *The Dying Rooms*, it caused a huge stir.

'No, the dying hill,' he repeated. 'Every village in our area had one, of course. It's where the women went with the babies they couldn't feed or had something wrong with them. Girls, of course. We children didn't like to go there, because we heard there were ghosts . . .'

He spoke in a very matter-of-fact tone, and I realised that the kind of practices which still produce headlines in the West were a commonplace in his childhood.

The slightest familiarity with Chinese proverbs turns up a long and depressing list of sayings on the subject of daughters: 'Girls are maggots in the rice. . . . It is more profitable to raise geese than daughters. . . . A stupid son is better than a crafty daughter. . . .' And so on. There is nothing ironic or amusing in these proverbs, just the trudge of tradition down the ages as Chinese women have been ordered to be obedient to fathers, husbands and sons, and their daughters have been seen as 'outsiders' and of no use to their families after marriage, 'like spilled water'.

Compared to many other societies until modern times, China was not particularly different in seeing women as inferior and having fewer rights than men. The huge institutions in Europe in the seventeenth and eighteenth centuries attest to similar attitudes, though for somewhat different reasons – poverty and social disapproval of single mothers, rather than downright contempt for girl children. However, the preference for boy children is much more starkly emphasised in China. Folk tales and superstitions abound of the misfortune of having female children, with a common theme being the box of clean ashes placed beside the bed if the newly born was a baby girl – so that the baby's face might be pushed into the ashes and smothered.

Even in ordinary conversation today girls are still sometimes referred to as 'relatives' rather than 'family', and when I first went to China I was always curious about the different style of questions and answers in what I thought were internationally standard exchanges. Working as a reporter with a television crew I expected to introduce myself, only to be confronted with the enquiry: 'Who is your group leader?' This produced giggles from the crew and a mock argument about who wanted to be boss for the day.

'Where is your work unit from?' The reply: 'The BBC' seemed somewhat inappropriate, the concept of work unit being as far removed from the newsroom as you can get.

'How many beds you have?' I was floored by this one – I mean, why? It turned out to be a perfectly sensible method of working out what sort of dwelling you inhabited. Any Chinese worker or peasant curled up on the *kang* knows instantly exactly how many bedrolls can be fitted on to it and how many the family own – and does an instant calculation on the size of your house. Our questioners rolled their eyes in amazement as we paused and mentally trekked through our rooms at home, counting our beds – and informed our interpreter of the number, which produced the reply: 'They so rich they don't know how many beds they got!' They did not ask us about families.

When we came to ask *them* for some standard details, there was naturally the answer 'One' as to the number of children they had, only for the interpreter to add that this wasn't always true, especially with older people. It seemed that their reply was not intended to conceal an illegal second child, but merely signified the omission of the existence of a daughter. For many, the girls just don't count and aren't worth a mention unless you specifically ask. Nor is this attitude just the legacy of Chairman Mao's regime.

In 1909, the reign of the Imperial family in Beijing was coming to an end. The Empress Cixi, known as 'The Old Buddha', died – amid the usual creepy shenanigans which attended any transfer of power in the Forbidden City within the capital. She may have been poisoned – and she probably ordered the poisoning of the man who was to succeed her, Kuang Hsu, who died the day before. Three-year-old Pu Yi – 'The Last Emperor' – came to power. Intrigue and rebellion were in the air.

Over a thousand miles south, near the walled city of Chaozhou (formerly Chowwan) in Guangdong province, another domestic drama was taking place in a grand mansion of over two hundred rooms. The house belonged to a local warlord, who'd made his fortune in the opium trade and been able to afford Western materials – blue Italian tiles, Moorish floors, beautiful glass – alongside the traditional lacquer paintings on wood, curly roof-ends and ancestral shrine. There was room for more than a thousand people to live in the warren of courtyards and secret doors: one man was employed solely to shut the doors and close the windows. Many of the rooms could only be entered by a trapdoor – a device which suited the family arrangements of Chen Ci-hong, who had ten wives and concubines and between forty and fifty children. Hierarchy and status were a constant source of tension among the women, with the lower-ranking concubines very conscious that they and their children could be discarded – especially the daughters. There were still many traditions in this near-feudal society, where women of any consequence had tiny bound feet and there was a well-established practice of selling off girls as servants or as *tongyangxi* – little prospective 'daughters-in-law'. Into this scenario of instability and domestic intrigue Sim Koh-wei was born.

'My mother talked about her background in China off and on over the years – and parts of it registered, but it's all a little sketchy. Basically, she was from a good family – in fact she never failed to impress upon me that she came from this "well-known family of good standing". But almost immediately after she was born she got smallpox.'

The speaker is May Prosser, whose family history I first heard in the unlikely surroundings of the Worshipful Company of Tallow Chandlers in the City of London. May's husband is a Past-Master of the Company, and amid the glitter of silver on polished tables lit by tall candles she mentioned to me that her mother had started life as a foundling in China.

'She was put in a basket by the side of a river, close to a place where the Han Jiang meets the South China Sea. She was left to die, because she had smallpox. I've been back to the spot – it's very beautiful. She was seen by a man who was a farmer on his way to work at the start of the day. He did his day's work and on the way back he heard this baby whimpering. He hadn't the heart to leave it, so he picked up the basket and took it home. She always told me that they knew who had abandoned her – but no questions were raised. And, as I said, she was immensely proud that she "came of a very good family". But she had a very good relationship with her foster-father – she adored him, the apple of her eye. But she lost him when she was sixteen. She never learned to read. She never learned to write. She gave her family name as Sim – a common name in the region, but *sim pu-a* in the Hokkien dialect is used for abandoned girls. . . . However, she remembered that, as she grew up, her beauty prompted the neighbours to call her Eagle Eyes.'

Sim Koh-wei was growing up in the chaos that convulsed China after the end of the Manchu dynasty: warlords, assassination, battles and riots, with the nearby town of Swatow seeing opium burning and demonstrations against foreigners. But in this traditional society there would have been an emphasis on hard work and survival. 'She told me it got very cold in the winter and as a young girl she made quilted jackets. And she talked about living in a house in a courtyard, in a small town which had four walls and four gates – and a river, where she'd been left. Her foster-mother died when she was very young – and of course, both her parents had been illiterate and they never adopted her formally.'

The economy, though growing rapidly and modernising in the cities, was unpredictable, and ordinary workers toiled in dreadful conditions – abandoned, exhausted and dead children were a feature of reports from China's visitors. Life on the land would hardly have been easy. 'She was married when very young – and probably had very little choice – in her late teens, to a farmer or fisherman. She had a little daughter and continued working in the fields, with the child strapped to her back. But her husband died soon after and she found life a struggle as a widow with a small child. China was going through tremendous tumult – and she saw a lot of violence.'

By 1935 Japanese military incursions, local warlords, famine and flood all contributed to a wave of emigration, with half a million leaving. At the time, Chowwan was very much the centre of commerce with the rest of the world, especially Europe – and Swatow was an international entrepot. When Sim Koh-wei went to trade her farm goods there she discovered that thousands of women were heading for domestic service in South-east Asia, to become amahs or nannies. 'She decided to make a new life for herself. When she discovered there were shiploads of local people leaving for Singapore, she decided to go. Her husband's family refused to let her take her child, Poh-kim. She decided to go on her own, got on one of the boats which were absolutely bulging, overflowing . . . a lot of people didn't survive the journey – one thousand miles and at least ten days' sailing to Singapore.

'When she arrived, there was a man from her local village already there, a village elder in what they called a *kong-si* – a clan association based on an area back in China. She went to live in their *kampong* [village]; along with two female cousins who'd travelled with her.'

Singapore was a diverse city, a hub of the British Empire, which attracted all kinds of entrepreneurs from around the world. It was glamorous and stately amid tropical vegetation, and hummed with dozens of languages.

'My mother went out to work as a maid, then a housekeeper, and ended up as housekeeper in my father's house. He was a Sephardic Jew whose father had left Mesopotamia [modern Iraq] in the nineteenth century, when Jews were being persecuted in Baghdad. He took the silk route. My father was born in India, and he then moved on to Singapore. He was married and had two daughters when my mother met him, and he was the best part of twenty years older than her – she was in her twenties. The first wife was also Chinese and had converted to Judaism. She was very ill with polio and my mother went to look after the two girls – but she sadly died. So my mother went back to her Singapore *kampong* – and my father pursued her. But she refused to return to the house, believing that he wanted more than for her to look after the children. But the village elder, after he'd met him, advised her that he was a good man: "A successful businessman – he'll look after you. Otherwise the alternative is working in people's houses for the rest of your life.'

'She married him – and I was born in February 1938, the first of six children, five daughters and a son. My mother had spoken only Hokkien, but she eventually learned to speak Malay in which she later conversed with my father, and with us – but she occasionally broke out in Hokkien. *His* original language was Arabic, but he also spoke English, which the rest of us used at home, Hindustani and Hokkien. He called himself a broker and he was in the spice trade, like his father before him. He also dealt in property – and was quite successful.

'From the earliest photographs I have of her, she had on a *sam-fu* – a high-collared Chinese white top – with black trousers. Her hair's done up in a bun. But gradually she took the bun down and wore a *lapan*, a voluminous Middle Eastern long dress, with lace round the neck and fluffy sleeves – rather like a kaftan. Then she moved on to Western dress, skirts and so on, then trousers as an old lady. She made a huge cultural leap. And she rarely cooked Chinese – it was Sephardic Jewish food with a taste of Baghdad:

saffron cabbage, kebbah and vegetables stuffed with rice and mincemeat.

'We were evacuated to India during World War II, just before the Japanese invasion – my father being Jewish. We were very lucky to be in one of the last troop ships to leave Singapore, with bombs dropping round us. We zigzagged all the way to Bombay, according to one of my step-sisters – where my father had been born and where he still had strong connections. He was a wonderful man; he was so jolly, singing in many languages – such a zest for life.

'We returned after the war and my mother fitted into my father's environment – an Orthodox Jewish community. She had converted to Judaism, but she wasn't Orthodox. She'd put her Chinese past behind her and she really wanted to become Jewish – she wanted to belong. Even so, she wore her jade bangle along with her Star of David and held on to her Chinese superstitions, with a very firm belief in ghosts. After she converted, when she'd had all her family, they were married in the synagogue in 1965!

'She stayed in contact with her family in China for many years, because she got a letter eleven years after she arrived in Singapore saying that Poh-kim was dead. But she herself never saw China again.

'She always talked about her Chinese background, and I went to see her in Singapore just before she died and was buried in the Jewish cemetery there, next to her husband. After his death she'd gone to live in Dallas of all places, with some of my sisters, before returning to Singapore. I think she had unhappy memories of the country and she said to me, "It's a pity I never went to school and I would love to be more educated." However, she was able to communicate on a very deep level – and it was an accepted fact that girl babies were *never* welcome, especially sick girl babies. And this was more than half a century before Maoist One-Child Policy. But at least, being brought up as a peasant girl, she escaped bound feet.'

May Prosser, who married a British army officer and has had a well-travelled life herself, went to Guang Dong province a couple of years ago with her younger son. 'We found this massive great house with about two hundred rooms in it which had been built by this very rich businessman who would have been there about the time my mother was born – though it's surmise on our part. It's an old Tang Dynasty city and very beautiful, built about two thousand years ago. The houses go back a couple of hundred years and they're exactly as she described them – lots of little houses with courtyards in the old Chinese style. Three of the city walls have disintegrated, but, extraordinarily, one wall is still standing. And all four gates into the city are in that one wall – all different from each other – and they look out on to the river.

'We were taken there by a guide who arranged for us to meet some of the occupants. They gave us tea and asked about my mother's surname – Sim – and said it was very common in that part of the world.' In the midst of chatting, her son realised that May was speaking in Hokkien – a language she hadn't thought she'd ever learned. And her mother's experience as a foundling never once seemed to shake her pride in her original family: 'She just loved the idea that she came of that blood-line. She was very proud of coming from that family – whatever they'd done!'

To most people, the number of people who live in your country is a slightly vague statistic that occasionally gets discussed in terms of an ageing population in the West, or a youthful population in a developing nation. Occasionally, as in Libya for many years, the statistic doesn't exist, all enquiries being evaded by mutterings of 'state secret' or 'confidential defence intelligence information'. One look at the Libyan Ministry of Information's chaotic offices, with sand-dusted files wedging doors open, indicated an administrative system that really couldn't be bothered to find out how many people there were between the Mediterranean and the Sahara as long as the oil money paid for them to be fed and housed. As one official told me: 'Why collect numbers about births and deaths, when that number will change every day? What's the point?'

Not a view that would have found favour in China in the last sixty years. When in 1982 the Chinese finally used United Nations experts, five million canvassers and twenty-nine mammoth computers to find out how many people were living in the Republic, they got the unpalatable answer of more than a billion – almost twice the figure arrived at in 1953. What particularly disturbed the authorities was the enormous pool of women of marriageable age. All those fecund daughters, ready to deliver ever-more-hungry mouths. And since 1979, the state had been very publicly interfering with the most private actions of its citizens: courtesy of the state there had been campaigns, contraception, abortion, sterilisation, coercion and infanticide. There were reports of women fleeing their villages as the One-Child Policy teams approached. And it should be no surprise that baby girls were the chief casualties of that policy.

The results of a nationwide application of state meddling in conception are still causing headaches today: affluence and a more independent-minded citizenry make control more difficult and the government is still unable to hit the targets it has carefully projected for the future. The sex ratio is appallingly skewed, with the latest assessment showing that for every 100 girls born there are 117 boys – and in rural areas, the ratio may be 100: 130. This compares to a world average of 105 boys for every 100 girls. In China, this sex ratio doesn't make girls more special. Instead, it has raised the spectre of an 'army of bachelors' or 'bare branches', willing and perhaps determined to acquire a wife at any cost – literally: selling daughters as wives has reared its head again, along with kidnapping.

The policy is quite complex in its consequences, for daughters are still valued and wanted; the One-Child Policy is increasingly flouted – particularly in rural areas – and a girl baby is for many a complement to the 'little emperor'. However, the historical preferences, coupled with the fact that sons carry on the family name, tend to inherit property and are thought more 'useful' in heavy farm work, are still in play. And most recently, worries about the future have made parents nervous about who will look after them in their old age: like many other societies, China is ageing, and boys earn more than girls – therefore . . .

. . . therefore, the orphanages are full of girl babies, nearly all of them abandoned new-borns. A considerable proportion are handicapped in some way, again the consequence of traditional prejudice, coupled with the modern state's exhortation: 'Fewer but *better* children.' Not that many foreigners get to see them. Since the *Dying Rooms* documentary there's been a great reluctance to have these institutions open to public view – the locals themselves are often unaware of the building's purpose. Even where conditions are good, a sense of pride also affects the desire of the Chinese to parade the fact that adoption by foreigners is something which solves a problem they can't seem to prevent.

In 1992 the law was changed to allow legalised international adoption. Since then, tens of thousands of hopeful foreign parents have gone through an orderly legal process which results in them taking a Chinese foundling home.

Gina Birch is a video director in the independent music business, a very energetic, lively woman who used to sing in an all-girl band called the Raincoats. She and her husband Mike, a New Zealander, have made the trip to China twice. The results are scattered around her living room, a colourful riot of toys and pictures, photographs and drawings.

'My best friend is adopted, and I'd had numerous fertility issues and she suggested adoption. I thought, "What a ridiculous idea!" Time went on, and I met another friend who was a Buddhist, and she said adopting was like having a partner. The closest relationship you have in your life is not necessarily a blood relationship, it's something else – it's like two souls spending their life together, and adoption is like a soul who's meant to spend their life with you. To me that makes a lot of sense – it suited me, and I still think so.

'Options in the UK are limited – and a long haul. Then I met Thereza Finzi, [the cellist] Jacqueline du Pré's niece, and she'd adopted a little boy from China – and it was very inspiring. I looked into adopting from other countries as well – Guatemala, for example. But after I'd met lots of people who'd adopted, the common thread of those who'd been to China was they talked very positively about it – though perhaps they hid the negative . . . but going through the process, you're so fed up with the negatives you want to emphasise the positive. I mean, our first meeting with social workers in this country was full of questions such as "How would you feel if both parents were schizophrenics? If they had Aids?" And you sink lower and lower in your chair and think, "I just want to nurture some little person and . . . er, yes, I suppose if I *had* to deal with . . .

'So, with China, ignorance is bliss. You don't know any of the genetic history of these children.'

Even during the first steps in the process Gina found some resistance, with a lot of to-ing and fro-ing between both British and Chinese bureaucracy, and social workers who had been trained here in the ethos that trans-racial adoption is a taboo. However, she persisted and finally got together with a very helpful social worker, though two years would pass before she finally achieved her desire. She started to learn Mandarin and began the Home Study process by Social Services, which took about four months.

'It's thought-provoking – whether it's necessary or not . . . you kind of have to write your autobiography, you know: "How did your parents make you feel about your body?" and "Do you ever intend to let your child see you naked?" It's interesting. I felt it's reasonably good preparation, full of self-reflection, though a lot of good stuff wasn't included . . . and I went on two weekend courses for people who wanted to adopt abroad. There were two of us who wanted to adopt from China. Then your paperwork, police checks, marriage certificate, passport, income, it all goes to the Department of Health and they take six to eight months to rubber-stamp it (though they've speeded it up a bit since). *Then* the paperwork goes to China – *then* that takes at least a year, perhaps fourteen months.

'When you're being assessed you write a letter, specifying an age range, boy or girl – but there are not many boys. I think you assume you get a girl. Some people say twins – and quite often they get them. The first time you do it you just can't bear the wait – it's just totally too long. You're desperate.

'Then one Saturday morning the doorbell rang and this big document arrived, registered post, and all the information was in Chinese. I phoned my best friend Petra to come – who's adopted – and we opened it and looked at this photograph: this sad little face, this baby. There were three photographs. She just looked so sad. And we ran out that minute to try and find someone to translate – and eventually I faxed it to my Chinese teacher. And unfortunately he translated and romanticised it completely – that she was "found by a little school – and her eyes began to sparkle like the stars blah-blah-blah" – completely embellished, I found out later. . . . In reality, it said she was found at two days old and was very sick, and then she went to the hospital. It's very hard, because part of you wants to take on the fiction, and it became my reality for a little while. . . . I was a bit disappointed when I found it wasn't true . . .

'From that point on, it was terrifying. I was both absolutely excited and absolutely scared. We set off for China – I'd never been before – flying to Beijing, then to Changsha, the capital of Hunan province. On the way we met another family – Christina, a single mum who was with her mother and already had a four-year-old. We booked into our hotel and the next morning we met to go to the official's office. And I was standing in reception frozen with fear. Christina, who'd done it before, was incredibly nice and when I said I was really terrified she didn't say, "Oh, don't worry. It'll be all right." Instead she said, "You will be, you will be!"

'It's incredibly tricky. You have a guide and he's a bit disconnected – perhaps a student who's translating. He's just doing a job. And there's an official line – they've also got a long list of things they've got to tick off. What they're *not* saying is, "What a marvellous person you are for taking one of our poor . . ." and so on. There's a kind of . . . blankness in a way.

'We got to the office – it's freezing cold, December 2000 – and we were led into a spartan building. There was so much building going on. . . . And Christina and Mike and I are left in a room and the officials rush off. So what do we do? Take a photograph? And we're freezing and we're scared and then: "This is the wrong room." So we rush to another. And then suddenly there's this woman with a little baby. And it's *Christine's* baby – and she's whisked off and I'm taken to this table to do my promises. You write a letter to the Chinese authorities saying you have respect for their culture and how much you want to adopt from their country. Then you make a lot of promises to love and to educate, and about their inheritance, and that you'll treat her as you would your birth-child. Fortunately you're writing this in English! And I hear Mike's name being called out and I'm thinking all the time, "Will I love this child? How will I love this little soul I plan to meet?" And I look round and I *see* her . . . and I go YES, I can love this child! And she had these little pink cheeks and she was so gorgeous . . . and she had no lips – she was biting them! All wrapped in this padded suit thing – and I knew it would be all right. She was eight and a half months – just a little thing. She never had any birth-mum time – she was abandoned immediately and she didn't like being touched by the carers very much. Some of the carers used to sleep with the babies and cuddle them, but they said she didn't like that very much.

'She was handed to Mike because I was still writing my promises. The carer was talking about her – but did I get much information? Just "She likes bright colours. Ooh . . . she likes warm milk. . . ." It's just so disappointing. In the original letter she'd been given the name Jiang Yong – Yong is an old word meaning a eulogy to a famous person or something like that, and Jiang is river. Basically she was found in a little village called Ma Tou – "Horsehead Village", in Wushi town. You really don't find out much more when you go to China. The carer, the director of the welfare institute – they don't really know much more either, I think. One of the officials said that the woman who had brought her was sobbing in the corridor. I didn't sense a great deal of closeness between them but I could never. . . . To this day I don't know whether she was sad to lose Honey or whether she was crying for her own self – if she'd perhaps been brought up in the orphanage and was wanting the freedom and opportunity that

Honey was about to get. I do know that sometimes – particularly in a village – the carers know whose baby this is . . . .

'You notice that batches of children seem to have the same birthday! You wonder. . . . Since the *Dying Rooms* TV programme they've become rather defensive – but through the door into the next room I saw a whole host of Americans with a whole number of babies – *they* do it in large numbers!'

Four days of formalities followed. The Chinese are meticulous about the paperwork, especially authorisation. However Jiang Yong was now with them, staying at the hotel. 'We spent the night with her at the hotel. Fantastic. A marvellous time. Two full years from when we started! We called her Honey – I'd been thinking about it for *two years*.'

After a roller-coaster of emotion and bringing Honey home, Gina and Mike might have left it at that, but. . . . 'Well, basically, I thought I wouldn't do it again. Honey was so brilliant. Then one day . . . if we don't start the ball rolling . . . so we started again. And from that day it was like being pregnant. And the funny thing was the second time, what I was really scared about was that she'd be unappealing. It sounds really heartless, doesn't it? Even my mother said, "You'll never get another one like Honey!" And this picture arrived of a little baby with a great big lump on her head, which migrated in the other photographs – so I was worried.

This time it was a different province – and the city of Hubei. 'And this time, Lei Lei was brought to us. We did two days of paperwork for the adoption, and she stayed with us that night. They'd sent me another picture previously – and the bump had gone. But they didn't tell me much about her. They just said she was a sweet and lovely little girl, that she yelled very loudly before falling asleep and they all loved her very much. Then I found out she had been abandoned at about four or five weeks old, found on a doorstep: "A certain number of a certain street and a man found her and took her to his friend, and his friend's wife, before they took her to the institute at Daye."

I wanted to go there – but they said, "No – too far." But this time we insisted on going to the welfare institute itself, not just the office. We drove over very bumpy roads for two hours and no one could find it. Our guide must have asked about thirty people – it was extraordinary how no one knew where it was. So we got there late, with a barrage of officials standing outside this new building (basically, all the 'donations' – voluntary, and 3000 dollars – that are made have to be spent on building, so you're always seeing these new ones), saying, "You're late, and you can take photographs here but nowhere else. So line everyone up, bring the baby, here's the director." And we're marched into the place and we go into this room and there are nine new-born babies in it, all swaddled up to the neck – and it's hot, it's May. Some awake, some asleep, some ill, and there's a carer holding one. And we look at all these babies, and think what's going to become of them . . . and Honey's looking at them with me. Then we go into an empty room, are shown the bed "where Lei Lei slept", and then we're marched off to a restaurant. But there's no more information.'

Lei Lei means Little Bud – Gina's grandmother was called Rose – and she hasn't got an English name. Nor is she old enough to start asking questions, unlike Honey. 'I haven't yet told Honey that she was left somewhere, or found. As far as she knows she was born in another lady's tummy, who was unable to look after her, and then she was looked after by lovely people in a place with lots of other babies.

'But she goes to a church school and she's already heard stories of Moses being found in a basket, and then there's *The Jungle Book* – so she's already heard stories of babies being found and reared by different people. And there are always enough negative aspects – all the girls in school going, "Why doesn't your mummy look like you – you're Chinese, aren't you?" And all the "Where's your *real* mummy . . . ?" We are obsessed with blood-lines, aren't we? I just want to sow seeds for her to feel and think positively about it.

'I tell them everything I can now. I keep everything I can – all the pictures, the videos, the documents, and a slip of paper for Lei Lei on which was written her birth-date. It's very fragile.

'They're very much in a community here of children with similar backgrounds – it's vital they have a support group around them. I can't change what happened to them, put a sticking plaster on it. All I can tell Honey is what I know, and I'm not going to tell her anything I don't know. I shall tell her a man told us a beautiful story and that I would like to believe little bits of it – but I don't know if it's true. And for all the things we don't know about her birth mother, we can paint a picture for ourselves – if we want to.

'And we will go and stand in Ma Tao village in Wushi town some time. We shall go on a detective trail. I would love somebody to go and find out more about them – but it's not easy in China. In some ways, I wish she'd been born in my tummy – but if she had, she and Lei Lei wouldn't be the gorgeous, fantastic girls they are.'

The contrast couldn't be greater for these children: a warm home, full of toys, with loving parents. And, eventually, knowledge of the sheer determination and hard work that went into two years' waiting by their parents.

The lack of information about the foundlings does not daunt prospective parents, nor the possibility that the first months of life are often spent in less than ideal surroundings. Twins Victoria and Elizabeth spread their 'baby clothes' on the floor: two tiny outfits of poor quality consisting of thin, faded trousers with a slit in the crutch, a skimpy jacket, and some rough unappetising grey nappies complete with large elastic band to hold them up. They've left off helping their mother bake cakes, and are heading for a session in front of the television watching their favourite video. Their younger sister Alexandra trots behind, all of them returning to hear what their parents are going to talk about, clambering joyfully over everyone and clearly adoring their parents, Karen, who's from New Zealand, and John Turland, who lectures at Cambridge.

The Turlands went through the same steps as Gina and Mike Birch. Again, they didn't find the atmosphere very encouraging and their Home Study took a year to complete. In the background to the very personal desire to adopt in China are the political shadows, and the fact that China never wishes to 'lose face'. Each time there is something in the West which offends – a TV programme, a newspaper article – the government becomes hyper-sensitive. But every so often the official system suddenly hiccups and a small gap appears in the official hedge, as Mike explains.

'Our situation was slightly odd – we'd been approved to adopt one child or twins and our papers were out in China. It's very stressful and takes months. Suddenly we got a phone call saying, "Is it true you've got approval to adopt twins? Well, we've heard about twins in an orphanage in Guilin." This was a call from a Canadian woman who already had adopted Chinese children and who was on holiday in the south of China with her family. She'd managed to blag her way into the orphanage, and when the policeman arrived to ask questions she said she was a teacher. He said, "OK, you can stay and talk to the officials – but you may not see the children.' Then the orphanage deputy director arrived and said, "Would you like to see the children?" She said Yes, and for no particular reason she asked, "Do you have twins?" And the director said, "As it happens, yes – in this room," and pointed to the mats on the floor. There were Victoria and Elizabeth lying on the floor, and Victoria was very poorly. When this woman went back to Canada she was very worried and made it her business to try and find someone very quickly who could adopt them.

'Now we're the only people we know who've done it this way round, because basically the Chinese officials usually – understandably – want to do the nomination. So *we* then nominated these children, and we did have a few lucky breaks. Normally the officials take you on a tour, with nice places to visit, but these Canadians wrote to officials and through their contacts we were assisted.

'We rang the people in Beijing – and they'd say, "Ring tomorrow."'

'You rang the next day,' interjects Karen, 'and they banged the phone down!'

'But eventually it all went through and we got the approval,' John sums up.

Having listened intently to the story so far, Victoria has rushed off to get the big red album with the photographs which were sent from Canada, showing the blue metal cots up against the wall and the mats on the floor – and the twins aged about three or four months. The Turlands set off for China in 1996 and stayed in a hotel in the provincial capital, Nanning, because the formal adoption process takes place there. There are the snaps in the album pointed out excitedly by the twins, showing the room, the guide, and the vice-president of the orphanage who'd made the ten-hour rail journey from Guilin. Then one with two women carrying the eight-month-old twins; one of the women had been the twins' foster-mother. (Pointing and squeals of 'Me . . . me!' from the girls.)

'This was the moment we saw them,' says Karen, 'with a little money tucked into one of the twins' socks!'

'It's a dramatic moment,' says John. 'You can't really believe what's happening.'

Karen adds, 'You try not to have too great expectations of anything – in fact, I felt very guilty taking the baby from the foster-mother . . . .'

'Victoria and Elizabeth . . .' says John, trying to hang on to the picture of that moment as the girls want to leaf on eagerly through their history, 'we knew that they'd been left at the Women and Children's Hospital in Guilin and then taken to the orphanage. And that's it. Sometimes, apparently, there are papers . . . and quite often a note that's been pinned to the child has also been kept – but it's kept in the files . . . you don't see them.'

'I think they're pretty reluctant to give you much information. They're very guarded,' adds Karen. 'I mean, we were warned that we mustn't necessarily believe everything we're told.'

John goes back to the photographs: 'Victoria was very poorly. There were a lot of small charities helping in this area and one of them had sent money for Victoria to go to hospital (which we later repaid), and apparently she wasn't doing very well. They had the idea that she was missing her twin – so Elizabeth joined her and she improved.

'You don't get to the orphanages. They're nervous after the big impact of the *Dying Rooms* TV programme – and they're afraid of cam-corders. We heard the Chinese government said that if it was shown again in Britain they would stop all adoptions.

'Guilin's in southern China, near the border with Vietnam. The orphanage director said, "May your children grow as beautiful as the mountains of Guilin," though I think that was a line that he'd used before – it sounded as if he'd been working on it for a few years! One young chap asked us, "What will you do if the children are naughty – will you beat them?" And we said, "No, no!"

'It was a very friendly atmosphere – you're signing forms, and there's a roll of toilet paper on the table and you wonder why. Then you realise the children have to sign the forms as well, and there's a large pad and the children ink their foot and sign with their footprint. . . . We went back to Guilin to get the passports and saw the city. In the hotel, the staff gathered round the children and couldn't grasp why all these white people were with Chinese children. When we explained, they all took photographs. We then went on a boat trip down the River Li – and were learning to know the children.'

'With hardly any information from the officials, it's a journey of exploration with the children,' says Karen. 'When you first meet the officials they're supposed to tell you what they've been eating, but of course all they get is milk powder with lots of sugar in it, and so you try to wean them off this as quickly as possibly. And I remember a lady on the boat offering them a banana – and they'd never had solids. So we just then fed them with all the wonderful food on the cruise – noodles and everything! There wasn't a nappy to buy anywhere, though!'

Then they managed to get to the places where the twins had first turned up – the hospital and the orphanage in Guilin – but were not actually allowed in. 'The director was a Party creature and he was interested in getting a little more money; but generally everything was very above board in China. However, our guide went in to look at the children in the orphanage (he said he was preparing a report on other children) and we got some snaps. And when we showed them to the Canadian lady she said, "Yes, this is the room I saw them in originally."

'We did a lot of travelling around with the babies. The guide was amazed, but we thought it a once-in-a-lifetime chance, carrying the children everywhere. Victoria, because she'd been so ill, hardly slept . . . they were both, though, beautiful, easy, gorgeous. . . . She had probably suffered from malnutrition because in the orphanages, because of the number of babies all gathered there, the staff up-end the feeding-bottles with the teat (which they've cut the end off) against the corner of the mouth – and that's it. Leave the baby with it propped there, and then on to the next one. They also put rice in with the milk and sugar, which in itself is dangerous. If the bottle slips, then the baby gets nothing. . . . And we almost lost Victoria – it's a pure consequence of the *number* of babies. But what we *do* know now from others is the moment they're adopted, they blossom and flourish very quickly.'

Nine-year-old Victoria is busy with the carrier bag of orphanage clothing, carefully folding the thin little garments with all the expertise of a Benetton veteran.

In 2000, the Turlands returned to collect their third daughter. This time, an actual Foundling Certificate was supplied:

This is to certify that female Mei Fang, born on April 8 1999, was found by Wu Ming, who is a resident of the precinct of Shangyunqiao, local police station of You county, at the gate of villager committee of Naiguqiao Cun and Shangyunqiao Town, You county on April 10 1999. Then she was transferred to our centre by Shangyunqiao local police station of You county on April 10 1999. After she was taken care of by our centre, we have made the notification for seeking her bio-parents in the newspapers for two months, but hadn't any information about her bio-parents, so Mei Fang is a Foundling. Signed You County Welfare Centre.

A red seal is attached.

'We had asked if we could have another child from the same region and Alexandra (Mei Mei) is from Changsha in Hunan province, where Chairman Mao came from. On the plane back, a Chinese man asked where she was from and wiggled his finger to his temple. I thought "stupid" or something? He said, "No, no – streetwise people!"'

'Our guide was the same one as before. Alexandra comes from an orphanage called You Xian, and it's one of quite a lot of these orphanages which is new and smart because the fees from foreign adopters go to the building rather than to the staff or care. She was called Mei Fang which means Fragrant Plum, and we called her Alexandra.'

The Turlands were also given more official bits of paper about her, which may or may not have been compiled with good impressions in mind. Her personality is 'open and active, she likes music, she likes to play with other children', and there's a whole list of meals she's been given: 'Breakfast: steam egg, apple, banana and biscuit; afternoon: milk, vitamin, cod liver oil and calcium tablet . . .' and a list of precise 'sleep times'. Believe this if you will, say the Turlands.

Back in Cambridge, the children have had some Chinese lessons – and a certain look passes over their faces when I mention this. They lasted about two years. However, they're extraordinarily articulate in English. Their parents watch their development with both pride and amazement, knowing their start in life. They look at them and wonder: does Alexandra belong to the Han Chinese majority? The officials said so, but it's an area of a lot of minorities. Are the twins identical? They were told they were, but Karen says 'every part of their bodies are, but if you put them together they look different! So we're not too sure.' None of this matters a jot – it's just a curiosity – and the future matters much more than the past. They may make a return trip but not while the girls are so young – however, they can't put it off too long, because the buildings which relate to their past may well be bulldozed soon, so great is China's pace of development. And the girls are asking questions.

'Elizabeth said two years ago, when she was seven, "Where were we born?" And we said, "We don't know if you were born at the Children's Hospital and then left – or if you were born somewhere else, and then somebody put you there to make sure you were safe, and then someone would find you and take you to a police station and then the orphanage." She said, "Why don't you find out?" We said, "Well, it's a bit difficult, really." And she said, "Why? Why is it difficult? If we were born there, then they would *know* – somebody must have seen us." And so we said, "Well, we'll see what we can do."

'And you know, you think you're always prepared for every eventuality, you think you know the answers. . . . So we said, "We don't know – but we're very lucky, aren't we? We're an international family – England, New Zealand and two girls who are Chinese – and so we're very lucky." And she said, "I don't know." I asked her, "What do you mean, you don't know?" And she said, "I don't know if we're lucky." I said, "Well, we're very happy and we love each other" and she said, "Yes, we do, Mummy. I don't know if I might have been happier in China. How do I know that?"

'For a seven-year-old . . . so I think that's why she wants to know as much as possible . . .' She turns to Elizabeth. 'Don't you, darling?'

She nods and the three of them tear off to play, hugely happy and endlessly running to their parents and laughing and asking questions.

The export of children is an ancient business: those who are 'surplus', 'unwanted' and plain 'destitute' have historically been seen as property that can be disposed of. Not always in a cynical manner, though, for many schemes involving emigration have been started with the good intention of giving children the chance of a better life. Today, adoption has taken the place of enforced migration and 'peopling the colonies' or 'new territories and frontier land'.

International adoption is big business. With all the rules in place, however distasteful the notion of financial involvement may be, countries should be able to alleviate the plight of unwanted babies by giving them a chance of a better future in another land if their own will not or cannot cope. Will not – because in many instances the children who are made available are often those who are shunned by society: the disabled in Russia, the Roma in eastern Europe and girls in China. Cannot – because of poverty: Guatemala and Brazil, for example. The countervailing view is that Western societies are using what they perceive to be anti-racist and benevolent theories to fill the void left by the dwindling supply of poor children in their own countries and 'rescue children from a miserable future'.

There are rules a-plenty these days, with governments embarrassed by the arrival of foreigners who highlight the national shortcomings and all kinds of bureaucratic hurdles in place in an attempt to ensure proper transactions. There's also a much greater understanding of the psychological factors involved, and a steady increase in the recognition of the rights of the child. However, where there's a demand that isn't met immediately, there will always be someone ready to supply. Baby-trafficking is big business, especially as citizens of the richer West can afford to search and find. And the tougher the rules become, the more the trade is driven underground.

Where it is above board the numbers are now in tens of thousands a year, with some countries remarkably efficient at the process. Over the last fifty years Korea has sent more than 150,000 children overseas for adoption, mainly in the United States. It began with the children of American GIs in the Korean War in 1950 and was encouraged by the activities of Christian fundamentalist organisations who wanted to 'rescue the seed from the East'. The South Korean government weighed in a decade later with a highly effective set of laws and speedy procedures which created a very efficient adoption industry. This then became the export vehicle for Korea's unwanted children, created by the upheaval of industrialisation and urbanisation and officially declared 'foundlings' by President Park Chung Hee. Korea holds the record for supplying for international adoption more children than any other country in the last half-century, with around two thousand a year still leaving, most for the United States. However, since the mid-nineties America has been adopting more children from China. And in Britain, there are now numerous Chinese adopted children – some of them forming unique families.

Peter Lighte works for an international bank and has a background in Chinese academia. His two daughters, Hattie and Tillie, were celebrating Christmas in London in front of a beautifully deco-rated tree and a roaring fire. However, they were painstakingly doing a little homework, egged on by Peter and his partner, Julian Grant, who's a composer and teacher.

'I always knew that I had to be a father, one way or the other, and Julian thought that he had to deal with that issue, because of dancing on one side of the ballroom. When we moved to Hong Kong in 1996 we were invited to a party by an old classmate of mine from university, and it turned out they were all old pals of mine from Princeton and Beijing. And there were two straight couples who had adopted children, and I was very happy for them and wistful at the same time, because I thought – if only I could do this. And they said; "You can." So it started immediately, and got me by the throat. And Julian – he was shell-shocked.'

Julian laughs and admits that they had to sit down and have a discussion about being prospective parents: 'Yes, and it had not crossed my mind for one second. But I realised it was something Peter wanted to do so very badly that I felt he would be perpetually dissatisfied with life if he never attempted it. So I think without taking into account the emotional ramifications of what it would all mean, I kind of said Yes without the emotional thunderbolt hitting.'

I wondered why they had chosen China, then looked around their wonderfully furnished living room, full of strange and elegant Chinese and Far Eastern objects.

'I read Chinese at university and I taught Chinese cultural history for five years and I have a natural affinity with that,' Peter responds. 'And as a Jewish kid growing up in New York, I had Chinese food every Sunday . . . so it seemed perfectly natural, and we were in Hong Kong at the time, and it seemed like *this* had to be.

'I don't think there's an easy path to it for anybody. What I understood quickly was that, in the eyes of American law, one could only adopt as a single parent, because unmarried people at that time – of either persuasion – could not adopt jointly. So there was no use in raising a red herring at that point in time, because I was not interested in making a political statement. I wanted a kid. So we decided it would be done that way. And there's a Confucian notion of the "rectification of names" – the idea of words having certain meaning. And if you're adopting as a single parent that means you're adopting as single parent, and what that means dictates procedures that flow from that classification.

'The most important thing is that one finds a bona fide agency that is empowered by the United States government to do a Home Study. There was one in Hong Kong that I was able to use and it had been recommended, and I thought they were these great experts in what I wanted to do, and subsequently we became friendly with them and they told me that I was only the second adoption they'd ever done, and they said that because I was the only single parent they'd ever done they'd learned a tremendous amount!

'It took fourteen months, and also about eight months into the process there was a glitch – the handover of Hong Kong in 1997. Suddenly there was a letter in the post from the agency saying there would be an unspecified delay, and we can't tell you how long it would take. I knew at that moment that there was a serious problem, and that if we did not adopt a child at that time it was not going to happen. So one had to be "resourceful" to deal with this situation.

'A fax came to my office with the baby's picture! I had a business meeting that day – this came right before lunch. And suddenly my baby gets Xeroxed to me – our child is there! And I had to go to this business lunch – people I knew pretty well – in a wonderful restaurant in Exchange Square, and I got there, and no one was there, and I was sitting there and they all arrived looking very "corporate" and I said, "Boys, forget it. This is the deal!" So we actually got pretty drunk on champagne because nobody knew about it, and they were quite shocked and surprised – and very happy.

'At that time she was about eighteen months old. We called her Hattie, short for Harriet. I also gave her a Chinese name, Xiao Qu, which means Little Song, and Qu can also mean "indirect" because I figured she came to us indirectly. She's from Hang Zhou, which is legendary for its beautiful women in Chinese history – concubines used to come from there, because of the beauty of the women. Originally, when I was interviewed by the agency, they said, "Do you have a preference?" I had originally requested a child from Yunnan which is in the south-west, where there are all the minorities. I wrote my thesis on Yunnan, so I had an affinity for that place. But because it was a minority area at that time there were no children available, because there were no orphans in minority areas – children were taken care of. And when we visited Yunnan and went to an orphanage it was wonderful and jolly and it was *not* open for business – also there is no One-Child Policy in the minority areas.'

'I saw the fax as well,' adds Julian. 'It was a very smudged fax and we didn't get the colour photograph until later. I remember thinking: "It's a picture of a child . . ." and it didn't mean anything, in a funny kind of way. My thunderbolt came a little later.'

Peter picks up the story again. 'I went to China on my own because I wanted no potential problems, and I took a cousin, a cool six-foot-one grandmother. I needed someone very unemotional, because my hormones were raging. We went to Hang Zhou – we went as appointed to the Ministry, across the street from the hotel, walked in . . . and we weren't supposed to meet Hattie that day . . . and walked into this room. It was a very Stalinist kind of building – cement thing, huge sofas, all this kind of stuff. And suddenly my cousin poked me and said, "She's over there" and this tiny, *tiny* child with a very runny nose was sitting there in this yellow and white stripy thing and I was immediately whisked off to do all this paperwork, and my cousin was left. And she was very good – she didn't go too close. And the romance began.

'The only thing we found out about her – inadvertently and I think it was because I read the file – was that she had not found her way into the system until she was seven months old. And that was it. We know absolutely nothing. This wasn't even told to me. Because we did this after the *Dying Rooms* programme and people were kept away from the orphanages.

'I had to write a little essay about looking after her, but it was very jolly, with loads of people around, and it was all very proper, and I was able to pick her up and took her out on to the balcony. She'd come from a rural place and she became immediately fascinated with the trucks and the cars and was quite excited. And then we were allowed to take her away.

'But there was an ensuing drama, because there was a fight at that time between two ministries – Justice and Civil Affairs – as to who had jurisdiction over these children. And the Ministry of Justice lost out in Beijing, so it took a while for the decision to be enforced in the provinces. And the provincial Justice officials made it very tough for the rest of the week. It was the documentation – there was a threat that we'd have to wait a good long while.

'What was at issue was they needed to know that I was single, and they said, "You need to go and get these documents 'notarised'." And I said, "What do you have in mind?" They replied, "Just go to the British government in Hong Kong and get them to say that you've never been married." I was then really naughty and said, very conspiratorially, "You know, the one thing we can really all agree on is that we really hate the British – so you're not going to send me to *them*?" So then I realised that they had my tax form, which said that I'm single on it. And I said, "Would you dare to lie to the tax authorities? I certainly wouldn't." And they said, "OK, if you can get this notarised by the American consulate in Shanghai . . . ."

'And a friend of mine was working in the US consulate in Canton and he knew what I was doing and I called him up, and he said, "Just fax it to me and I'll stamp it." It came back immediately and one of the dragons there (who are actually really rather appealing!) was very impressed: "Fabulous," she said, "you must really be very well connected! Make sure you bring the original back when you come to pick up the rest of the documentation." And it arrived by express post, and when I went to get the final documentation and sort out the passport I thought they didn't ask for the original, so I didn't give it to them. And when I got back to the hotel the woman was waiting in the lobby, and she said, "OK, where's the original?" and I said, "Here."

'They're so meticulous. I think they're torn. On the one hand, they're really ashamed of having to do this. On the other, they think it accounts for a great amount of goodwill. Just think of all those people in America who are pro-China now, just because China gives away its babies. You have a cadre of American people now who have more to say of value about the Chinese people than the Chinese people do about themselves!'

Julian: 'I came to Guangzhou and the hotel room door opened and there was Peter and his cousin with this little tiny baby. And at this point he'd asked his cousin, "Does she walk?" And she said, "Put her down." And she ran away! They knew *nothing* about her.'

Peter: 'But you know, however it comes to you, that's the deal.'

Julian: 'I really didn't know how to hold a child, and I was a complete novice. I took her off to the bird market in Guangzhou, which was completely noisy and probably the filthiest place on the planet – and I thought, if she touches something she's going to get something horrendous. And she just beamed and smiled. And *then* I dropped her on her head in the hotel lobby . . . .'

Peter: 'Both of us are only children, and Julian didn't mind and I did. So we were thinking it would be nice to have a sibling for the kid. And several months after Hattie came we were throwing out documents and I came across the original permission granted by the American government to adopt, and I noticed that it had a few weeks until it expired – so it was still valid. And I said, "Hey, Julian, let's put on a show! Wouldn't it be nice if we didn't have to go so intensively through things again – you know, police checks and fingerprints and all those things?" So I called someone at the US consulate in Hong Kong and they said, "Sure. Fine. Just get the agency to send us a message saying you had always intended to adopt a second child." And they did the business and we went again, and this time Julian came along in our group of friends.

'We asked for Hangzhou again, and they said there was no child available, so we said, "Let's go for a northern lass this time." An area I felt more comfortable with – I'd studied in the north and I speak Mandarin. So to Luoyang in Henan province, way up on the Yellow River, the heartland of China. So, one child from the Yellow, one from the Yangtse, River. This time it was easier. The local jurisdiction were lovely. They took us out to supper with their great dumpling chef, and they put on a show for us – "the smallest dumplings in China". It was a scream.

'Our second daughter is called Tillie – short for Ottilie – and we gave her a Chinese name, Xiao Ti, which means Little Beauty, and it is also made up of the character for "woman" and the verb "to be" – so it seemed a very strong name, and God knows we weren't disappointed! It was interesting. Hattie was tiny when we got her. Tillie was enormously pudgy at fourteen months when we got her, and she was sunny from the moment we saw her. But because she was so sunny she was fed a lot, and never taken out of her cot. So we went on to discover that she seemed to have developmental problems – and her muscles had never developed. She couldn't walk! She couldn't even crawl at fourteen months! It seems like she'd never been moved.'

Julian: 'She couldn't even sit up.'

Peter: 'We had to put pillows around her – so we faced all that when we got back to Hong Kong. I don't think we were apprehensive – we didn't think like that. It was all very present: "The kid's here, we have to get on with this."

At this, two perfectly normal-shaped girls whiz in and out of the room, avoiding the argument about going to bed.

Julian: 'I think we had known enough about how the Chinese system worked, and we had already had Hattie – a profoundly malnourished child. Some people did say, "Oh, well, the skills are so absent, do you think there's a neurological problem?" But when we got to Hong Kong, we took her to the Mathilda Child Development Centre, who prescribed some exercises. And over time, it became clear that her absent skills only needed to be taught.'

Peter: 'The doctor said it was the first time he'd ever thought it would be a good thing if a kid who came out of China *lost* weight.

What we did learn very quickly was that if you throw 'em around and hug 'em and kiss 'em, they just take off like rockets. We knew nothing, absolutely nothing about Tillie.'

Julian: 'There are newspaper adverts placed about them . . . .'

Peter: 'But it's nonsense, because they don't know anything about the child – it's a tick in the box.'

I asked if the girls spoke Chinese, because they'd been chattering to us without any trace of a Chinese word, and Peter speaks Mandarin.

'When Hattie first came I spoke to her only in Mandarin. And she learned English and answered me in English, and clearly understood what I was saying, but she just didn't want to speak Chinese. And in the Montessori we signed her up for a Mandarin module, and when the class met the teacher asked Xiao Qu to identify herself, and she put up her hand and said, "Only my papa can call me that. I do not want to speak Chinese." And after that, I never spoke to her in Chinese. When Tillie came, the last thing we wanted to do was to drive a linguistic wedge between the two sisters. Who knows, maybe some day they might want to learn. It's their shout, though.'

There's quite a lot of noise coming from upstairs as bed is being avoided, and another energised appearance downstairs.

'They surprise us. Constantly, constantly.' And Julian adds, 'And people say constantly: "They're learning so much from you." And we say, "Oh, no, it's the other way round!"'

I suggested that they're a family unit, but with two people from unknown backgrounds, to which Peter answers passionately, 'But they both know exactly where they come from. The thing is to avoid secrets and also to avoid projecting on to the children what *you* think they need to know – we just answer their questions. We keep it tidy, and we address their needs, not ours – that's so important.'

I wondered if they had questions about who their two mothers were, and Peter replies, 'They have two *fathers*. I'm Papa.'

'And I'm Daddy,' says Julian.

And Peter goes on: 'But it's all so interesting. When Hattie asked some questions once, the thing that was of greatest concern to her was not motherhood in her life, but did she come out of a lady's tummy? That was the great equaliser!'

Julian: 'We want them to be happy and well adjusted.'

Peter: 'And to go their own way. It's funny, from the day we got them we encouraged them to be independent – and then the *last* thing a parent wants is to have independent children! And there's a Chinese expression which means "inner conflict" – is there a spear that can pierce any shield, and is there a shield that cannot be pierced by any spear? I mean, they're real critters, these kids, normal . . . and it was very sweet, about a month ago Hattie wanted to have a play-date arrangement and she called up her friend and the answer machine was on, and she whispered to me, "What do I say?" And I said, "You know the people. Leave a message, tell them what you want." And she left a message: "Please call my parents." And I had never heard her use that expression before, so I think she really does understand what her parents are – the people who love her.'

Will adoption from China continue? China now has a population of 1.3 billion – officially. The real number is thought to be higher. It is undergoing breathtaking change, yet traditional attitudes remain. The kind of situation which is summed up in a little note attached to a baby girl in Hunan province in 1992 is likely to persist:

> This baby girl was born on XX-X-1992 at 5.30 a.m. and is now 100 days old. She is in good health and has never suffered any illness. Owing to the current political situation and heavy pressures that are too difficult to explain, we, who were her parents for these first days, cannot continue taking care of her. We can only hope that in this world there is a kind-hearted person who will care for her. Thank you. In regret and shame, your father and mother.

20

New York-Boston
What is the purpose of your visit?

Being with the New York cops sounds glamorous. Streaking through the concrete canyons with lights flashing, looking like a TV trail for an action-packed hour of mindless mayhem. Tim Jaccard takes another view. He's a police medical officer and spends a good deal of his time literally scraping the remains of human beings off pavements and from burnt-out cars. He's a tough cookie. At the same time he's got bottomless wells of humanity and energy which would beat a greyhound past the hare.

For a man who spends a good deal of his time crawling through crack houses past spaced-out addicts and hookers looking for someone raving, in a bad way or possibly dead, he's very matter-of-fact. But he is a man with a mission, and it turns on the simple fact that he got fed up burying babies.

'I'm a medical officer with Nassau County Police Department, and in 1998 I had a series of calls to respond to "babies not breathing" – that's what I basically do in my job. And within a ninety-day period I responded to five separate neo-naticide cases. The first one I ever responded to was a "baby not breathing" in a courthouse. I found a baby in a toilet bowl drowned by her mother, with over five hundred people in the courthouse at the time. And it was in the main bathroom of the main hall of the district court. And she just walked out, disappeared. We were unable to see her on the cameras – they interviewed hundreds of people. And this baby was born and died there. And that was baby Angelica – that was the first child that we buried. And right after that, two weeks later, I responded to a "baby not breathing", and I found a baby wrapped up in a plastic bag in Louiston Park at the side of a building. And three weeks after that responded again to a town called Hempstead on Long Island, and I found a baby that was dug up by a dog in the back yard of a house and that baby had been asphyxiated the night before in that back yard. And two weeks after that, I responded to the same call in Lawrence, and found a baby in a recycling bin, asphyxiated in a plastic bag, and right after that we were called to another house to find a baby in a trash-can.'

Tim Jaccard rattles off the calls and the details with machine gun-like emphasis. He can describe each scene, can remember getting to the site, the medical details and the few clues as to what happened. It's factual, precise and unemotional. He sees murder and misery on a daily basis, so why did he suddenly begin to notice these cases?

'At the time, my step-daughter was having difficulty trying to become pregnant, and she had had a miscarriage. She was cold, she was crying and my wife called saying Mary had just lost the baby – and that call came in while I was called to that first courthouse. I was just about to take off and go home and there I was worrying about my daughter – then I was responding to a call about a full-term 6 lb 7 oz baby drowned in a toilet bowl. So I sat down and asked, "Why is this happening?"

'I went to the library and looked things up and found out that a woman could not safely give birth to a baby – go to a hospital, give birth – *and* walk away, no questions asked. She would be charged with abandonment and endangering the welfare of a child. And in doing that she would then be labelled as a child abuser. And – say she was to get her life together, two years down the road, and to give birth in a loving, wanted pregnancy, the Children and Family Services would come in and take the child away from her into foster care, until it was proved that she was able to take care of that child. So I wrote a bill, and presented it to local politicians here in New York, and every single one of them threw me out of their office. They thought I was *nuts*.'

Tim Jaccard thought the law ought to be changed. He had no knowledge of legal work other than what he needed as a police surgeon.

'I went to the law library at the Police Headquarters and learned how to write a bill, and I wrote the presentation, and they still thought I was a nut. "You want us to sponsor a bill that will allow a woman just to hand a baby over to you?" "Not just to me," I said, "but to any responsible person, so that we don't have doctors finding dead babies any more." So they said, "Well, we really hate to see these babies found, but we don't think that that's the way we're going to be able to do this, so we're not going to be able to support this." So, one by one, they rejected and rejected, until a senator in Syracuse decided to support the bill.

'My own fears were that I was a little crazy, so I was debriefed – because they thought that, maybe, having so many of these calls in such a short period of time, maybe I was flipping out on this, so there was concern that perhaps I was having a problem. But I was focussed not on the death of these children but on trying to *stop* the death of children in the future. Even so, I could still not get support.

'What I did then was, the next babies that came along, I had enough support from all of my men and women who I work with to get them to "please help me bury these children". I went to Holy Rood cemetery, and I bought several plots on what is now called the Island of Hope. I bought eleven funeral plots, so that if any children died *I* would be able to bury them. Otherwise they would be put in Potter's Field, with just a number. I didn't want that – I wanted the children to have an identity.

'So we had our first funeral – police in full dress uniform, the bagpipers, all volunteers, and an escort of police motorcycles with permission of the Commissioner, and the local funeral home gave us the hearse. Then I had to go to Family Court to get technical custody of the child – which was going to take years! I went back to the medical library and realised that I could become a Health Proxy. I went to a judge to give me power of attorney over the child – a lot of legal stuff – and then I got custody of the child under my name. Except that all the children who are buried in that grave site have the name "Hope" – so they've become known as the Children of Hope.

'We had two babies born either end of the Williamsburg Bridge in April 2000, found by two separate precincts of police, one right near a fence and the other in a garbage can. Initially we thought they were twins, but they turned out to be unrelated. We had over fifteen hundred people show up for the funerals, with a police escort of motorcycles and flags and bagpipers.

'Cardinal Archbishop O'Connor was originally not going to do the Mass. But the numbers grew and the cathedral in Manhattan was packed. Then there'd been a "quiet word" from his assistant, Bishop Murphy, that we should go round to the side door rather than use the main entrance on Fifth Avenue! But I've never brought any of my babies to the side door of any church, so we had a little bit of a stand-off – with the coffins waiting in Fifth Avenue. And then the Cardinal himself came out and opened the door . . . .

'It was then, as we were burying these babies, which was averaging one a month – we had sixteen that first year – I lambasted the politicians. How can they allow us to do this when all I'm asking them to do is support a bill which will allow us to give mothers the right to be able to relinquish these children into the arms of a loving person, and ask no questions? I went on talk shows and finally got a local politician to be a co-sponsor – and then another senator joined in.'

As Tim Jaccard was getting his legal proposal off the ground in New York State, others were becoming more aware of legislation which still prosecutes women who abandon babies – regardless of their circumstances. And in the United States, foundlings are much more common than might be expected in an affluent, developed country which offers contraception, abortion and adoption. The figures are hard to quantify accurately: there is no central register and newspaper cuttings are the only source of detail. At the end of the twentieth century, there was one unpublished national report which assessed the number of abandoned babies at 108 in 1999 – with the inference that this was almost double the number at the beginning of the decade; the figures were definitely on the rise, year by year. However, individual states reported much higher numbers – thirty-eight in California in 2001, with the city of Los Angeles alone estimating that it dealt with a dozen a year, and Texas where fifty babies were found in rubbish bins in 1999. On average, a third of the children were already dead when found and more died later despite immediate medical care. The statistics are complicated by the number of children up to teenage 'left alone', 'lost', 'mislaid', 'neglected', 'missing', 'runaway' and 'abandoned for a period' – a figure of about forty thousand a year for a myriad of social and health problems. Added to this are the number of babies relinquished in hospitals by drug-addicted or ill mothers – another thirty thousand. But with new-borns, the causes of abandonment have not changed: poverty and social problems – particularly drugs, and religious and moral disapproval both within and outside the family. And although foundling fiction continues to flourish – American literature is very fond of the fantasy child from nowhere, full of magic and happy endings – the reality is one of the meaner aspects of life.

Step by step, in the last decade activists across the United States have argued at local level for the law to stop prosecuting mothers and start providing a way for them to leave a baby safely, under specific conditions. While Tim Jaccard was writing letters to all the thirty thousand medical journals and organisations in the country to find out how many deaths of new-born babies they had recorded, a couple in Boston, Massachusetts were running their own campaign.

Mike and Jean Morrisey run a counselling service, modelled on a charity called Bonny Babes in Australia, which helps people who've lost a baby through miscarriage or still-birth. Jean herself organises the burial rites for such babies and in November 2000 had just left some information about her work with the local medical examiner's office – the equivalent of the Coroner in the UK – when a baby's body was reported as having been found in St Mary's cemetery in Rochester, a tough district of Boston. The office rang Jean and asked if she could help. A group of eight-year-olds had been playing in the cemetery, which is a hundred yards from their school. The graveyard is hardly ever used these days and it's a hang-out for local teenagers sneaking off to drink beer.

Under a tree the children had found an 8lb baby wrapped in a towel, and it had been there for some time. Even after extensive publicity, no one came forward to claim it. Jean can't forget that baby.

'It haunts me. The smell of formaldehyde which came from the open casket which the police lieutenant had chosen. The baby looked beautiful – well, her face did, but the rest of her was highly distressing, with the effects of being left exposed for at least forty-eight hours to the elements and the cemetery crows. It was this which came back again and again to spur us on. And when we were literally lowering the coffin into the ground, we kept saying two words: "No more." And we made a vow to get a law passed, so that hopefully this wouldn't happen again. Obviously you can't say absolutely that it won't happen again, but at least this would be one solution to the problem.'

The Morriseys are a quietly spoken couple, but with a great deal of determination. We're discussing these highly emotive matters – which reflect some of the regular occurrences in the poorer parts of Boston – in the noisy Cheers bar, home of the popular TV series. This is the image many people have of Boston: one which portrays a large group of people who find easy friendship and camaraderie in a big city and which is on a different planet from the world we're discussing. Mike decided there were two ways to tackle the law.

'You can either wheel and deal in the political maze, or you can go directly to the people – the public – and let them decide. We didn't want "Beacon Hill back-room deals". However, we had media contacts – I used to be a sports journalist – and I could get to local papers and I stacked up the column inches on the subject. We went on local cable TV and radio stations, and the more people knew about what we were doing the greater the pressure on the state.'

'It was hard,' says Jean, 'but we knew a law would be passed if we kept at it. I have to say that our friends said, "Oh, no, not again!", because we'd done some legislative work in other areas. But we weren't going to give up.'

While they were getting their campaign off the ground they were

acutely aware that Massachusetts, which prides itself on being a
forward-looking, sophisticated and liberal state, was dragging its
heels, having been trounced by – of all places – George W. Bush's
Texas, hardly the home of the pinko progressives. As Governor,
Bush had already signed a bill in 1999, and Texas had become the
first state to enact a Safe Haven law.

The local media in this conservative state had had to concede
that Houston led the *country* in what they called 'dumpster baby'
cases: in ten months thirteen infants had been found, three of them
dead. None of the professionals involved in abandonment could
give a reason for the rise in foundlings, though some pointed to the
state's porous border with Mexico and the uncounted number of
illegal migrants. But nor were they able to detect a common thread,
either ethnically or economically. So, with much teeth-grinding
from those who opposed the legislation, whose main objection is
that a Safe Haven actually encourages women to have babies and
then give them up, Mr Bush signed the bill and the Texas landscape sprouted large posters proclaiming the message: 'Don't
abandon your baby. Call 1–877–904–SAVE.'

The reformers in Boston had expected to meet opposition from
the immensely powerful Catholic lobby in Massachusetts – one of
the richest Catholic communities anywhere. But suddenly there
was a message from the Boston Cardinal's staff. The hierarchy
were engaged upon a different battle and did not have the
resources to fight on two fronts: an appalling scandal of priestly
abuse of children was engulfing the Cardinal. It ultimately cost him
his job, with the archdiocese paying out $85 million in compensa-
tion claims. The powerful machinery of Catholic influence was
discreetly left idle in the face of the Safe Haven campaign. So the
Morriseys continued to plug away at the grass roots and spent two
years on town meetings and poster campaigns.

'We went to a lot of the sites where babies had been abandoned.
When we went back to the site of that first baby in St Mary's
cemetery, we looked across the street and just 300 yards away was
a fire station where she could have been left. And you always try to
put yourself into the position of the person – you know – what did

they think when they walked up there? They're probably scared, they're panicked, they're looking up the street to see if cars are coming . . . .'

Fire stations would not be the first port of call for help for a pregnant mother, you might think. However, this is to under-estimate the iconic status of US firefighters, who are a *rescue* service, who are trusted, and who – unlike hospitals – don't demand payment. And the local fire station is the ultimate Safe Haven, though most states' new laws also list hospital emergency rooms and police stations. Even if it's a volunteer fire station, possibly unmanned, there now has to be a notice next to the bell explaining where the nearest Safe Haven is, with the words: 'Go and see them.'

While the passage of the law was still being blocked, one of Jean's friends who ran a phone hotline connected to the Safe Haven law already passed in neighbouring Connecticut took a call and put it through to a cable TV show.

'A man's voice (probably the father) spoke to a paramedic in the TV studio and said that he was with a "preemy" – a premature baby – in a car. It was the middle of winter and freezing. He was told how to stabilise the child, to warm up the car so it didn't go into shock and to get it to the nearest hospital. He was in Connecticut, just south of the border with Massachusetts, so he headed for the nearest hospital – which happened to be over the state border. The Massachusetts hospital reported that a man came in and said, "My girlfriend's outside – she's just delivered a baby. I'm going to go and get it and leave it with you." "Er, well," said the staff. "You have to know it's still illegal to do that here." So he turned and ran out the door, and no one knows what happened to them.'

Just as they were beginning to run out of steam a Boston City Councillor, John Tobin, joined the fray – his adopted son had been abandoned at birth under a motorcycle in a hallway. Tobin gave his full support and the bandwagon got going. Not ones to ignore the importance of the dollar, the campaigners pointed out that states which had already passed Safe Haven laws were saving money! Prosecutions of mothers mean jail time, defence lawyers, appeals and court costs running into millions of dollars per state. New York State was thought to have saved $5 million and more than twenty lives. Mike Morrisey calculated that Massachusetts had just wasted $3 million while dithering about whether or not to pass the bill; meanwhile, six babies had been found dead. Even so, Boston was still cautious: under his letter about financial savings printed in the *Massachusetts News* was the Editor's comment: 'Although this sounds like common-sense at first-blush, we note that there are pro-lifers who believe this is injurious to the saving of lives. We do not yet have an opinion on the matter.'

Tim Jaccard in New York was very aware of the commitment of the US anti-abortion campaigners, some of whom are quite wont to take their protests to the point of fire-bombing clinics and shooting doctors. He was treading a fine line through sex education, public information and fundamentalist attitudes to single parenthood: antagonise the religious right and you get fire and brimstone, which today turns up in the form of strident denunciation and people with guns. All the time he kept emphasising that this legislation was about babies *already* born – and the need for humane treatment of both mother and child. So, to complement the proposed Havens and allay fears about encouraging women to abandon, Tim had set up a hotline, calling his organisation the Children of Hope Foundation.

'My first crisis centre was a toll-free number, 1–800 877796 HOPE, and I manned that myself, seven days a week, twenty-four hours a day for the first six months. This was a number anyone could call if they needed advice, if they were desperate. And when we buried the babies, we buried them as heroes, for we knew the media was covering these stories and that the message would get out there about the crisis hotline centre. And the first year, 1999, before the bills were even passed, I had fifty-two calls on the hotline.

'My youngest birth mother was twelve years old and later on we prosecuted the father of the child – a Baptist minister! My oldest was forty-four years old. All with a range of backgrounds – from a seventeen-year-old girl on a Christmas break up in Upper Brookville area in a house valued at maybe $6 or 7 million, to a house where there were six or seven people living in one room; or a pregnant stripper about to give birth in Grand Central Station; or [a woman] living in a car – I delivered the baby in the back seat of the car, took the child to hospital, and managed to get her to a shelter.

'I delivered a baby in the back seat of an abandoned car under elevated subway tracks in Jamaica, and another baby in a rat-infested basement in the same area of Queens. In Bedford-Stuyvesant – a ghetto area – in an abandoned basement I met a young girl who was strung out on drugs, who was a premature birth – lots of premature births because of drugs, also foetal alcohol syndromes. I went to a prostitute in a rat-infested basement in a crack house. There were three guys on the floor unconscious and me with a flashlight and her on the floor next to them giving birth. These are the circumstances I run into.

'Then there was Baby Headia Hope – all our babies get the name Hope. If you want to use your real name that's fine, but otherwise we give them the family name Hope. She was one of our first babies. Her mother called the crisis hotline, she saw the news coverage of a funeral we had a few days before. I promised her I wouldn't ask any questions, and she'd already given birth to the baby. She saw my poster on the side of the garbage trucks in Hempstead which the union president there had helped me with, and after she saw the poster she called and I met her on a corner with the baby wrapped up in a green towel, and she handed it to me. And we took it to a Safe Haven – the medical centre – even though the law had not yet been passed then.'

In 2000 Tim Jaccard saw his hard work pay off, with the law being signed and his Children of Hope Foundation playing a big part.

'I hoped originally the Foundation was going to be state-funded – the Governor of New York did all the signing for the law and so on, with $500,000 to go to the Foundation – *big* ceremony and we were photographed, and he handed the pen to me that he'd signed the bill with! But in the small print, it said that we'd get that funding if there was a *surplus* in the Children and Family Services funds. And there hasn't been a surplus in those funds for twenty-five years . . . so I knew where we were going. Now I have sponsorship, corporate support, and about a $250,000 budget.

'It's very tight, because I need around a million dollars to operate. But we're now at a position that we've gone from a hotline where I could just say, "You've got the right to relinquish a baby" to where I have forty-six special hospitals which have made agreements with me that, if a mother calls our crisis hotline and we counsel her, they can come into that hospital and give birth under the name of Hope, and get pre-natal care, give birth, then leave. And the baby stays there and comes into the baby Safe Haven programme. And the mother can have post-natal treatment if necessary, and she has thirty days to change her mind: And then Children and Family Services take custody of the child – and the legal process takes over.'

And across the country, from the grass roots up, small-town lobbying meetings and local lobbying groups were managing to nudge their state governments towards new legislation. And being the United States, every state that has passed Safe Haven laws has managed to produce something different – but in broad outline they are similar, addressing Safe Haven locations, the maximum age of the child, anonymity, father's rights and whether a parent should be immune from any further prosecution.

Eventually, at the end of 2004, Massachusetts became the forty-seventh state to pass the law, with Mike and Jean Morrisey at the ceremony in Boston. States such as Hawaii and Nebraska and Alaska have rejected the idea – mainly because of complications regarding local minorities' rights ('sovereign nation issues') which are different in respect of extended families and adoption.

So what's been the effect of the law? Difficult to assess without a campaign of education and publicity, say its supporters – and often there isn't enough money allocated for a programme of public information.

In California, as in many other states, the money provided for education and publicity was pretty measly. Mothers just didn't know about Safe Havens. Then the unexpected happened. Since 1996 Debi Faris-Cifelli had made it her mission in life to bury foundlings in her Garden of Angels in the town of Calimesa. She helped pass the California law, but despaired of ever getting it more widely known. 'This law does work, but it works when there is some kind of campaign going along with it,' she said. The state allocated about $1.5 million for advertising: 'Not enough for a state-wide TV spot.' She's buried seventy babies since she began her work, but there are fewer each year since the new law has been in place. Meanwhile, in December 2004, for only the third time in her life she played the state lottery. Debi won $27 million. A vast education programme is now under way.

In Nevada, support came from a stunning young woman who was crowned Miss Nevada in Carson City in 2004: Elizabeth Muto had been found twenty-four years earlier on top of a check-in counter at Reno-Tahoe Airport. Nevada passed the law in 2001 after two babies were found in rubbish bins in Harrah's Casino in Las Vegas. However, Elizabeth felt that there was still a lot of work to do.

'I don't know my birthplace, my birth mother or my birth date. They figured I was about ten days old, give or take two days, when I was abandoned. Two pilots found me and took me to the Lost and Found! I don't think enough people know about our Safe Haven law. Young women don't know they can leave a baby at a fire station, a police station or a hospital and not get into trouble.'

Miss Nevada – also Miss Black America – has been photographed at a raft of fire stations and headed for the Miss America contest with the specific intention of using it to publicise the law. Her own state is now targeting high schools, has printed two hundred thousand brochures and fifty thousand pamphlets and has stuck bumper stickers on fire trucks and ambulances. Who said beauty contests were pointless?

Interestingly, Nevada's experience disputes the notion that it's mainly young or drug-addicted women who leave babies. One of the nurses in charge of the publicity effort told the *Las Vegas Review-Journal* that 'Most women who abandon babies are middle-class white women, not all of whom are young. Often they go into denial that they are pregnant. If we save one baby, it is worth it. We want to get out [the message] that there is no shame or blame if you give up your baby.'

In Georgia, there was considerable opposition until Ron Sheppard reversed his rubbish truck into the car-repair yard of Backus Cadillac in Savannah. It was January, 3.30 in the morning and dark. He looked in his mirror as a load of fenders and metal and oil cans was rising up behind him about to be tipped in. Then, as he put his hand on a lever to jolt the rubbish into the compacter, he saw a tiny hand sticking out. Ron leaped out of the cab, dug into the trash and found 7lb 14 oz of silent baby which he wrapped in his T-shirt. He put her next to the heater in his truck and was rewarded with a loud howl before he drove his truck to a hospital, where the child was named Grace. Tony Pagan, Ron Sheppard's colleague at Atlantic Waste Services, wasn't in the least surprised because in the USA this is the most frequent place where aban-doned children are found: 'We're used to finding raccoons, cats and homeless people in trash bins. Finding babies isn't as much of a shock as it used to be. Used to be they just left babies on a doorstep with a note. These girls out there, they're getting bolder. They just throw them in dumpsters.'

The bill entitled A Safe Place for Newborns had been stuck in the Georgia House of Representatives for two years, unable to get voted through in the Senate. The legislation now goes by the name of the Baby Grace law – in the nine months after it was passed fourteen babies were dropped off in hospitals or clinics, and none found in rubbish tips.

Because the laws have fought their way up from local level there's been a lot of debate and discussion, with suspicion that women will gallop towards fire stations with new-borns under their arms countered by relief that little hands won't stick out of rubbish heaps so often. The professional modern analysis of abandonment recognises that through history there have been all kinds of motives and circumstances which have affected women and caused them to give up their babies. The numbers today vary hugely across the world, but it's clear that even in countries with adoption, birth control and legal abortion there are still women who cannot or will not keep their children. And it's more logical, humane – and practical – to regard them as being either in the grip of fear and despair or in denial, rather than monsters and criminals.

Those who are tracking the impact of the Safe Haven laws report an uneven response, and many states are keeping no specific records. However, anecdotally, those who are at the sharp end seem to be dealing with fewer 'trash-can' babies – and everyone agrees that more publicity and education are needed to reach those women who are not happy about the fact that they are pregnant. The rights of fathers are another moot point: some American states address the issue, others do not. Anonymity is also a problem. The amount of information asked of a mother is variable, for there are major concerns about unknown medical history. But most states require the baby to be handed into the arms of a person at the Safe Haven, rather than just being left at the location, thus giving the opportunity for some contact and information while maintaining the mother's anonymity. This is something Tim Jaccard recognises.

'Over the years we've realised that you have to have three scenarios: a parenting plan, an adoption plan, or a final relinquishing plan – under this you walk away within five days, no questions asked. And you can fluctuate from one plan to another while you're calling us on our hotline. We want the mothers to realise they have options – and what they say initially can be changed. They often say, "I don't want anyone to know, I want to hide this", and then you can go into that last resort – relinquishment. But in the counselling you can also say to them that they can have an adoption plan, with no one knowing about it – a lot of them don't realise this. I can tell them that I can arrange for them to choose the adopted couple – "somewhere you want your child raised". Now think what a relief that is for them. I also say to them, "I want you to sit down and write a letter to your child, and put it in a sealed envelope – I don't want to read it. Tell your baby what you're going through, and what your emotions are right now, why you're doing this . . . .' I've had a lot of letters. These letters are kept until that child grows up and it's appropriate for them to read them. When I talk to the adopting couples, I want them to understand that it's better that the child does know they are adopted – and what their mother felt.'

Across America there were issues raised about fathers' rights, Native American rights, the rights of adopted children to access their files and the lack of medical records. However, Jaccard stuck to his original aim. 'My concern was the mother's rights to proper medical treatment, that she should give birth safely and then be able to leave. And that the child would be safe. What I'm able to do is walk the fine line between Planned Parenthood and Birthright – two opposing groups who are sometimes even involved in violence. But I'm saving a new-born infant from abandonment and death, so I'm offending neither of the groups.

'You know, it's an adrenaline high. You turn around and hold this new-born infant in your arms and say, "Timmy, you've picked 'em up dead, but this child's alive – you're going to be able to move forward and have this baby adopted and have a good life." I look at it like a volunteer fireman: the Safe Haven programme I established here is like the Fire Department in the suburbs. The men and women in the suburbs volunteer and come in and put fires out. I'm putting out the fire of *fear* in unwanted situations. Changing an uncontrollable situation and creating a controlled environment. The hospitals are now finally set up so that I can walk in with a mother and they can ask, "What's your name?" and she can say, "My name is Hope" and not have anybody question that.

'Between 1996 and 1999, we averaged sixteen babies a year found dead; in 2000, when the law was passed, we got the number down to eight, but with twenty-three babies alive, relinquished into the programme, with seventy-six mothers making adoption or parenting plans. In 2002 it was the first time in eleven years in the New York Metropolitan area that we had no dead babies found.'

Tim Jaccard is in his late fifties and was about to retire 'before all this happened'. Now his entire family is involved in the Children of Hope Foundation and he lectures and fund-raises as well as doing the 'day job'. He targets schools in particular, because there are a large number of girls who get into trouble round the time of the 'Senior Prom' in the spring. After the celebrations, these sixteen-to seventeen-year-olds find themselves pregnant just as they're off to college in September. So they wear studenty baggy clothes, and in the New Year the entire country sees the peak in the annual number of babies found dead. He's dealt with many of these girls, and one in particular remains in his mind.

'Baby Molly Hope: I met her mother at a health fair in the Bronx, near the university, three months before she called. She was a college student. She kept coming back to our information table and saying, "I have a friend of a friend who is pregnant" – and it's always a third party! So I kind of joked about it and we hit it off pretty well.

'And I said, "Does your friend who knows your friend who knows your friend know how many months pregnant she is?"

' "She thinks she thinks she might be four or five months."

' "So could you tell that friend to tell that friend . . . ." So by doing that I'm breaking down the tension, and eventually I said, "Just tell your friend to call me any time she wants – and your friend can feel completely confident."

'Three months went by and nothing happened. Then all of a sudden, September 9th, I received a phone call at around 3.30 in the morning asking for Tim or Grandpa Noise – my handle came from my granddaughter who was learning her first words when I was redoing the kitchen and making a big racket. So she asked for me, and I got on the phone, and the voice seemed familiar, and I said, "Is this Maria?" and she said, "Yes."

'So I said: "I'm glad the friend of your friend called." And she laughed, even though she was in labour and in pain. She was giving birth. I told her I'd come. She said she didn't want anyone to come near her. I said I'd come personally – and wouldn't let anyone else near her. I notified the local medical team. She was on the south end of Central Park on 59th Street and Sixth Avenue. I went into the Park, and I ended up delivering her on a rock in Central Park.

'She'd meanwhile befriended an older man in the Park – an alcoholic, and he was there and he was intoxicated. So I got on and delivered the baby and she refused to go to the hospital. But the baby needed to go, so she had the ambulance meet her – with the homeless drunk! – on the corner and they took the baby to hospital.

'I took Maria to a local hotel and put her up for the night. I monitored her for a time, because she was bleeding a bit, and she stayed there. And the last I heard of her was thirty-six hours later, she was seen walking out of the hotel down town early in the morning. And that was 9/11, the morning the Twin Towers crashed. And she disappeared, never to be seen again. And all we have is a story which appeared the next morning which said a mother had given birth on a rock in the Park – and that's Baby Molly. She's been adopted – by a young couple in Long Island – and she became the baby on my posters.'

21

Do you have a criminal record?

'Never darken my door again' is a phrase which would have to be explained (thank goodness) to today's young women. Even my generation heard it, and though it sounded Victorian it had real meaning, especially when heard right after the announcement: 'I'm going to have a baby.'

In the twenty-first century the foundling and adoption landscape has changed. There are no longer nurseries and Baby Homes taking in hundreds of the 'illegitimate'. Since the late sixties, with the combined effect of the contraceptive pill, legalised abortion and the gradual acceptance of single motherhood, the flow of unwanted babies has shrivelled to a trickle. Welfare payments, more tolerant social attitudes and the increased confidence of women in a more equal society have made it possible for women to make their own choices. Bullying by family, Church and state has decreased.

Though there are still areas of deprivation and poverty in Britain, no one would expect to walk home – as Thomas Coram did – past little bundles abandoned to fate in the streets. Adoption is now a very regulated process in Britain and in most developed countries. Indeed, so great is the inspection of prospective adoptive parents in this country that many are daunted by the attention to detail and the bureaucracy. Professional theories abound and social agendas influence decisions. If you wish to adopt, you will have to pass tests that most ordinary parents would fail. The casual acceptance of a child into a family that was practised for centuries would make most of today's social workers faint.

Sometimes the paperwork and lengthy scrutiny are quietly bypassed – the wealthy and well-connected pull a few strings and acquire a fast-track child. The German Chancellor Schröder has a word with his friend the President of Russia and swoops down on a St Petersburg orphanage. Celebrities discreetly donate to threadbare foreign institutions. Public figures use their clout to cut through the niggling paperwork. And, inevitably, desperate couples sneak through passport control with forged papers, usually taking a child from poverty to a life in the richer West.

But there are still foundlings in Britain. It's difficult to find out precisely how many cases occur every year. They're classified along with children whose parents merrily hop off for two weeks in Benidorm and are discovered by neighbours to be fending for themselves at home while the adults get a tan. These stories figure prominently in the national news, an opportunity for much tut-tutting about modern life. Abandoned new-borns rarely get such prominence, their discovery handled by the local media on a collaborative basis with the police and hospitals: a photograph, a paragraph about the circumstances and the hope that either the mother will return or someone may have witnessed her leaving the child. A very rough guess, trawling through the regional press for the last decade, might suggest that around fifty babies are abandoned per year.

It's a guesstimate. Some mothers return and are reunited with their children very discreetly with the help of Social Services – and often this doesn't get reported. Others are complicated cases, such as under-age girls or women from minority communities whose religions are intolerant of those who stray outside the traditional limitations imposed on their behaviour. It may well be that the mother's life may be in danger from relatives wishing to inflict punishment – possibly death.

The very young and those living in communities where knowledge of English law is limited may not realise that the law is going to be invoked until they see mention of the police in the newspaper, under a picture of their baby. At which point fear takes over and the urge to go back on their actions is thwarted. What may have been an act of desperation which – on reflection – they wish to rescind suddenly gets a nasty tinge of criminal behaviour and society appears to threaten the mother rather than put out a helping hand. It's logical that because of this some mothers don't return to acknowledge their child. And with the influx of illegal and transient workers into Britain in the last few years, women – many in the commercial sex business – who become pregnant and who are either ignorant of or apprehensive about the options open to them are also at great risk of abandoning their infants.

One consequence of the arrival of the press at the hospital is the pressure to give the baby a name: a headline will be more appealing if it's Baby Noel or Little Lucy. And what is sometimes decided on the hoof, with the reporter and photographer and TV news crew needing quick access before a deadline, resonates in the foundling's life. It matters what someone first calls you; and though these days it's only a first name that is chosen it becomes *your* name. And perhaps naming shouldn't be undertaken lightly.

The Coram children at first received the names of distinguished patrons and famous individuals. Babies taken to nineteenth-century institutions followed the tradition of using saints' names, with a local street name as surname. For this reason, there are still a number of Piazza families in London, many no doubt thinking that their Italian heritage is assured. In reality they were found in Covent Garden, which happens to have . . . a piazza. Though many children go through life gritting their teeth that their parents decided to give them a bizarre name 'on a whim', it's hard to beat the naming of baby Apec in Thailand in 2003. The policeman who found him in a rubbish bin gave him the name in honour of the Asia-Pacific Economic Co-operation forum – the grand motorcade to the Bangkok summit was about to cruise past the bin at the time.

Newspapers the world round have stories about foundlings – though, rather than concentrate on the sad and complex social problem, they tend to highlight the odd-ball tales: the scavenging crows who seized a bag in a Bangladeshi town and fought over its contents – a new-born girl; the pack of stray dogs in Romania who curled up under a picnic table all night in freezing temperatures, for villagers to find a 6lb baby girl nestled among them the next morning. The run-of-the-mill abandonments – numerous in both countries – hardly merit a line. Some nations, such as Russia and China, have foundling problems on the scale of eighteenth- and nineteenth-century Europe. Others are new to the phenomenon. South Africa has the nightmare of Aids and has seen an explosion in the number of foundlings: prejudice and desperation and poverty are combining to produce thousands of abandoned children in addition to the multitude of Aids orphans. Kenya has seen a large increase and the majority are boys, with a Nairobi orphanage matron explaining that 'boys need to be schooled while girls don't. A boy needs to inherit while girls don't, girls can be prostituted, they can work young, you can get a dowry for them – girls are "cheaper" to hold on to.'

In Europe, a century after the turning wheels were finally dismantled in Italy, they've reappeared in modern form in several countries. 'Baby hatch', 'baby drop' or 'baby box': they come in various guises, but have the anonymity and secrecy which were common to their medieval forerunners.

One of the reasons why Hungary and the Czech Republic have initiated them is the continuing discrimination against the Roma, the gypsies of eastern Europe who are barely tolerated even on the fringe of society. I remember, from the Balkan war in the early 1990s, Bosnian villages where the last few houses at the end of the long main street seemed markedly different from the rest. Instead of small, balconied villas with window-boxes and gardens full of apple trees, there were tumbledown houses surrounded by a jumble of junk in the mud where scruffy children played. The communal rubbish tip appeared to mark the territory. Most Bosnians were sniffy when asked about them: 'Roma,' they said, shrugging. As the fighting lurched up the valleys and over the mountains, individual villages took up arms against their neighbours and everyone knew exactly who lived where: Bosnian Muslim, Croat or Serb. Every so often, such is the fall-out of war, the Roma were included in the damage. Wondering which faction they belonged to – in a war where 'ethnicity' was all – I got the reply that the Roma didn't *qualify* for the war. They were not worthy of inclusion – and if they were hurt or killed, then tough: they shouldn't have been there in the first place.

Sarajevo had four orphanages which more or less functioned throughout the years of near-siege by the Serbs. I went frequently to one, which was a bleak place, devoid of home comforts. Having seen several Bosnian asylums and institutes – usually under shell-fire, with the inmates running around the grounds after the staff had fled, utterly unhinged by the explosions – I was conscious that the care system was old-fashioned by Western standards, and the war merely added real deprivation. However, in the Sarajevo orphanage the baby room was particularly bleak: what staff had remained were also not particularly concerned about the foundling new-born: 'Look at them,' they said with a shrug. 'Dark, aren't they?' Nearly all in the room were from Roma families, with no chance of adoption but a childhood ahead in some Home.

For this reason, foundlings are viewed with some disdain by many eastern European authorities, conscious that little sympathy is to be gained by spending public money on an unpopular section of society. Nevertheless, as the old Eastern Bloc begins to acquire Western-style economies the Roma are squeezed even more, hardly managing to be counted officially as citizens. Put poverty and the high price of contraceptives together and add a tradition of young motherhood – and dead babies result. So Budapest and Bratislava now have baby hatches. Antwerp in Belgium has a hatch, and so does Vienna. Since the start of the new century Germany has calculated that as many as sixty babies are abandoned every year, more than half of them dead. The high number of foreign workers, traditionally Turks, now swollen by the new influx from eastern Europe, plays a part – there is a notice in German, Polish, Turkish and Russian next to the hatches in Berlin, and one in Turkish, French, German and English in Hamburg.

The German *Babyklappe* translates as 'baby hatch' or 'baby flap'. It's a non-judgemental term, even friendly. But many of the

English headlines which followed the introduction of the first one in Hamburg contained the phrase Baby Dump, indicating immediate disapproval, and it turns up in myriad newspaper stories. If you dump a baby, you are clearly just tossing it out like last week's rubbish, without a thought. And that's the feeling among many even today: that women could be in full possession of their faculties, and just decide to pop a child into a hatch without a second thought. Selfish, lazy members of the throw-away society. It conjures up the ancient spectre of the wanton woman, who's had her pleasure and can't be bothered with the consequences. And there are still lots of commentators queuing up to wag their fingers in righteous outrage.

I've been trying to find a single case in which it has been proved that this indifferent creature exists: one who readily justifies relinquishing a baby for someone else to find, without suffering any emotional concern and angst. I was fascinated to hear a lawyer tell me when I was researching this book that 'if abandonment was decriminalised, then women would go around leaving children willy-nilly'.

One of the German baby hatches is in the outer suburbs of Hamburg. I've driven past a Roma camp – a clutch of wretched wooden houses surrounded by a jungle of junk – then a grim high-rise housing development where women enveloped in headscarves and long coats trail through muddy sparse grass, the landscape dominated by a power station and the thump-thump of a wind farm. The sign saying '*Babyklappe*' stands on the pavement outside a handsome three-storey villa with bright butterflies and flowers stuck to the windows. Small children shriek in the courtyard – few speak German, and there are words of Turkish, Albanian and Serbo-Croat in the air. A door in the villa's side wall is lit up – even in daylight – and has another large sign above it. The door is made of toughened glass and halfway up is a metal hatch with a handle. Inside you can see a clear plastic cot attached to the flap – a standard hospital baby's bed, its mattress permanently heated to 37 degrees C. There's a small yellow teddy bear in the corner of the cot.

It's in a tiny room, warmed with another large radiator, in a pre-school building and the head, Ulrike Kaatze, also doubles as a volunteer responsible for the baby hatch. She's energetic and immensely well informed about the problem of abandoned children in a modern European society and she radiates kindness.

The *Projekt Findelbaby* grew out of the work of a German non-denominational charitable society called Sternipark working with disadvantaged children. It has six pre-schools in Hamburg and a girls' home in the countryside. In 1999 there was a major outcry when workers discovered a dead baby in a massive heap of rubbish at a waste-sorting centre, and Sternipark decided that 'something must be done'. It started a nationwide helpline, free and manned day and night, to give women someone to turn to if they were pregnant and desperate. Its staff found themselves listening to women who had managed to conceal their pregnancies right up to the eighth month – and who were scared witless. Advice and help were offered, including the possibility of staying in a country farmhouse well away from prying eyes where the mothers can choose to give birth – or they can arrange to go to a hospital anonymously.

The first call came in January 2000, from a woman who said she had just had a baby – could they come and get it? She said she didn't dare go anywhere she might be seen. She arranged to meet a volunteer in a parking lot, handed her new-born baby through the car window and drove off. Abandonment is illegal in Germany if the child is left in a 'helpless situation' – which includes doorways in public places. However, as Sternipark takes care of the baby the police are helpful.

When this incident happened, Sternipark had already been thinking about setting up somewhere permanent for babies to be left: somewhere warm where the baby could be found quickly – a 'not helpless' location. So the organisation designed the *Baby-klappe* and installed the first one in central Hamburg in April that year, with the second at the pre-school two months later. The whole arrangement is meant to be both simple and secure – and during the day, the door from the baby room leads directly into Ulrike's office.

'There's a bell that automatically sounds in the school as well, but of course I'm not here in the evenings and weekends, so there's also an alarm which sounds in a service agency. So they call a mobile number which is always someone who can get here within five minutes. They just run – don't bother getting dressed if it's the middle of the night, just rush round. "Get the baby!" – because babies cool off way too fast.

'There's a letter in the hatch, a "Letter to the Mother" and a little stamp-pad, so they can make a little hand or foot-print. There's all the information about us in the letter, our helpline number, and we tell them that they have eight weeks in which they can come back if they have second thoughts. No problem, we can help – the mother can live with us, if she needs.' Total anonymity is possible with this system. Up to now, a few mothers have left notes or letters or a name pinned to clothes – but not many. Only the mothers with whom they have contact via the helpline can be encouraged to write a note about their child – health, background and so on – or to write a letter to be kept with a lawyer for their child to open when he or she reaches eighteen.

In the 1990s, over sixty children a year were known to be abandoned in Germany – either in the forests or in rubbish dumps, and usually dead. As in Britain, there's no central collation of the number of children found abandoned, but the regional news reports consistently produced such a number – and the police estimated the number *not* found to be at least two or three times higher. So who leaves their baby? The area we're in has a high number of impoverished immigrant families – including Turkish *Gastarbeiter* and Roma. However, Ulrike's experience is that the net is cast much wider.

'The thing is, we don't see the mothers who leave their babies, but we do know the women who come to live with us. And they're not really young. No. They're between sixteen and forty-two – and the average is somewhere in the late twenties. You have the very young who think their life is over and that they can't go to school any more. You have Muslims, where the girl can't have a baby outside of marriage and they're forbidden to use contraceptives. You have prostitutes, whose pimps won't tolerate a baby. There are older women in stable relationships, in a nice home, but they have three kids and the husband says, "No, not one more – we can't do it." And these women don't dare talk about the fact that they're pregnant to anyone. People with their own house, she works, he's in full-time work and they have three beautiful kids and it happens. And you wonder, how can the husband not notice that she's eight and a half months pregnant? But it happens. And they come to us – and we can talk to them and we're able to work something out.

'And it's not just the poor, the young drug addict or the prostitute, the Russian and Polish "sex workers" – it's every sort of person. In this area the babies are usually just wrapped in a towel, but at the hatch in central Hamburg they have a nappy and proper baby clothes.

'Some mothers who leave their babies in the hatch come back to us. And if they come and live with us, the percentage who keep their babies is much higher – 60 or 70 per cent. The rest arrange through us to put the babies up for adoption. But we don't get involved – we leave that to the state.'

That all this has happened in the twenty-first century raises the question as to whether abandonment is on the rise again. In Germany, it's hard to make historical comparisons – records of abandonment existed until World War II and then were discontinued, though the war and post-war years abounded with reports of babies dead in ditches. There were a number of high-profile stories at the end of the nineties – but possibly, because one newspaper story leads to another, a mere highlighting of something which has been going on for a long time. The baby hatches were the response, and the idea was quickly taken up across the country. There are now nearly seventy hatches, run by charities, the Catholic Church and hospitals. Not everyone's happy, though, says Ulrike.

'The opposition has come from an organisation which represents adopted people, and they say that kids don't have a chance to find their roots. It's true, they won't. And we can't change it. At least they're alive. But they respond by saying that every child has a *right* to know their roots. But what is that worth without being alive? So it's a choice.

'Often the mothers tell us: "I was about to go and put the baby in a rubbish bin. I read about you, so I called you. I brought it to you." They were ready to throw it away. They're frightened, just thinking, "I can't go on with this."

'Other people opposed to what we're doing have said that we're making it too easy for women to get pregnant – and just throw their baby away! I sometimes wonder if these people have ever been pregnant . . . and know what it's like . . .'

For the last five years, via the helpline, the Sternipark volunteers have enabled nearly sixty women a year to give birth anonymously, and the hatch gets a baby about once every six months. 'The first Hamburg baby hatches have had nine or ten babies left in five years. But compared to the number found abandoned now it's amazing – it's gone down so much. In 2000 there were over sixty that we knew of abandoned all over Germany, and in January 2003 we had a month – the first since the war – that *no* baby was abandoned.'

They are not inundated with children – nor do they receive all the children who are abandoned. But they represent a legal way of last resort for a mother who can think of no alternative. In the affluent West, life is now more precious than it was when 'God's Will' took a large number of your brood before they even attained their teens. And when women have access to contraception and abortion, and can make informed decisions without interference from Church or state, the mother who gives birth and then abandons must surely be in special circumstances which have to be understood.

In France, the baby hatch was pre-empted more than half a century ago by the consequences of the Nazi occupation in World War II. Women who became pregnant by German soldiers were seen as collaborators, leading to their children often being called '*Boche* bastards'. It's estimated that up to two hundred thousand such children were born – often fatally blond and easily singled out. In 1941 the pro-Nazi Vichy Government passed a law making it possible for women to go to a public hospital for an '*accouchement sous X*': they could withhold their names and personal history and leave the children at the hospital to become wards of court, available for adoption. Since 1966 it's been possible for the mother to leave personal details in a sealed envelope for the child to open when of age, but it's not compulsory. This law is still in force, despite numerous arguments taken as far as the European Court of Human Rights, which ruled in 2003 in favour of upholding total anonymity – still haunted by the view that more babies would be killed or abandoned if it was removed – but frustrating those adopted French adults who want to know their origins.

Why is a Vichy-inspired law still on the statute book? The answers vary, ranging from a charge that unwanted children can be quietly disposed of by the embarrassed middle class to the argument that the Catholic Church prefers this situation to abortion. But in an age where the right to discover one's origins is increasingly encouraged, there's disquiet that these children (more than a million people are now descended from those born '*sous X*' since 1941) are unable to know anything about their roots. However, this system of legal abandonment is what is now being introduced through the Safe Haven laws in the United States (though it only involves potential foundlings, the majority of children relinquished by their mothers being born in hospitals and known to the staff). And each American state has different rules about information – whether or not to coerce the mother into giving some details of health and background, or to allow her to abandon her baby without any information being given.

The UN Convention on the Rights of the Child states that the child shall have 'as far as possible, the right to know and be cared for by his or her parents'. However, there is no global consensus on putting this into practice, and Europe is full of argument about it. Luxembourg, Italy and Greece have laws to conceal identity – but allow an adopted child to search for information. In Ireland, there's continuous debate about the difficulty of digging out the records of abandoned and adopted children: the Church has been obdurate in its opposition, arguing that sin and shame are involved and that a child should not know these things, nor the mother be 'exposed'. Reformers are pushing for more information to be made available, and they're on the path to change.

In Britain, the situation is complicated because the law of the land treats the mothers of foundlings under two years of age as criminals. The Offences Against the Person Act of 1861 was introduced at a time when women had fewer legal rights compared to men and illegitimacy was perceived as shameful. Industrialisation and urbanisation had made the population more mobile and less under the thumb of village busybodies, and by the mid-nineteenth century, as the law was being framed, probably well over fifty thousand children a year were born out of wedlock, most ending up in the workhouse – if they survived.

In 1861, the *Times* of London reported: 'During the last five years in the London area were found the bodies of two hundred and eighty murdered babies. Over sixty were found in the Thames and in canals, over one hundred under railway arches, in staircases, in rubbish dumps, in cellars and similar places.' When Sir Joseph Bazalgette created the new sewerage system, after 'The Great Stink' in 1858 when the Thames overpowered even Parliament, the number of bodies increased dramatically. The huge majority of abandoned children were merely seen as dying 'naturally', and the indifference to the discovery of small bodies in public places hadn't really altered since Thomas Coram walked the city's streets a century previously.

However, the concept of women and sex had been through the puritan mangle of Victorian attitudes, with the basic premise that women should 'lie back and think of England' rather than dare to extract some pleasure from the occasion. Producing a bastard was tantamount to an admission that you'd selfishly had some fun. Seduction, rape and betrayal were not matters of interest to the courts. A woman was to be punished for abandonment – but with the underlying accusation of 'kicking over the traces' and failing morally. And the law still stands.

The result is the involvement of the police at an early stage in the discovery of any foundling. The infant is usually taken to a hospital for health checks, and if no one comes forward immediately the press are alerted and a picture appears in the local papers. Nevertheless, there is always the phrase: 'The police are anxious to trace the mother, because she may be in need of medical treatment.' Which poses the interesting question: since when were the constabulary interested in gynaecology?

The aim is to get the mother to come forward. But if she does she runs the risk of prosecution, which would mean that eventually she'd be separated from her baby if she got a custodial sentence – which could be up to five years in prison.

'Bloodhounds assisted the police yesterday, in a search on the South Downs for the person who abandoned a 12-months-old baby girl in a thicket, naked and with hands tied behind her.' In 1937, the police were on the trail of someone they wanted to charge with attempted murder. 'The whole of the British Isles is being combed by the police in an effort to clear up the mystery,' reported the *Worthing Herald*, agog with a national story on its doorstep and countrywide coverage of 'Baby Ann'.

Nowadays, the bloodhounds would be unlikely to be snuffling around the Downs behind Sompting. The men with the DNA kit would be crawling through the blackberry thicket. However, the purpose would be the same: to track down someone who had committed a crime – though this would probably be downplayed in favour of statements expressing concern about the mother's welfare and the child's need for her.

Even so, the 1861 Act is still in force, carrying with it a possible jail sentence, and 'Baby Ann's' mother – if she is still alive – might well find that she could still be prosecuted. Even the House of Lords had no idea in 2002 whether or not there was a statute of limitations in such a case: they were discussing whether to set up a contact register for adopted children and birth parents looking for them. The intention was humane – to make it easier for children to trace their roots and for parents to search as well. But the Lords spotted that a *foundling*'s parent agreeing to a DNA test would, if it was positive, actually make them liable to prosecution for the original abandonment.

It's a thought which bothers the Worthing baby, no longer Baby Ann but Anthea Ring. She's a pretty woman with open features and a ready smile, whose husband is making us coffee in their Wiltshire home while a black and ginger cat is head down inside my handbag, tail twitching with excitement.

'I sometimes wonder: did my parents try to kill me? Or did someone kill my parents and couldn't kill *me*? But I'm not angry – I just want to *know*.' She speaks without a trace of vindictiveness or condemnation. Unlike many foundlings she has a wealth of detail about the circumstances of her finding, but nevertheless a complete void as to what went before.

'I didn't know I was adopted until I was nine. I was a perfectly happy child of older parents in Surrey – well looked after and privately educated. When I was nine I was playing with some boys and, when it came to the crunch, I said to this boy Peter, "I'm going to tell my mother!" And he said, "She's not your mother." And I said, "'course she's my mother." And he said, "No, she's not – you're adopted."

'I went stomping home, absolutely certain that my mother was going to say, "Rubbish!" And when I opened the door and said, "Peter says you're not my mother . . ." I remember her reaction – the way that something had changed for me. . . . But the next thing I remember was that in the evening we all sat down with my father – who was a travelling salesman – and they told me they had adopted me because I had been found in a doorway of Worthing Hospital, "a brand-new baby". I knew that there had been a child in the family who'd been killed. I'd been told she'd been my sister Veronica, who'd been knocked down by a motor car – and so they told me they'd so wanted a baby because Veronica had died. And that I accepted.

'I was very happy to be adopted and remember thinking, "Ooh, tomorrow at school I can tell them I'm adopted!" It shows how secure I was. In fact, I met a school friend years on and she thought I'd been telling stories, I'd been so pleased and proud of it.

'When I was thirteen, we were staying with Aunt Flora in Bexhill and I asked if we could go and see the hospital in Worthing. But my parents said it had been bombed in the war.

'When I was about sixteen or seventeen my mother took me to Germany – she was half German – and I had to have a passport. There was a little hiccup – and I didn't know quite what that was. At seventeen I went to London to work in Bourne and Hollingsworth in Oxford Street, and thought, "I'll go and see about this thing about not having a birth certificate." I didn't understand why they'd kept it from me. And off I went to Somerset House, only to be shown that all I had was an Adoption Certificate. I'd been adopted at sixteen or seventeen months – and that was that. So I did no more about it. I then went into nursing, and my parents moved back to the West Country, where my mother came from, and . . . .'

There's a pause. The cat is extracting itself from the bag and demanding to go out, and Anthea is catching her breath and looking thoughtful. 'It does affect me,' she says quietly, then takes up the story again.

'When I'd married and had a son and a daughter, it occurred again: my daughter was *exactly* like me. I took some photos and went on the bus to Bristol to show them to my parents. My father sat there and said, "You'll have to show her now, Peggy." I didn't know what they were talking about, and my mother went very reluctantly upstairs and came down with a newspaper cutting. A picture of me in the paper, with the writing torn off. And this picture was identical to Christine, my daughter. I said, "Who's that?" And they said, "It's you."

' "But this isn't a new-born baby," I said, "on a doorstep."

'And she went upstairs again. Then she gave me another cutting . . . .'

She breaks off again. The cat has decided that, after two minutes, Out is boring, and is staring huffily through the glass door. It gives Anthea a couple of moments to collect herself. She apologises, for she's talked about this many times in the last decade but is still not detached from the emotional rhythm of her history and the moment she read her own story.

'My parents said, "That was how you were found, pinioned in a thicket. Wearing a pink dress, hands tied together." I was twenty-four when I read the cutting – I was in the middle of having my children. I went home, just sat on the bus, and when I got home went upstairs and just cried all night long. But it's the hands tied together, that's what affects me.

'Anyway . . . I went on to have Juliet – and I didn't do anything at all about it. Just got on with life – three children to bring up. And when they were about ten to thirteen Francis, my husband, said to me, "Why don't we go down to Worthing?" Anyway, we went down to Worthing. Curiously, it had always been avoided on summer holidays – we'd been to a caravan at Selsey, Chichester, Bognor, Brighton, but never to Worthing: I suspect my mother felt that somebody would recognise me. I felt very sad for them, because I think they always had the thought at the back of their minds that someone might come forward one day. I think that's partly because of the circumstances in which I was found – and their kindness, and partly that, if I did anything about it, would anyone come forward?

'But the night she told me, I remember my mother insisted, "Nobody will ever come forward. You will never find who did it."

'Francis and I went through the Worthing papers with a fine tooth-comb, and we found nothing that had been hidden from me.

'The people who found me were from London. Every year they went for a fortnight and stayed in the same flat on the seafront at Worthing – the father, Arthur Dodd, had been in World War I and had a lot of mental problems. He had this second family, two daughters of eleven and fifteen, Elizabeth and Jane, and methodically he took them for walks over the Downs every day. And this is the miracle! On this particular day he planned this tour and – and I've met the daughters, they're still alive – suddenly he thought, "This is not a very interesting walk, so we'll go back over the top the other way." And as they went over the top the mother said, "There's a baby up here." It was all low gorse and scrub and blackberry bushes.

'"There's a *baby* up here," she said. She'd heard the cry. And the father said, "Can't be a baby up here – there's no grown-ups up here." And she said, "It's a *baby*" – like a mother knows. And they followed my cries. I'm quite a loud person and my mother said, "That was your salvation – that you were loud!"

'And I'd been crying evidently for hours, and so they came over and found me in a scooped-out area of a blackberry bush, with my hands tied together, with this little pink silk dress on, which was ridden right up around me, no nappy, and covered in scratches. They picked me up and took me to the nearest place, which was a lodge. But there was no phone there, so they took me to this farm where they were having a tennis party. It was a gentleman-farmer who owned all this land I was found on – I didn't know that until recently – and the farmer's daughters were twenty-two and twenty. I've met both of them.

'Joy, one of the daughters, told me, "Mother said, as we wrapped you in a blanket and took you into the kitchen, fed you warm milk and brown sugar – and you gulped it – she said as she smelt your hair: 'What's a baby like this doing up on the Downs?'"

'That really makes me feel I wasn't just a baby that was dragged up somewhere – something *happened*. I was eight to nine months. And then the police were called and I was taken to Worthing Hospital. No shoes on, no nappy, just a dress. Round my wrists was a strip which had been ripped off from the bottom of the dress, according to the elder daughter, and used to tie my wrists. It's important to me, because it seems this wasn't premeditated, just ripped off and done at the time. Because the newspapers reported that it was string or rope – I suppose it sounded more dramatic.

'And there are two main ways of looking at it. One: I was on top of the Downs, so maybe it was to stop me crawling and rolling down and killing myself. And Two: to tie me so that I would stay there. It was then a very remote area.

'The father of the girls who found me was an analytical chemist and he actually marked the area with four feathers where I was found, so the police could find the exact spot. So the police went there, they had bloodhounds out and did get some sort of track to a local station. But they weren't certain, because I would of course have been carried. So they were on somebody's tracks . . .

'There were all sorts of suggestions, but once the police got involved everyone backed off. I was in every national daily – I've got piles and piles upstairs. It's inconceivable that the woman who did it didn't know that I'd been found. But the police are looking for someone. It's a crime – in this case, attempted murder.

'After finding this out I went on bringing the children up. Then Father, then Mother died, and I rarely talked about it. It's funny, but I told people my father was Scottish, my mother half-German, but then some days it hit me – they're not, they're not my parents.

'I went to Norcap, the foundlings group, and they suggested I try the Worthing Hospital and the police records. The police were wonderful; a police inspector went into the archives and found that only one policeman had survived from that time of the eight who'd been on the case. He was still drawing a pension and I went to see him and told him, "One of your previous cases has turned up!" And so I met this lovely man, Edward Adamson. He had never seen me, he said, but he was the village policeman in Sompting and he was given the job of door-to-door enquiries.

'He said: "I never saw you but" – and this is what really touched me – "I carried your photo in my wallet for about ten to fifteen years, just in case one day somebody said . . . ." And occasionally he used to ask, "Did you ever know this baby? Ever see this child?" But *he* doesn't think I was born in Worthing at all. He said, "You've come from outside."

'But that opened everything, because he then wrote an article for the local police publication in Sussex, and next thing the TV companies were on the phone, then the local newspapers, then local TV, and that all led to Liz, the (then) fifteen-year-old daughter of the people who found me. And she told me that the rest of the holiday had been terrible for them, because she wanted to adopt me: "Why can't we take the baby we found?"

'Then there was an article in a national newspaper, and after that a nurse wrote from a hospital in Kent and said that she was in the hospital when I was brought in. She remembers me being on the ward and being looked after. But she had a friend who actually worked on the children's ward at that time and she would contact her. And this proved unbelievable! This woman – called Betty – she wrote to me and said *I* actually called you Ann . . . it's . . . it's . . . *she* calls me Baby Ann. "Because I felt that you had to be called something, and I was on the ward all over that weekend when you were found, and after forty-eight hours you were settled and you were lovely, despite being on a busy ward – no problems."

'I was clearly a confident, happy baby. I feel something happened in my family, obviously I don't know what . . . and the lovely thing was, she told me that when my adopted mother came to see whether she would have me, because she had this great scar with Veronica being killed (Mother was forty), she said, "You came to the end of the cot, and put out your arms just like this." She spreads her arms up and wide in anticipation. "And your mother said, I thought, '*You* want *me.*'"

'I was called Baby Ann for six months. I was Anthea Shannan while I was at school, and I was Anthea Ring when I got married – but I'm not any of those people. Which *is* me? But I'm not. I'm somebody else.

'I'm probably registered in St Catherine's House because I don't think this was premeditated. I don't think you bring up a child, and in the condition I was found – in fact "well-reared" was how they described me. . . . And I don't think she was a teenage mother: I was clean, well nourished, in a silk dress.

'My mother told me, "They took out everything that could connect you to anything. The label was cut out of the dress."

'Having met Betty and Mabel, the two nurses, I've also since found the farmer's elder daughter. She said to me, "I could tell that if you hadn't been found that night, the foxes would have eaten you. You wouldn't have survived."

'My mother had given me the pink dress and a nappy, saying, "This came out of Worthing Hospital with you." And the nappy had "Worthing Hospital" embroidered on it. But the dress she didn't even explain to me – I had to wait until just about ten years ago, when I met the elder daughter. And she said, "You had a pink dress on." And you know, it took me ten days to realise that *I* had the pink dress. It didn't even click – I'd always wondered: was I naked . . . did I have clothes on?

'Everyone has turned up who's important: the nurse who named me, the other nurse, the people who found me . . . where I was taken . . . and a photo, a wonderful photo came from Mabel . . . I've got a case full of stuff here . . . Here's the first photo the police took – you see, I'm not unhappy, am I?'

A chubby, serious baby lies propped up, clearly unbothered by the attentions of the photographer and the national hue and cry in progress.

'My adoptive parents chose my birthday – and beautifully, too. My mother was the 5th July and my father was the 25th October. The hospital told them to choose between October and December 1936 and they chose November because it was the middle month, and I remember my mother saying, I'm the 5th, you're the 15th and Daddy's the 25th. But I don't think I *am* that date – I think I'm a month younger.

'We've been up and searched through *every* baby born from September 1936 through to March 1937 to see if there's a child who doesn't turn up somewhere, and we've been to all the schools in Worthing to see if a child didn't turn up at the right age – you see, I think I've got a birth certificate and another name.

'My worst scenario would be that I was left to die – and I have faced that. The other is that there was something going on whereby "I shall leave the baby, if you don't do such-and-such" – and I was meant to be picked up. I stand back and sometimes think it's such an extraordinary story – it's not me. And then, suddenly, you're in it.'

And all the players have come on stage – except one.

'And I want to know three things: where I was born, what I was called, and who are my family. I don't really *need* my family unless they need me – if I find them. Because I've had a lovely family – husband, children, grandchildren.

'When we were at this conference for foundlings we were all

more or less the same age, and I said it's as if we're all perfectly normal – but there's a wound there, and if that wound is touched then suddenly it's alive and raw. But other than that, we can cope.'

Anthea Ring's many newspaper cuttings about her abandonment feature comments from the police and possible prosecution of her mother. Most foundlings today know that the law still looks upon their mothers as criminals, and many find it uncomfortable and inappropriate. I've asked lawyers and judges involved in child protection for their views. They all wrinkle their brows and begin by remarking that it's a very obscure bit of law and they can't recall it ever being used. Social Services would intervene, they say.

This is true, but the most recent cases show that any mother watching local television or seeing a newspaper headline would be fully aware that the police were looking for her. And there is evidence from mothers who do come forward that they're frightened 'they'll be punished'. And others who make calls to hospitals or the papers and then don't appear, are clearly scared or distressed. In these cases the possibility of the law bearing down on them serves no practical purpose whatsoever.

Admittedly there are all kinds of bewhiskered and mildewed statutes cluttering the law which are never invoked in practice, but they law's very existence steers a mother towards the courts initially, instead of towards help and support. And it cannot be denied that some mothers fail to return their babies because of this threat.

Surely it needs crossing off the criminal list? The last time this was tried was in 1999, when the Home Office and the Department of Health were approached for their views. The Midland Family Placement Group – an association of adoption professionals – had discussions with civil servants that resulted in a letter which stated that 'they could not envision prosecution, but they *reserved the right to be able to prosecute, depending on the circumstances*'. The case they cited? The Worthing Baby in 1936.

The Worthing Baby herself isn't particularly impressed. What good would have come of such a prosecution, she told me, if her mother had ever appeared? Perhaps the civil servants should consult the foundlings themselves.

If the law was scrapped, there would still be adequate safeguards, relating to infanticide and neglect residing in the laws. And there are several professional bodies eager to discuss how best to coordinate plans for dealing with abandoned babies. At the moment, though, there is still no national policy. One of the suggestions from Norcap is to hold an appeal for the mother to come forward so that her child can be named, so replacing the threat of prosecution with the offer of further contact, practical and confidential – and possibly leading to fewer instant Noels in December. A change in the law would alter the status of a foundling so that they would no longer be the child of a suspected criminal.

No one wants new-born babies to die a death of lonely neglect. No one wants to encourage infanticide. But everyone has to acknowledge that there will always be mothers who, for reasons that seem overwhelmingly imperative and crushing to them at the time, leave their babies to be found by others. Anonymity and secrecy used to be thought the overriding virtues of any system that was prepared to deal with these babies, based on the need to protect women from 'shame' – even though that 'shame' was often attached to the foundlings themselves. Today we have become more open-minded and humane, and the patronising attitudes to women's sexuality are on the wane, though not extinct. Stigma is giving way to understanding – and for the foundling, perhaps it's time to take the criminal shadow out of the picture and change the law. A woman who leaves her baby should not have to scuttle away trying to leave no trace, through fear of prosecution. She should be able to leave the child somewhere safe, perhaps at a hospital. It may be that the only way to guarantee that the baby lives is to allow the mother to relinquish it anonymously. However, it is possible to devise a system with at least the option of leaving sealed information, so that in the child's unknown future, it will still be able at some point to learn about its past.

For we all need roots. And we need to know about our past so as to be sure of who we are. Not just when we have to fill in the shoal of forms which are increasingly penetrating into our lives. The information an official reads on our passport or driving licence, or application for a bank account or credit card, is very much for public consumption, and these days may end up stored in a data bank into which almost anyone can stick their nose. It needs to be consistent in public, yes, but it may not be precisely and entirely matched to the knowledge you have about yourself.

The foundlings I talked to often had a birthday which had been written on a certificate when they were a few days old. Further research had shown that the certificates were often a day or two adrift of their real age. 'So what?' they said. '*I* know about it – that's what matters.'

Place of birth – well, my passport carries a lie. It was convenient at the time, a minor adjustment, and what I wanted to acknowledge. And I've never bothered to change that information, in all the hundreds of forms I've since filled in.

Names come and go. Victor Banks is mightily relieved that he lost his name, courtesy of his adoptive parents; the Victoria Embankment is not something he wants to drive down with a deep sense of belonging. And as I've learned more about my own past, having met my own mother, I've thought about what goes on paper and into the public domain, stating who I am. I could change my name, to reflect my moment of birth; alter some details, to confirm my history; add a little detail, to clarify events.

But I don't want to invent a different identity, so I stick to what I've always used. And there are millions of us, all slightly at variance with our official paperwork. Each with some inner knowledge of who we are, which completes the picture of our tiny space on this earth.

So, all the demands on application forms for personal details can be coped with – with a little private flexibility. It isn't deceitful, it's practical. However, when it comes to the names of mother and father, the immense worries that society used to have about revealing further information are abating. Adopted people have proved over the past thirty years that information about their past is essential to them – and that they can handle it. And they've

undertaken the research not from idle curiosity, but for a fundamental understanding of who they are.

What may be discovered or revealed may be a blessing – like my
own – or it may be painful. But it tells you where you came from
and why you were adopted, satisfying a deep need to know,
whatever the circumstances. It gives you the fuller picture, and
you play a part in it. But for foundlings, this is where they hit a
brick wall. Everyone I spoke to had little hope of discovering the
parent who had left them. Nevertheless, for nearly all of them, it
was a wall that cast no shadow. Life began this side of it, and
though they longed for a titbit of news from the other side, such
longings were not by any means a constant blight on their lives.

'Life is what you make it', I heard over and over again. No
common thread of guilt or disaster ran through their stories. Just a
profound desire to know more about the family tree and to hear
why they had been broken off it.

All accepted that their present identity was 'who they are now'.
Any news from the past would be highly unlikely to change that.
'Life is to be got on with,' they all said, adding quietly, 'though it
would be nice to know . . .'

For we all need roots, and we are all somebody's child.

Useful Addresses

Norcap (National Organisation for Counselling Adoptees and Parents) (includes the Norcap Foundling Group)
112 Church Road
Wheatley
Oxfordshire
OX33 1LU
Tel: 01865 875000
enquiries@norcap.org
www.norcap.org.uk

BAAF (British Association for Adoption and Fostering)
Skyline House
200 Union Street
London
SE1 0LX
Tel: 0207 593 2000
mail@baaf.org.uk
www.baaf.org.uk

The Family Records Centre
1 Myddelton Street
London
EC1R 1UW
Tel: 0208 392 5300
enquiries@nationalarchives.gov.uk
www.familyrecords.gov.uk

The General Register Office
Smedley Hydro
Trafalgar Road
Southport
PR8 2HH
Tel: 0845 603 7788

Child Migrants Trust
28A Musters Road
West Bridgford
Nottingham
NG2 7PL
Tel: 0115 982 2811
enquiries@childmigrants.com

The Foundling Museum
40 Brunswick Square
London
WC1N 1AZ
Tel: 0207 841 3600
enquiries@foundlingmuseum.org.uk

AMT Children of Hope Foundation
1490 Franklin Avenue
Mineola
NY 11501
USA
Tel: (001) 516 781 3511
www.amtchildrenofhope.com

Picture Acknowledgements

Kate Adie: page 8 top. © AMT Children of Hope Foundation – Safe Haven, NY, USA: page 5 centre right. Associated Newspapers: page 6 centre left and right. *Belfast Telegraph*: page 6 centre below right. © Bettmann/Corbis: pages 4, 5 top left. Bibliothèque Nationale, Paris/photo Bridgeman Art Library, London: page 2 bottom. © Richard Cohen/Corbis: page 5 bottom. Coram Family in the care of the Foundling Museum, London: pages 2 centre left and right, 3 top left and right. Colin Dalley: page 6 bottom. © Getty Images: page 1. © Julian Grant: page 7 top. © M. Holdsworth: page 7 bottom. © Hulton-Deutsch Collection/Corbis: page 3 bottom. © Reuters/Corbis: page 8 bottom. Anthea Ring: page 6 top. © Scala Picture Library, Florence: page 2 top.